THE ASSOCIATION FOR SCOTTISH LITERARY STUDIES

NUMBER NINETEEN

THE COMIC POEMS
OF WILLIAM TENNANT

THE ASSOCIATION FOR SCOTTISH LITERARY STUDIES

ANNUAL VOLUMES PUBLISHED BY SCOTTISH ACADEMIC PRESS

1971 James Hogg, *The Three Perils of Man*, ed. Douglas Gifford.
1972 *The Poems of John Davidson*, vol. I, ed. Andrew Turnbull.
1973 *The Poems of John Davidson*, vol. II, ed. Andrew Turnbull.
1974 Allan Ramsay and Robert Fergusson, *Poems*, ed. Alexander M. Kinghorn and Alexander Law.
1975 John Galt, *The Member*, ed. Ian A. Gordon.
1976 William Drummond of Hawthornden, *Poems and Prose*, ed. Robert H. MacDonald.
1977 John G. Lockhart, *Peter's Letters to his Kinsfolk*, ed. William Ruddick.
1978 John Galt, *Selected Short Stories*, ed. Ian A. Gordon.
1979 Andrew Fletcher of Saltoun, *Selected Political Writings and Speeches*, ed. David Daiches.
1980 *Scott on Himself*, ed. David Hewitt.
1981 *The Party-Coloured Mind*, ed. David Reid.
1982 James Hogg, *Selected Stories and Sketches*, ed. Douglas S. Mack.
1983 Sir Thomas Urquhart of Cromarty, *The Jewel*, ed. R. D. S. Jack and R. J. Lyall.
1984 John Galt, *Ringan Gilhaize*, ed. Patricia J. Wilson.
1985 Margaret Oliphant, *Selected Short Stories of the Supernatural*, ed. Margaret K. Gray.
1986 James Hogg, *Selected Poems and Songs*, ed. David Groves.
1987 Hugh MacDiarmid, *A Drunk Man Looks at the Thistle*, ed. Kenneth Buthlay.
1988 *The Book of Sandy Stewart*, ed. Roger Leitch.
1989 *The Comic Poems of William Tennant*, ed. Alexander Scott and Maurice Lindsay.

THE ASSOCIATION FOR SCOTTISH LITERARY STUDIES

GENERAL EDITOR — DOUGLAS S. MACK

THE COMIC POEMS
OF WILLIAM TENNANT

Edited by
Alexander Scott
and
Maurice Lindsay

SCOTTISH ACADEMIC PRESS

EDINBURGH

1989

First published in Great Britain, 1989
by Scottish Academic Press Limited
139 Leith Walk, Edinburgh EH6 8NS
for
The Association for Scottish Literary Studies

ISBN 0 7073 0539 1

Introduction and Notes © 1989, Alexander Scott and Maurice Lindsay

British Library Cataloguing in Publication Data

Tennant, William, *1784–1848*
The comic poems of William Tennant. – (Annual volumes)
I. Title   II. Lindsay, Maurice, *1918-*   III. Scott,
Alexander, *1920–*   IIII. Series
821'.5

ISBN 0-7073-0569-1

The Association for Scottish Literary Studies
acknowledges subsidy from the Scottish Arts Council
towards the publication of this volume.

Typeset in Ehrhardt by Speedspools, Edinburgh
Printed by Aberdeen University Press

CONTENTS

Introduction	ix
Anster Fair	1
Papistry Storm'd	101
Tammy Little	204
The Tangiers Giant	207
Appendix: Maggy Lauder	212
Notes	214
Glossary	223

THE ASSOCIATION
FOR
SCOTTISH LITERARY STUDIES

The Association for Scottish Literary Studies aims to promote the study, teaching and writing of Scottish literature, and to further the study of the languages of Scotland.

To these ends, the ASLS publishes works of Scottish literature (of which this volume is an example), literary criticism in *Scottish Literary Journal*, scholarly studies of language in *Scottish Language*, and in-depth reviews of Scottish books in *SLJ Supplements*. And it publishes *New Writing Scotland*, an annual anthology of new poetry, drama and short fiction, in Scots, English and Gaelic, by Scottish writers.

All these publications are available as a single 'package', in return for an annual subscription. Enquiries should be sent to:

ASLS
c/o Department of English
University of Aberdeen
ABERDEEN
AB9 2UB

INTRODUCTION

The most original Scottish poet of his period, in the generation follow-
ing that of Scott and Hogg, William Tennant was born in the thriving
seaport of Anstruther, a small burgh on the southern coast of Fife, on 15
May 1784. His father, a merchant and farmer in a small way, belonged
to the Burgher sect of the Church of Scotland (see below), but both
in his personality and his poetry Tennant was entirely free of the
narrow illiberalism which is traditionally associated with sectarian
religion in Scotland. Lamed in early childhood, he became a dedicated
scholar, and although his parents' poverty compelled him to leave the
University of St Andrews at the age of seventeen, after only two years'
residence, without a degree, he went on without tuition to make himself
the master not only of Greek and Latin but also of Italian, German,
Portuguese and Hebrew. Yet all this massive early accumulation of
international learning was accompanied by an interest in his native
tongue, Scots, and in native traditions of verse, one of his earliest
compositions, 'The Anster Concert', being a piece of Scots light verse
in the style, and in the stanza, of the influential medieval poem that
celebrates a communal occasion, 'Christ's Kirk on the Green'.

For some years in the first decade of the new century, Tennant
acted as a clerk to his elder brother, a corn merchant, while employ-
ing his scanty leisure on the writing of his first major work, *Anster
Fair*, until the businessman went bankrupt and the poet was seized at
the instance of the creditors. After his release, *Anster Fair* was com-
pleted and published (anonymously) in Anstruther in 1812, and its
favourable reception, together with the revelation of its authorship,
led to Tennant's appointment as schoolmaster at Dunino, a village
half-way between Anstruther and St Andrews, in the following year.
Consequently gaining access to the university library, Tennant ex-
tended his linguistic range to even further fields, including Arabic,
Syriac, Persian, Sanskrit and Hindustani.

A second edition of *Anster Fair* (1814) was favourably noticed
by the most influential of contemporary critics, Francis Jeffrey, in *The
Edinburgh Review*, and subsequently Tennant was promoted to a big-
ger school at Lasswade, near Edinburgh, in 1816, while three years
later he was appointed teacher of classical and oriental languages at
Dollar Academy. During his period in the latter post, he produced
two further extended poems: in English *The Thane of Fife* (1822;

ix

unfinished), and in Scots *Papistry Storm'd; or the Dingin' Down o' the Cathedral* (1827). He wrote, as well, two dramas in English blank verse, *Cardinal Beaton* (1823) and *John Baliol* (1825), the former being diversified by some well-handled prose dialogue in Scots. From 1830 he contributed articles and verses to the *Edinburgh Literary Journal*, and two of these poems, in Scots, are sufficiently entertaining to warrant inclusion here. In 1834 he was appointed Professor of Oriental Languages in the University of St Andrews on the recommendation of the Lord Advocate for Scotland, who was none other than his erstwhile favourable reviewer, Francis Jeffrey, now serving in the Whig government which had passed the famous Reform Bill of 1832. During his incumbency of the chair, Tennant's scholarship was acknowledged by a Fellowship of the Royal Society and a doctorate from Marischal College, Aberdeen, but his *Hebrew Dramas* (1845) added little, if at all, to his poetical reputation. At his death in 1848, he was buried in his native place, Anstruther, which he had celebrated as the scene of his best-known work, *Anster Fair*.

In location, then, as in content, *Anster Fair* is a local poem; but it is far from being local in style. However provincial Tennant's experience of life may have been, his experience of literature was wide, and his first major work is a brilliant example of literary cross-fertilisation, with Fife folk-poetry wedded to Italian art-poetry. The principal characters, and part of the theme of the poem, are derived from the celebrated Fife folk-song, 'Maggie Lauder', probably best-known in the version first printed by David Herd in his *Scots Songs* of 1776. It describes how Maggie, a local beauty, accosted by a piper, at first rebuffs his advances, but when she learns that he is the famous Border piper, Rob the Ranter, and has danced a jig to his playing, she invites him to attend Anster Fair and enquire for her there ('Gin ye should come to Enster Fair,/ Speir ye for Maggie Lauder'). From this Tennant has taken the notion of the power of the heroine's beauty to conquer all hearts ('Wha wadna be in love/ Wi' bonnie Maggie Lauder?'), the idea of the power of the hero's playing to create the desire to dance ('The lasses loup as they were daft,/ When I blaw up my chanter'), and the association of those two characters with the fair at Anstruther. On the other hand, he ignores the information given in the song that Maggie is an incomer to the county and a married woman ('I've lived in Fife, baith maid and wife,/ These ten years and a quarter'), preferring to regard her as a native of his own native county and as an unmarried girl. In so doing, he not only associates her with his strong sense of local patriotism, he makes her a more promising – or at least a more respectable – subject for a love-affair with Rob the Ranter.

Out of those largely traditional elements, Tennant has created a narrative poem which is at once new and individual and yet still redolent of 'folk' atmosphere. Playing a variation on a theme made fashionable by Scott, the medieval tournament where the winner receives his prize from the hand of the lady elected 'Queen of Beauty', the younger poet presents a contest where the Queen of Beauty's own hand – in marriage – is the prize. That Queen, of course, is 'bonnie Maggie Lauder', and the contest, which takes place at Anster Fair, consists of a donkey-race, a sack-race, a piping-contest, and a competition in story-telling. Interwoven with those themes of bucolic revelry and rivalry, Tennant spins a thread of supernatural fiction – for the idea that Maggie should settle the argument among her countless suitors by means of a contest in various skills is first suggested to her by a fairy figure, Puck, whom a spell has imprisoned in the heroine's mustard-pot. Again, Rob the Ranter is stimulated to leave his Border haunts, and to travel to Anster Fair to seek Maggie's hand, by a female fairy, Puck's wife, who has been similarly imprisoned in his pepper-pot; and the story Rob tells at the contest is the tale of how those two were made captive by the wicked enchantments of the wizard Michael Scott (whose notoriety had recently been renewed through his appearance in Walter Scott's *The Lay of the Last Minstrel*).

Such elaboration of plot requires considerable space, and the poem extends to no less than six cantos, an approach towards epic proportions. The subject-matter, however, for all its charm, is entirely lacking in the dignity of epic. On the contrary, *Anster Fair* is a completely comic creation, and Tennant writes it in the style not of epic proper but of mock-epic, to which his scholarly reading of Italian literature introduced him in the work of the greatest writer of romantic verse comedy of the Renaissance period, Ariosto, the author of *Orlando Furioso*. From this source derives even Tennant's stanza, for he uses *ottava rima*, Ariosto's eight-line stanza of iambic pentameter rhyming *ababab cc*, modified by making the last line an Alexandrine of six strong accents in order (says Tennant) 'that its close may be more full and sounding'. In using *ottava rima* for comic poetry in English, or in Scots-English ('in a humorous poem, partly descriptive of Scottish manners, it was impossible to avoid using Scottish words'), Tennant anticipated Byron, another student of Italian poetry, who was to employ the stanza for all the finest work of his final period, *Beppo*, *The Vision of Judgment*, and *Don Juan*.

Tennant's temperament was sunnier than Byron's, and his verse does not attempt the same critical cutting edge, the tone being gay rather than ironical, the effect more often one of burlesque rather than satire. Yet both poets often adopt a similar method of achieving comedy by building up a scene or a situation or an idea in the first seven lines of a stanza and then dissipating it in the last, a conscious exercise in the art of 'sinking'.

'Twas on a keen December night; John Frost
   Drove through mid air his chariot, icy-wheel'd,
And from the sky's crisp ceiling star-embost,

xi

Whiff'd off the clouds that the pure blue conceal'd;
The hornless moon amid her brilliant host
Shone, and with silver sheeted lake and field;
'Twas cutting cold; I'm sure, each trav'ler's nose
Was pinch'd right red that night, and numb'd were all his toes.

There the fanciful picture of Jack Frost as a kind of pagan god careering
through the night sky modulates into the beautiful naturalistic picture
of the 'hornless moon' and the 'brilliant host' of stars, which is inter-
rupted by the abrupt statement of brutal fact, "'Twas cutting cold',
leading to the ludicrously prosaic concern with the redness of the
traveller's nose and the numb condition of his feet. This kind of comic
effect through bathos, through the juxtaposition of the sublime and the
ridiculous which has been called 'the reductive idiom', is characteris-
tic of much eighteenth-century Scots comic verse, and Tennant uses
it with apparently easy brilliance – as when, discussing poetical inspi-
ration, he writes 'My pulse beats fire – my pericranium glows, / Like
baker's oven with poetic heat', counterpointing the plain vigour of 'my
pulse beats fire' against the pompous pseudo-scientific inflation of 'my
pericranium glows', and then pricking the bubble of pomposity with the
sharply prosaic simile, 'Like baker's oven', and the odd association of
that workaday object with the esoteric 'poetic heat'.

The best criticism of *Anster Fair* is still that written by Jeffrey in 1814,
when he referred to it as 'gay or fantastic' and as 'extravagant rather than
ridiculous'. While describing the narrative aspect of the poem as 'this
homely foundation', Jeffrey credited Tennant with having built upon
that 'a vast superstructure of description . . . and a great treasury of
poetry'. For this critic the poem's 'great charm' lay 'in the profusion of
images and groups which it thrusts upon the fancy, and the crowd and
hurry and animation with which they are all jostled and driven along',
while he admired even more 'the perpetual sallies and outbreakings of
a rich and poetical imagination, by which the homely themes are con-
stantly ennobled or contrasted . . . the power of connecting grand or
beautiful conceptions with the representation of vulgar objects or ludi-
crous occurrences'. (Here we are given a vivid exemplification of the
so-called 'Caledonian antisyzygy', more than a century before Gregory
Smith invented the term.)

It may be invidious to single out, from all of the poem's many
and various illustrations of Tennant's ability to create a profusion of
'images and groups' and to whirl them along in 'hurry and animation',
one particular episode that seems to be the most evocative of all, but it
is difficult not to insist on the last twenty stanzas of Canto IV. These
provide the climax as well as the conclusion of this part of the work,
describing the wild beauty of Rob's piping and the frenzy of dance into
which it impels each and every one within its range, humans on land,
birds in the air, and even such supernatural beings as mermaids in the

sea, with the presentation of the mermaids providing an opportunity for the 'perpetual sallies and outpourings of a rich and poetical imagination'.

And eke the mermaids that in ocean swim,
  Drawn by that music from their shelly caves,
Peep now unbashful from the salt-sea brim,
  And flounce and plash exulting in the waves;
They spread at large the white and floating limb,
  That Neptune amorously clips and laves,
And kem with combs of pearl and coral fair
Their long sleek oozy locks of green redundant hair.

As for the 'grand and beautiful conceptions' which Tennant was able to connect with the 'ludicrous occurrences' of his general narrative, the most impressive example may well be found in the description of morning which shines through the first five stanzas of Canto III. There the image of dew sparkling in early sunlight – 'on ten thousand dew bent leaves and sprays,/ Twinkle ten thousand suns, and fling their petty rays' – is in itself enough to show that Tennant possesses the capacities of the poet as well as the capabilities of the humorous versifier.

Achieving success in mock-epic with *Anster Fair*, Tennant was tempted to try epic itself in his next extended work, *The Thane of Fife* (1822), a story of the Norse invasion of his native county during the Dark Age of Scottish history, but here he was much less successful. Striving for seriousness, he was often only grandiloquent; and however hard he fought against his natural trend towards the ridiculous, he failed to render his description of the Norse gods other than grotesque, an incongruous effect in epic. Publication of the first part of the poem was so poorly received that Tennant never issued the remainder, returning instead to another mock-epic, *Papistry Storm'd: or the Dingin' Down o' the Cathedral* (1827), a work which its sub-title describes as 'Ane Poem, in Sax Sangs'. Unlike *Anster Fair*, where the language is English – although a number of Scots terms are employed throughout – *Papistry Storm'd* is written in a literary Scots which not only looks back towards the medium of the medieval makars but also forwards in the direction of the so-called 'synthetic' Scots written by Hugh MacDiarmid and his followers in the present century.

Tennant's poem is the one extended work in Scots verse produced during the Regency period, and in order to find another original Scots poem of corresponding length – some four thousand lines – it is necessary to go back, bypassing Alexander Ross's derivative *Helenore* (1778), as far as the sixteenth-century Sir David Lyndsay. It is all the more appropriate, then, that *Papistry Storm'd* is dedicated to Lyndsay as 'Poetae Fifensis Celeberrimi' (Fife's most celebrated poet), while

xiii

Tennant in his preface to the poem expressly avows his indebtedness to the sixteenth-century writer with regard to style, manner and metrical form – 'the author has borrowed the style and manner and diversified strophes of Sir David Lyndsay'. Among all the diversifications, the strophe or stanza most frequently used is an eight-line sequence rhyming *aaabcccb*, the *a* and *c* lines being of four strong accents and the *b* lines of three, a measure with a movement similar to that of the Standard Habbie or Burns stanza, which Tennant derived from Lyndsay's famous verse play *The Three Estates*.

While Tennant realised that, at the time of composition, it was 'daring . . . to write a long poem in Scottish', he was very far from apologising for making the attempt. On the contrary, he calls 'Scottish' (or Scots) 'that language, the richest, perhaps, and most flexible for humorous purposes, of any dialect of modern Europe', and refers approvingly to 'the facetious strength, fluency and vivacity of our native speech'. His own handling of literary Scots has all the qualities he praises.

Papistry Storm'd, like *Anster Fair* and *The Thane of Fife*, is to some extent a product of Tennant's notable local patriotism, since the subject is the destruction of the Catholic Cathedral of St Andrews by the Protestant mob during the Reformation riots of 1559. Such a subject, however, is of more than merely local interest and relevance, and Tennant, although writing in Scots, and in the stanzas (and, sometimes, in the vocabulary) of an earlier Fife makar, also draws on his knowledge of European literature. When he introduces 'one or two allegorical personages', such as the god of Mirth and the goddess of Learning, he excuses their presence by citing the 'example of the poets of southern Europe', the Italian poets Pulci and Ariosto, who also 'employ such actors, and . . . mix up their shadowy and symbolical names in the same stanzas with those that are real and historical'. The appearance of the classical deities in allegorical guise is customary in mock-epic, and their introduction into the Scottish scene by Tennant adds a further element of the grotesque to the events described.

But if Tennant, on his own admission, was 'daring' in publishing a mock-epic in Scots in 1827, he may be thought even more temerarious in attempting a comic poem on a subject which his countrymen for generations had been accustomed to regard with deadly seriousness (or awful solemnity), the Reformation. That he was able to write humorously on his chosen aspect of that subject would seem to show the liberalising influence that his literary education had had upon a religious background of strict sectarianism. For Tennant had been born and brought up as a member of the Burghers, a sect which had separated from the parent Church of Scotland on the vexed question of patronage, and such sects are under the temptation to take a 'holier-than-thou' attitude towards the unenlightened who fail to share their views. But the sectarian tendency to confuse sanctity with sanctimoniousness finds no place in Tennant's work.

At the same time, however, the poet takes great care to avoid the theological aspects of his theme, and those Catholic clerics who appear in *Papistry Storm'd* are presented as clowns, or ignorant fools, rather than as purveyors of unsound religious doctrine. Again, the actual destruction of St Andrews Cathedral is presented as 'an extraordinary achievement of popular excitement . . . condemned or at least disclaimed by the principal Protestant leaders', rather than as a praiseworthy act of faith.

The whole poem is one long crescendo of comic action, growing ever faster and more furious – the mustering of the mob from every village in Fife, the march to St Andrews, the mock-tournament between the Catholic and Protestant champions, the taking of the town, and the final 'dingin' down o' the cathedral', when the wrath of a stormy sky eventually destroys an edifice so mighty as to defy all human attempts to lay it low. Tennant diversifies his theme, which might otherwise become monotonous in its repeated violence, with episodes on the humorous exploits of his allegorical deities, and other passages which provide moments of rest – in Sang First, Fisher Willie's dream, a wonderfully vivid, and highly comic, parody of the medieval dream-sequence, about the bishops who tried to levy tithes on his catch; and in Sang Third, the luxuriant description of the scrumptious spread with which the Catholic prelates consoled themselves after their first defeat at Protestant hands, a passage which represents Tennant's variation on the theme of Nero fiddling while Rome burns. For all its general atmosphere of unrestrained action, the poem does build up to a climax, the description of the 'dingin' down o' the cathedral' at the end of Sang Saxt being expressed in the most evocative lines of the whole work.

The medievalism which is a notable element in *Papistry Storm'd*, affecting its setting and characters, its techniques and metrical forms, and its linguistic borrowings from Lyndsay, also influences the most entertaining of the poems that Tennant contributed to the *Edinburgh Literary Journal* in 1830. These extravaganzas, 'Tammy Little' and 'The Tangiers Giant', are in direct descent from medieval Scots farcical verse, sharing what C. S. Lewis has called 'the northern wildness, the grotesque invention, the eldritch audacity'[1] of their predecessors. Yet they look to the future as well as the past, anticipating the farcical 'whigmaleeries' which are the most appealing poems produced by the modern Scots makar, William Soutar (1898–1943), during the last decade of his life.

Another twentieth-century Scottish poet, Norman MacCaig, has written about his contemporary, Robert Garioch, another effective farceur, in words which could be applied equally well to Tennant – 'There's a common heresy that art can be great art, or even serious art, only if it's dealing with a tragic experience, or at least a painful one, in a serious manner. This seems nonsense. If a comic manner is used as craftily as Garioch uses his, the result is true poetry. It may not be "sublime", thank God. But it is the real stuff' (*New Gambit*, Winter 1966). Tennant too is 'the real stuff', a never failing source of delight.

The editors wish to acknowledge the kind assistance of Professor Ian Cowan, the University of Glasgow; Professor Ian Kidd, the University of St Andrews; Mr S. M. Simpson, the National Library of Scotland; Mr R. Gillespie and the Staff of the Mitchell Library, Glasgow; Mr A. G. Mackenzie, Librarian, the University of St Andrews; and Mrs Sadie Douglas, the Administrative Director of The Scottish Civic Trust.

NOTE

1 'The Close of the Middle Ages in Scotland', *English Literature in the Sixteenth Century Excluding Drama* (Oxford, 1954).

ANSTER FAIR

A POEM IN SIX CANTOS

Nec pol ego Nemeæ credo, neque ego Olympiæ,
Neque usquam ludos tam festivos fieri,
Quam hic intus fiunt ludi ludificabiles.
Plauti, Casina.
— sane leve
Dum nihil habemus majus calamo ludimus.
Phaedri Fab.

PREFACE

The following Poem is presented to the Public with that diffidence and anxiety which every young Author feels when the good or bad fate of his first production must check his rashness and vanity, or enliven his future efforts with the confidence arising from popular approbation.

The Poem is written in stanzas of octave rhime, or the *ottava rima* of the Italians, a measure said to be invented by Boccaccio, and after him employed by Tasso and Ariosto. From these writers it was transferred into English Poetry by Fairfax, in his Translation of 'Jerusalem Delivered', but since his days has been by our poets, perhaps, too little cultivated. The stanza of Fairfax is here shut with the Alexandrine of Spenser, that its close may be more full and sounding.

In a humorous Poem, partly descriptive of Scottish manners, it was impossible to avoid using Scottish words. These, however, will, it is hoped, be found not too many. Some old English words are likewise admitted.

The transactions of ANSTER FAIR may be supposed to have taken place during the reign of James V, a monarch, whom tradition reports to have had many gamesome rambles in Fife, and with whose liveliness and jollity of temper the merriment of the FAIR did not ill accord. Yet a scrupulous congruity with the modes of his times was not intended, and must not be expected. Ancient and modern manners are mixed and jumbled together, to heighten the humour, or variegate the description.

EDINBURGH
5th May 1812.

ANSTER FAIR

Canto I

ARGUMENT

The subject being proposed, and Invocation made as usual, the poet is on a sudden hurried away by an irregular fit of inspiration, till, checking himself, he proceeds with method to relate his story. On a cold winter evening, as Maggie Lauder sits in her chamber at supper, she begins to muse upon the propriety of choosing a husband from the multitude of her suitors. After having in a soliloquy run over their names and characters, she is surprised by the spontaneous motion of her mustard-pot, that begins on a sudden to leap before her on the table – It stops, and from its cavity rises Puck the fairy, who advises her, in order to procure the husband destined to her hand, to dispatch criers and messengers through all the shires of Scotland, proclaiming that on next Anster market-day, (in April) there should be held, in the loan there, four games, or trials of ability and merit: the first to be an Ass Race, the second a Sack Race, the third a Competition in Piping, and the fourth a Competition in Story Telling; and that he who goes through all these trials with good fortune and success, is the man fated to receive her hand. Maggie Lauder sends away her messengers next morning accordingly; they pass through Scotland and rapidly publish her proclamation. The bustle and merry alarm caused thereby; and the great preparation in providing Asses, Sacks, Bagpipes, and Stories, made by those who design to engage in the Games.

3

I.

While some of Troy and pettish heroes sing,
    And some of Rome, and chiefs of pious fame,
And some of men that thought it harmless thing
    To smite off heads in Mars's bloody game,
And some of Eden's garden gay with spring,   5
    And Hell's dominions terrible to name,
I sing a theme far livelier, happier, gladder,
I sing of ANSTER FAIR and bonny MAGGIE LAUDER.

II.

What time from east, from west, from south, from north,
    From every hamlet, town, and smoky city,   10
Laird, clown, and beau, to Anster Fair came forth,
    The young, the gay, the handsome, and the witty,
To try in various sport and game their worth,
    Whilst prize before them MAGGIE sat, the pretty,
And after many a feat, and joke, and banter,   15
Fair MAGGIE's hand was won by mighty ROB the RANTER.

III.

Muse, that from top of thine old Greekish hill,
    Didst the harp-fumbling Theban younker view,
And on his lips bid bees their sweets distil,
    And gav'st the chariot that the white swans drew,   20
O let me scoop, from thine etherial rill,
    Some little palmfuls of the blessed dew,
And lend the swan-drawn car, that safely I
Like him may scorn the earth and burst into the sky.

IV.

Our themes are like; for he the games extoll'd   25
    Held in the chariot-shaken Grecian plains,
Where the vain victor, arrogant and bold,
    Parsley or laurel got for all his pains;
I sing of sports more worthy to be told,
    Where better prize the Scottish victor gains;   30
What were the crowns of Greece but wind and bladder,
Compared with marriage-bed of bonnie MAGGIE LAUDER?

V.

And O! that king Apollo would but grant
    A little spark of that transcendant flame,
That fir'd the Chian rhapsodist to chant   35
    How vied the bowmen for Ulysses' dame,
And him of Rome to sing how Atalant
    Plied, dart in hand, the suitor-slaught'ring game,
Till the bright gold, bowl'd forth along the grass,
Betray'd her to a spouse, and stopp'd the bounding lass.   40

4

VI.

But lo! from bosom of yon southern cloud,
   I see the chariot come which Pindar bore;
I see the swans, whose white necks, arching proud,
   Glitter with golden yoke, approach my shore;
For me they come – O Phœbus, potent god!   45
   Spare, spare me now – Enough, good king – no more –
A little spark I ask'd in moderation,
Why scorch me ev'n to death with fiery inspiration?

VII.

My pulse beats fire – my pericranium glows,
   Like baker's oven with poetic heat;   50
A thousand bright ideas, spurning prose,
   Are in a twinkling hatch'd in Fancy's seat;
Zounds! they will fly out at my ears and nose,
   If through my mouth they find not passage fleet;
I hear them buzzing deep within my noddle,   55
Like bees that in their hives confus'dly hum and huddle.

VIII.

How now? – what's this? – my very eyes, I trow,
   Drop on my hands their base prosaic scales;
My visual orbs are purg'd from film, and lo!
   Instead of ANSTER's turnip-bearing vales,   60
I see old Fairyland's mirac'lous show,
   Her trees of tinsel kiss'd by freakish gales,
Her ouphes, that cloak'd in leaf-gold skim the breeze,
And fairies swarming thick as mites in rotten cheese.

IX.

I see the puny fair-chinn'd goblin rise   65
   Suddenly glorious from his mustard pot;
I see him wave his hand in seemly wise,
   And button round him tight his fulgent coat;
While MAGGIE LAUDER, in a great surprise,
   Sits startled on her chair, yet fearing not;   70
I see him ope his dewy lips; I hear
The strange and strict command address'd to MAGGIE's ear.

X.

I see the RANTER with bagpipe on back,
   As to the fair he rides jocundly on;
I see the crowds that press with speed not slack   75
   Along each road that leads to ANSTER loan;
I see the suitors, that, deep-sheath'd in sack,
   Hobble and tumble, bawl and swear, and groan;
I see – but fy, thou brainish muse! what mean
These vapourings, and brags of what by thee is seen?   80

XI.

Go to – be cooler, and in order tell
  To all my good co-townsmen list'ning round,
How every merry incident befel,
  Whereby our loan shall ever be renown'd;
Say first, what elf or fairy could impel   85
  Fair MAG, with wit, and wealth, and beauty crown'd,
To put her suitors to such waggish test,
And give her happy bed to him that jumped best?

XII.

'Twas on a keen December night; John Frost
  Drove through mid air his chariot, icy-wheel'd,   90
And from the sky's crisp ceiling star-embost,
  Whiff'd off the clouds that the pure blue conceal'd;
The hornless moon amid her brilliant host
  Shone, and with silver sheeted lake and field;
'Twas cutting cold; I'm sure, each trav'ler's nose   95
Was pinch'd right red that night, and numb'd were all his toes.

XIII.

Not so were MAGGIE LAUDER's toes, as she
  In her warm chamber at her supper sate,
(For 'twas that hour when burgesses agree
  To eat their suppers ere the night grows late).   100
Alone she sat, and pensive as may be
  A young fair lady, wishful of a mate;
Yet with her pearly teeth held on a picking,
Her stomach to refresh, the breast-bone of a chicken.

XIV.

She thought upon her suitors that with love   105
  Besiege her chamber all the livelong day,
Aspiring each her virgin heart to move,
  With courtship's every troublesome essay,
Calling her, angel, sweeting, fondling, dove,
  And other nicknames in love's friv'lous way;   110
While she with heart more cold than new-caught herring,
Was hum'ring still the beaux, and still not one preferring.

XV.

What, what, quo' MAG, must thus it be my doom
  To live a spouseless never-wedded maid,
And idly toss away my body's bloom,   115
  Without a partner, on my joyless bed,
Giving my kisses to my pillow's plume,
  Cold, unresponsive kisses, void and dead?
Fool that I am, to live unwed so long!
More fool, since I am woo'd by such a clam'rous throng!   120

For e'er was heiress with much gold in chest
   And dowr'd with acres of wheat-bearing land,
By such a pack of men, in am'rous quest,
   Fawningly spaniel'd to bestow her hand?
Wheree'er I walk, the air that feeds my breast   125
   Is by the gusty sighs of lovers fann'd;
Each wind that blows wafts love-cards to my lap;
Whilst I – ah stupid MAG! – avoid each am'rous trap!

XVII.

Then come, let me my suitors' merits weigh,
   And in the worthiest lad my spouse select: 130
First, there's our ANSTER merchant, Norman Ray,
   A powder'd wight with golden buttons deck'd,
That stinks with scent, and chats like popinjay,
   And struts with phiz tremendously erect;
Four brigs has he, that on the broad sea swim; –   135
He is a pompous fool – oh no! I'll not have him:

XVIII.

Next is the Master Andrew Strang, that takes
   His seat i' the Baillies' loft on Sabbath-day,
With paltry visage white as oaten cakes,
   As if no blood runs gurgling in his clay;   140
Heav'ns! what an awkward hunch the fellow makes,
   As to the priest he does the bow repay!
Yet he is rich – a very wealthy man, true –
But, by the holy rood, I will have none of Andrew.

XIX.

Then for the Lairds – there's Melvil of Carnbee,   145
   A handsome gallant, and a beau of spirit;
Who can go down the dance so well as he?
   And who can fiddle with such manly merit?
– Ay, but he is too much the debauchee –
   His cheeks seem sponges oozing port and claret;   150
In marrying him I should bestow myself ill,
And so, I'll not have you, thou fuddler Harry Melvil!

XX.

There's Cunningham of Barns, that still assails
   With verse and billet-doux my gentle heart,
A bookish Squire, and good at telling tales,   155
   That rhimes and whines of Cupid, flame, and dart;
But, oh! his mouth a filthy smell exhales,
   And on his nose sprouts horribly the wart;
What though there be a fund of lore and fun in him?
He has a rotten breath – I cannot think of Cunningham.   160

7

XXI.

Why then, there's Allardyce, that plies his suit
   And battery of courtship more and more;
Spruce Lochmalonie, that with booted foot
   Each morning wears the threshold of my door;
Auchmoutie too, and Strang that persecute   165
   My tender heart with am'rous buffets sore: –
– Whom to my hand and bed should I promote? –
– Eh-la! what sight is this? – what ails my mustard-pot?

XXII.

Here broke the lady her soliloquy,
   For in a twink her pot of mustard, lo!   170
Self-moved, like Jove's wheel'd stool that rolls on high,
   'Gan caper on her table to and fro,
And hopp'd and fidgeted before her eye,
   Spontaneous, here and there, a wondrous show:
As leaps, instinct with mercury, a bladder,   175
So leaps the mustard-pot of bonnie MAGGIE LAUDER.

XXIII.

Soon stopp'd its dance th' ignoble utensil,
   When from its round and small recess there came
Thin curling wreaths of paly smoke, that still,
   Fed by some magic unapparent flame,   180
Mount to the chamber's stucco'd roof, and fill
   Each nook with fragrance, and refresh the dame;
Ne'er smelt a Phœnix-nest so sweet, I wot,
As smelt the luscious fumes of MAGGIE's mustard-pot.

XXIV.

It reeked censer-like; then (strange to tell)   185
   Forth from the smoke, that thick and thicker grows,
A fairy of the height of half an ell,
   In dwarfish pomp, majestically rose:
His feet, upon the table stablish'd well,
   Stood trim and splendid in their snake-skin hose;   190
Gleam'd, topaz-like, the breeches he had on,
Whose waistband like the bend of summer rainbow shone.

XXV.

His coat seem'd fashion'd of the threads of gold,
   That intertwine the clouds at sunset hour,
And, certes, Iris with her shuttle bold   195
   Wove the rich garment in her lofty bower;
To form its buttons were the Pleiads old
   Pluck'd from their sockets by some genie-power,
And sew'd upon the coat's resplendent hem;
Its neck was lovely green; each cuff a sapphire gem.   200

XXVI.

As when the churlish spirit of the Cape
  To Gama, voyaging to Mozambique,
Up-popp'd from sea, a tangle-tassel'd¹ shape,
  With mussels sticking inch-thick on his cheek,
And 'gan with tortoise-shell his limbs to scrape,   205
  And yawn'd his monstrous blobberlips to speak;
Brave Gama's hairs stood bristled at the sight,
And on the tarry deck sunk down his men with fright.

XXVII.

So sudden (not so huge and grimly dire)
  Uprose to MAGGIE's stounded eyne the sprite,   210
As fair a fairy as you could desire,
  With ruddy cheek, and chin and temples white;
His eyes seem'd little points of sparkling fire,
  That, as he look'd, charm'd with inviting light;
He was indeed as bonny a fay and brisk,   215
As ever on long moon-beam was seen to ride and frisk.

XXVIII.

Around his bosom by a silken zone
  A little bagpipe gracefully was bound,
Whose pipes like hollow stalks of silver shone,
  The glist'ring tiny avenues of sound;   220
Beneath his arm the windy bag, full-blown,
  Heav'd up its purple like an orange round,
And only waited orders to discharge
Its blasts with charming groan into the sky at large.

XXIX.

He wav'd his hand to MAGGIE, as she sat   225
  Amaz'd and startled on her carved chair;
Then took his petty feather-garnish'd hat
  In honour to the lady, from his hair,
And made a bow so dignifiedly flat,
  That MAG was witched with his beauish air;   230
At last he spoke, with voice so soft, so kind,
So sweet, as if his throat with fiddle-strings was lin'd.

XXX.

Lady! be not offended that I dare,
  Thus forward and impertinently rude,
Emerge, uncall'd, into the upper air,   235
  Intruding on a maiden's solitude;
Nay, do not be alarm'd, thou lady fair!
  Why startle so? – I am a fairy good;
Not one of those that, envying beauteous maids,
Speckle their skins with moles, and fill with spleens their heads. 240

9

For, as conceal'd in this clay-house of mine,
    I overheard thee, in a lowly voice,
Weighing thy lovers' merits, with design
    Now on the worthiest lad to fix thy choice,
I have up-bolted from my paltry shrine,   245
    To give thee, sweet-ey'd lass, my best advice;
For by the life of Oberon my king!
To pick good husband out is, sure, a ticklish thing:

XXXII.

And never shall good Tommy Puck permit
    Such an assemblage of unwonted charms   250
To cool some lecher's lewd licentious fit
    And sleep imbounded by his boisterous arms;
What though his fields by twenty ploughs be split,
    And golden wheat wave riches on his farms?
His house is shame – it cannot, shall not be;   255
A greater, happier doom, O MAG, awaiteth thee.

XXXIII.

Strange are indeed the steps, by which thou must
    Thy glory's happy eminence attain,
But fate hath fix'd them, and 'tis fate's t'adjust
    The mighty links that ends to means enchain,   260
Nor may poor Puck his little fingers thrust
    Into the links to break Jove's steel in twain;
Then MAGGIE, hear, and let my words descend
Into thy soul, for much it boots thee to attend.

XXXIV.

To-morrow, when o'er th' Isle of May the sun   265
    Lifts up his forehead bright with golden crown,
Call to thine house the light-heel'd men, that run
    Afar on messages for ANSTER Town,
Fellows of sp'rit, by none in speed out-done,
    Of lofty voice, enough a drum to drown,   270
And bid them hie, post-haste, through all the nation,
And publish, far and near, this famous proclamation;

XXXV.

Let them proclaim with voice's loudest tone,
    That on your next approaching market-day,
Shall merry sports be held in ANSTER loan,   275
    With celebration notable and gay;
And that a prize, than gold or costly stone
    More precious, shall the victor's toils repay,
Ev'n thy own form with beauties so replete,
– Nay, MAGGIE, start not thus! – thy marriage-bed, my sweet.   280

XXXVI.

First, on the loan shall ride full many an ass,
  With stout whip-cracking rider on his back,
Intent with twinkling hoof to pelt the grass,
  And pricking up his long ears at the crack;
Next o'er the ground the daring men shall pass,   285
  Half-coffin'd in their cumbrances of sack,
With heads just peeping from their shrines of bag,
Horribly hobbling round and straining hard for MAG;

XXXVII.

Then shall the pipers groaningly begin
  In squeaking rivalry their merry strain,   290
Till Billyness shall echo back the din,
  And Innergelly woods shall ring again;
Last, let each man that hopes thy hand to win
  By witty product of prolific brain,
Approach, and, confident of Pallas' aid,   295
Claim by an hum'rous tale possession of thy bed.

XXXVIII.

Such are the wondrous tests, by which, my love!
  The merits of thy husband must be try'd,
And he, that shall in these superior prove,
  (One proper husband shall the Fates provide)   300
Shall from the loan with thee triumphant move
  Homeward, the jolly bridegroom and the bride,
And at thy house shall eat the marriage-feast,
When I'll pop up again: Here Tommy Puck surceast.

XXXIX.

He ceas'd, and to his wee mouth dewy-wet,   305
  His bagpipe's tube of silver up he held,
And, underneath his down-press'd arm he set
  His purple bag, that with a tempest swell'd;
He play'd and pip'd so sweet, that never yet
  MAG had a piper heard that Puck excell'd;   310
Had Midas heard a tune so exquisite,
By heav'n! his long base ears had quiver'd with delight.

XL.

Tingle the fire-ir'ns, poker, tongs, and grate,
  Responsive to the blithesome melody;
The tables and the chairs inanimate   315
  Wish they had muscles now to trip it high;
Wave back and forwards at a wondrous rate
  The window-curtains, touch'd with sympathy;
Fork, knife, and trencher, almost break their sloth,
And caper on their ends upon the table-cloth.   320

XLI.

How then could MAGGIE, sprightly, smart, and young,
　Withstand that bagpipe's blithe awak'ning air?
She, as her ear-drum caught the sounds, up-sprung
　Like lightning, and despis'd her idle chair,
And into all the dance's graces flung 325
　The bounding members of her body fair;
From nook to nook thro' all her room she tript,
And whirl'd like whirligig, and reel'd, and bobb'd, and skipt.

XLII.

At last the little piper ceas'd to play,
　And deftly bow'd, and said, my dear, goodnight 330
Then in a smoke evanish'd clean away,
　With all his gaudy apparatus bright;
As breaks soap-bubble, which a boy in play
　Blows from his short tobacco-pipe aright,
So broke poor Puck from view, and on the spot 335
Y-smoking aloes-reek he left his mustard-pot.

XLIII.

Whereat the furious lady's wriggling feet
　Forgot to pelt and patter in such wise,
And down she gladly sunk upon her seat,
　Fatigu'd and panting from her exercise; 340
She sat, and mus'd a while, as it was meet,
　On what so late had occupy'd her eyes;
Then to her bed-room went, and doff'd her gown,
And laid upon her couch her charming person down.

XLIV.

Some say that MAGGIE slept so sound that night, 345
　As never she had slept since she was born,
But sure am I, that, thoughtful of the sprite,
　She twenty times upon her bed did turn,
For still appear'd to stand before her sight
　The gaudy goblin, glorious from his urn, 350
And still, within the cavern of her ear,
Th' injunction echoing rung, so strict and strange to hear.

XLV.

But when the silver-bitted steeds, that draw
　The car of morning up th' empyreal height,
Had snorted day upon North-Berwick Law, 355
　And from their glist'ring loose manes toss'd the light,
Immediately from bed she rose, (such awe
　Of Tommy press'd her soul with anxious weight,)
And donn'd her tissued fragrant morning vest,
And to fulfil his charge her earliest care addrest. 360

XLVI.

Straight to her house she tarried not to call
  Her messengers and heralds swift of foot,
Men skill'd to hop o'er dikes and ditches; all
  Gifted with sturdy brazen lungs to boot;
She bade them halt at every town, and bawl   365
  Her proclamation out with mighty bruit,
Inviting loud, to ANSTER loan and FAIR,
The Scottish beaux to jump for her sweet person there.

XLVII.

They took each man his staff into his hand;
  They button'd round their bellies close their coats;   370
They flew divided through the frozen land;
  Were never seen such swiftly-trav'lling Scots!
Nor ford, slough, mountain, could their speed withstand;
  Such fleetness have the men that feed on oats!
They skirr'd, they flounder'd through the sleets and snows,   375
And puff'd against the winds that bit in spite their nose.

XLVIII.

They halted at each wall-fenc'd town renown'd,
  And ev'ry lesser borough of the nation;
And with the trumpet's welkin-rifting sound,
  And tuck of drum of loud reverberation,   380
Tow'rds the four wings of heav'n, they, round and round,
  Proclaim'd in Stentor-like vociferation,
That, on th' approaching day of ANSTER market,
Should merry sports be held: – Hush! listen now and hark it!

XLIX.

Ho! beaux and pipers, wits and jumpers, ho!   385
  Ye buxom blades that like to kiss the lasses;
Ye that are skill'd sew'd up in sacks to go;
  Ye that excel in *horsemanship* of asses;
Ye that are smart at telling tales, and know
  On Rhime's two stilts to crutch it up Parnassus;   390
Ho! lads, your sacks, pipes, asses, tales, prepare
To jump, play, ride, and rhime, at ANSTER loan and FAIR!

L.

First, on the green turf shall each ass draw nigh,
  Caparison'd or clouted for the race,
With mounted rider, sedulous to ply   395
  Cudgel or whip and win the foremost place;
Next, shall th' adventrous men, that dare to try
  Their bodies' springiness in hempen case,
Put on their bags, and, with ridic'lous bound,
And sweat and huge turmoil, pass lab'ring o'er the ground.   400

13

LI.

Then shall the pipers, gentlemen o' th' drone,
  Their pipes in gleesome competition screw,
And grace, with loud solemnity of groan,
  Each his invented tune to th' audience new;
Last shall each witty bard, to whom is known   405
  The craft of Helicon's rhime-jingling crew,
His story tell in good poetic strains,
And make his learned tongue the midwife to his brains.

LII.

And he whose tongue the wittiest tale shall tell,
  Whose bagpipe shall the sweetest tune resound,   410
Whose heels, though clogg'd with sack, shall jump it well,
  Whose ass shall foot with fleetest hoof the ground,
He who from all the rest shall bear the bell,
  With victory in every trial crown'd,
He (mark it, lads!) to MAGGIE LAUDER's house   415
That self-same night shall go, and take her for his spouse.

LIII.

Here ceas'd the criers of the sturdy lungs,
  But here the gossip Fame, (whose body's pores
Are nought but open ears and babbling tongues
  That gape and wriggle on her hide in scores),   420
Began to jabber o'er each city's throngs,
  Blaz'ning the news through all the Scottish shores;
Nor had she blabb'd, methinks, so stoutly, since
Queen Dido's peace was broke by Troy's love-truant prince.

LIV.

In every Lowland vale and Highland glen,   425
  She nois'd th' approaching fun of ANSTER FAIR;
Ev'n when in sleep were laid the sons of men,
  Snoring away on good chaff beds their care,
You might have heard her faintly murm'ring then,
  For lack of audience, to the midnight air,   430
That from Fife's East Nook up to farthest Stornoway,
Fair MAGGIE's loud report most rapidly was born away.

LV.

And soon the mortals, that design to strive
  By meritorious jumping for the prize,
Train up their bodies, ere the day arrive,   435
  To th' lumpish sack-encumber'd exercise;
You might have seen no less than four or five
  Hobbling in each town-loan in awkward guise;
E'en little boys, when from the school let out,
Mimick'd the bigger beaux, and leap'd in pokes about.   440

LVI.

Through cots and granges with industrious foot,
  By laird and knight were light-heel'd asses sought,
So that no ass of any great repute,
  For twenty Scots marks could have then been bought;
Nor e'er before or since the long-ear'd brute,   445
  Was such a goodly acquisition thought.
The pipers vex'd their ears and pipes, t'invent
Some tune that might the taste of ANSTER MAG content.

LVII.

Each poet, too, whose lore-manured brain
  Is hot of soil, and sprouts up mushroom wit,   450
Ponder'd his noddle into extreme pain
  T' *excogitate* some story nice and fit;
When rack'd had been his scull some hours in vain,
  He, to relax his mind a little bit,
Plung'd deep into a sack his precious body,   455
And school'd it for the race and hopp'd around his study.

LVIII.

Such was the sore preparatory care
  Of all th'ambitious that for April sigh;
Nor sigh the young alone for ANSTER FAIR:
  Old men and wives, erewhile content to die,   460
Who hardly can forsake their easy chair
  To take, abroad, farewell of sun and sky,
With new desire of life now glowing, pray
That they may just o'erlive our famous market-day.

NOTE.

1 Tangle-tassel'd, hung round with tangle (sea-weed) as with tassels. I observe
tangle in Bailey's Dictionary, though not in Johnson's.

ANSTER FAIR

Canto II

ARGUMENT

Approach of Spring described. Arrival of vessels from Holland and France, with commodities for Anster Market. Great crowding of people to the loan as the day of the Fair approaches. They come from St Andrews – Crail – Kingsbarns – Pittenweem – St Monance, and neighbourhood – Dysart – Pathhead – Kirkcaldy – Leslie – Dunfermline – Kinross – Cupar – Dundee – from Nairnshire – Banffshire – Sutherlandshire – from the Western Isles – from Ayr – Glasgow – from the Border – Rob the Ranter proceeds from this quarter, not, as is vulgarly supposed, a strolling piper, but a Border Laird – They sail down from Edinburgh in pleasure boats – from Dunbar in Fisherboats – Many skiffs arrive from Denmark and Norway. Among the number of visitants is King James the Fifth, who, with his Court, comes from Holyroodhouse to enjoy the merriment of the Fair. Having landed at the East-pier, he goes, attended by his Nobility and the Fife Lairds, to Anster-house. Feast and revelry there. Tumultuous joy and diversion through the town and loan. Tents up-rearing; bagpipes playing; fiddling, gaming, and serenading.

I.

Last night I dream'd that to my dark bedside
  Came, white with rays, the poet of the "Quhair",
And drew my curtain silently aside,
  And stood and smil'd, majestically fair;
He, to my finger, then a ring apply'd,   5
  (It glitter'd like Aurora's yellow hair)
And gave his royal head a pleasant wag,
And said, Go on, my boy, and celebrate thy MAG!

II.

The sun, upcharioting from Capricorn,
  Had 'tween the Ram's horns thrust his gilded nose;   10
And now his bright fist drops, each April morn,
  O'er hill and dale the daisy and the rose;
Wantons the lewd Earth with the god unshorn,
  And from her womb the infant verdure throws,
Whilst he, good paramour! leaves Tithys' valley,   15
Each morn by five o'clock, with her to sport and dally.

III.

Old Kelly-law, the kindly nurse of sheep,
  Puts on her daisy-tissued gown of green;
On all her slopes so verdurous and steep,
  The bleating children of the flock are seen,   20
While with a heart where mirth and pleasure keep
  Their dwelling, and with honest brow serene,
The shepherd eyes his flock in mood of glee,
And wakes with oaten pipe the echoes of Carnbee.

IV.

And see how Airdrie woods upshoot on high   25
  Their leafy living glories to the day,
As if they long'd t' embrace the vaulty sky
  With their long branchy arms so green and gay;
Balcarras-craig, so rough and hard and dry,
  Enliven'd into beauty by the ray,   30
Heaves up, bedeck'd with flow'rs, his ruffian-side,
Like giant hung with gawds, and boasts his tricksy pride.

V.

Ev'n on the King's-muir jigs the jolly Spring,
  Scattering from whin to whin the new perfume;
While, near the sea-coast, Flora tarrying   35
  Touches the garden's parterres into bloom;
With joy the villages and cities ring;
  Cowherd and cow rejoice, and horse and groom;
The ploughman laughs amid his joyous care,
And ANSTER burghers laugh in prospect of their fair.   40

17

VI.

For lo! now peeping just above the vast
    Vault of the German Sea in east afar,
Appears full many a brig's and schooner's mast,
    Their topsails strutting with the vernal harr;[1]
Near and more near they come, and show at last   45
    Their ocean-thumping hulks all black with tar;
Their stems are pointed toward ANSTER pier,
While, flying o'er their sterns, the well-known flags appear.

VII.

From clear-sky'd France and muddy Zuyder-zee,
    They come, replenish'd with the stores of trade;   50
Some from the Hollander of lumpish knee
    Convey his lintseed, stow'd in bag or cade;
Heav'n bless him! may his breeches countless be;
    And warm and thick, and ever undecay'd!
For he it was that first supply'd the Scots   55
With linen for their sarks and stout frieze for their coats.

VIII.

Some bring, in many an anker hooped strong,
    From Flushing's port the palate-biting gin,
Th' inspirer of the tavern's noisy song,
    The top-delight, the nectar of each inn,   60
That sends a-bounding through the veins along
    The loit'ring blood when frosty days begin,
The bev'rage wherein fiddlers like to nuzzle,
The gauger's joy to *seize*, and old wife's joy to guzzle!

IX.

Some from Garonne and bonny banks of Seine,   65
    Transport in pipes the blood of Bacchus' berry,
Wherewith our lairds may fume the fuddled brain,
    And grow, with bousing, boisterously merry;
And whereby, too, their cheeks a glow may gain,
    Abashing ev'n the red of July's cherry;   70
O, it is right; our lairds do well, I ween;
A bottle of black wine is worth all Hippocrene!

X.

Soon, hurry'd forward by the skittish gales,
    In ANSTER harbour every vessel moors;
Furl'd by the seamen are the flapping sails;   75
    Fix'd are the halsers to the folk-clad shores;
Their holds discharge the wealth of Gallia's vales,
    And Amsterdam's and Flushing's useful stores,
All to augment, with commerce' various ware,
The bustle and the trade of famous ANSTER Fair.   80

XI.

Nor distant now the day; the cream-fac'd sun,[2]
    That, rising, shall engild to-morrow's air,
Shall shine with courteous beams upon the fun
    And frolic of the celebrated fair;
And, now, already, have the folk begun,   85
    (So eager are they the delight to share)
In flocks to MAGGIE's borough to resort,
That they may all, betimes, be present at the sport.

XII.

Each hedge-lin'd high-way of the king, that leads
    Or straightly or obliquely to the loan,   90
Seems, as the muse looks downwards, pav'd with heads,
    And hats and cowls of those that bustle on;
From Johnny Groat's house to the border-meads,
    From isle of Arran to the mouth of Don,
In thousands puffingly to Fife they run,   95
Gold in their pockets lodg'd, and in their noddles fun.

XIII.

Say, Muse, who first, who last, on foot or steed
    Came candidates for MAGGIE to her town?
St Andrews' sprightly students first proceed
    Clad in their foppery of sleeveless gown;   100
Forth whistling from Salvador's gate they speed
    Full many a mettlesome and fiery lown,
Forgetting Horace for a while and Tully,
And mad t'embag their limbs and leap it beautifully.

XIV.

For ev'n in Learning's cobweb'd halls had rung   105
    The loud report of MAGGIE LAUDER's fame,
And Pedantry's greek-conning clumsy tongue
    In songs had wagg'd, in honour of her name;
Up from their mouldy books and tasks had sprung
    Bigent and Magistrand to try the game;   110
Prelections ceas'd; old Alma Mater slept,
And o'er his silent rooms the ghost of Wardlaw wept.

XV.

So down in troops the red-clad students come
    As kittens blithe, a joke-exchanging crew,
And in their heads bear learned Greece and Rome,   115
    And haply Cyprus in their bodies too;
Some on their journey pipe and play; and some
    Talk long of MAG, how fair she was to view,
And as they talk (ay me! so much the sadder)
Backwards they scale the steps of honest Plato's ladder.[3]   120

XVI.

Others, their heels of weariness to cheat,
  Repeated tales of classic merriment,
How the fool Faunus, on his noiseless feet,
  At midnight to the cave of Tmolus went,
Scorch'd as he was with Venus' fiercest heat,   125
  On cuckold-making mischievous intent,
Till from the horny fist of hairy Hercules,
He got upon the cheek a most confounded jerk, alas!

XVII.

Nor only come the students down; in gig
  Or chaise, their sage professors lolling ride,   130
Their heads with curl'd vastidity of wig
  Thatch'd round and round, and queerly beautify'd;
In silken hose is sheath'd each learned leg;
  White are their cravats, long and trimly ty'd:
Some say they came to jump for MAGGIE too,   135
But college-records say they came the sport to view.

XVIII.

See, as their coachwheels scour the Eastburn-lane
  Rattling as if the pavement up to tear,
How men and women, huddling in their train,
  And hallooing shouts of loud applause appear;   140
Red-cheek'd, and white-cheek'd, stout and silly men
  With staff or staff-less, draw to ANSTER near;
And such a mob come trampling o'er King's-muir,
They raise a cloud of dust that does the sun obscure.

XVIIIa.

Next from Deninos, every house and hut,   145
  Her simple guileless people hie away;
That day the doors of parish-school were shut,
  And every scholar got his leave to play;
Down rush they light of heart and light of foot,
  Big plowmen, in their coats of hodden gray,   150
Weavers despising now both web and treadle,
Collier and collier's wife, and minister and beadle.

XIX.

Next, from the well-air'd ancient town of Crail,
  Go out her craftsmen with tumultuous din,
Her wind-bleach'd fishers, sturdy-limb'd and hale,   155
  Her in-kneed taylors, garrulous and thin;
And some are flush'd with horns of pithy ale,
  And some are fierce with drams of smuggled gin,
While, to augment his drowth, each to his jaws
A good Crail'scapon4 holds, at which he rugs and gnaws 160

20

XX.

And from Kingsbarns and hamlet⁵ clep'd of boars
  And farms around (their names too long to add)
Sally the villagers and hinds in scores,
  Tenant and laird, and hedger, hodden-clad:
Bolted are all the East-nook houses' doors;   165
  Ev'n toothless wives pass westward, tott'ring glad,
Propping their trem'lous limbs on oaken stay,
And in their red plaids drest as if 'twere Sabbath day.

XXI.

And bare-foot lasses, on whose ruddy face
  Unfurl'd is health's rejoicing banner ᵤeen,   170
Trick'd in their Sunday mutches edg'd with lace,
  Tippets of white, and frocks of red and green,
Come tripping o'er the roads with jocund pace,
  Gay as May-morning, tidy, gim, and clean,
Whilst, joggling at each wench's side, her joe   175
Crack's many a rustic joke, his pow'r of wit to show.

XXII.

Then jostling forward on the western road,
  Approach the folk of wind-swept Pittenweem,
So num'rous that the highways, long and broad,
  One waving field of gowns and coat-tails seem;   180
The fat man puffing goes, oppress'd with load
  Of cumb'rous flesh and corpulence extreme;
The lean man bounds along, and with his toes
Smites on the fat man's heels, that slow before him goes.

XXIII.

St Monance, Elie, and adjacent farms,   185
  Turn their mechanics, fishers, farmers out;
Sun-burnt and shoeless schoolboys rush in swarms,
  With childish trick, and revelry and shout;
Mothers bear little children in their arms,
  Attended by their giggling daughters stout;   190
Clowns, cobblers, cotters, tanners, weavers, beaux,
Hurry and hop along in clusters and in rows.

XXIV.

And every husbandman, round Largo-law,
  Hath scrap'd his huge-wheel'd dung-cart fair and clean,
Wherein, on sacks stuff'd full of oaten straw,   195
  Sits the Goodwife, Tam, Katey, Jock, and Jean;
In flow'rs and ribbands drest the horses draw
  Stoutly their creaking cumbersome machine,
As, on his cart-head, sits the Goodman proud,
And cheerily cracks his whip, and whistles clear and loud.   200

21

XXV.

Then from her coal-pits Dysart vomits forth
　Her subterranean men of colour dun,
Poor human mouldwarps, doom'd to scrape in earth,
　Cimmerian people, strangers to the sun;
Gloomy as soot, with faces grim and swarth,　　　　　　　　205
　They march, most sourly leering every one,
Yet very keen, at Anster loan, to share
The merriments and sports to be accomplish'd there.

XXVI.

Nor did Path-head detain her wrangling race
　Of weavers, toiling at their looms for bread;　　　　　　210
For now their slippery shuttles rest a space
　From flying through their labyrinths of thread;
Their treadle-shaking feet now scour apace
　Through Gallow town with levity of tread;
So on they pass, with sack in hand, full bent　　　　　　215
To try their sinews' strength in dire experiment.

XXVII.

And long Kirkcaldy from each dirty street,
　Her num'rous population eastward throws,
Her roguish boys with bare unstocking'd feet,
　Her rich ship-owners, gen'rous and jocose,　　　　　　220
Her prosp'rous merchants, sober and discreet,
　Her coxcombs pantaloon'd and powder'd beaux,
Her pretty lasses tripping on their great toes,
With foreheads white as milk, or any boil'd potatoes.

XXVIII.

And from Kinghorn jump hastily along　　　　　　　　225
　Her ferrymen and poor inhabitants: –
And th' upland[6] hamlet, where, as told in song,
　Tam Lutar play'd of yore his lively rants,
Is left dispeopled of her brose-fed throng,
　For eastward scud they now as thick as ants;　　　　230
Dunfermline, too, so fam'd for checks and ticks,
Sends out her loom-bred men, with bags and walking-sticks.

XXIX.

And market-maids, and apron'd wives, that bring
　Their gingerbread in baskets to the FAIR,
And cadgers with their creels, that hang by string　　　235
　From their lean horse-ribs rubbing off the hair,
And crook-legg'd cripples, that on crutches swing
　Their shabby persons with a noble air,
And fiddlers with their fiddles in their cases,
And packmen with their packs of ribbons, gauze, and laces.　　240

XXX.

And from Kinross, whose dusty streets unpav'd
   Are whirl'd through heav'n on summer's windy day,
Whose plats of cabbage-bearing ground are lav'd
   By Leven's waves, that clear as crystal play,
Jog her brisk burghers, spruce and cleanly shav'd,   245
   Her sullen cutlers and her weavers gay,
Her ploughboys in their botch'd and clumsy jackets,
Her clowns with cobbled shoon stuck full of iron tackets.

XXXI.

Next ride on sleek-man'd horses bay or brown,
   Smacking their whips and spurring bloodily,   250
The writers of industrious Cupar town,
   Good social mortals skill'd the pen to ply;
Lo! how their garments as they gallop down,
   Waving behind them in the breezes fly;
As upward spurn'd to heav'n's blue bending roof,   255
Dash'd is the dusty road from every bounding hoof.

XXXII.

And clerks with ruffled shirts and frizzled hairs,
   Their tassel'd half-boots clear as looking-glass,
And Sheriffs learn'd, and unlearn'd Sheriff-mairs,
   And messengers-at-arms, (a fearful class!)   260
Come strutting down, or single or in pairs,
   Some on high horse and some on lowly ass;
With blacksmiths, barbers, butchers, and their brats,
And some had new hats on, and some came wanting hats.

XXXIII.

Astraddle on their proud steeds full of fire,   265
   From all the tree-girt country-seats around,
Comes many a huffy, many a kindly squire,
   In showy garb worth many a silver pound;
While close behind, in livery's base attire,
   Follows poor lackey with small-bellied hound,   270
Carrying, upon his shoulders slung, the bag
Wherein his master means to risk his neck for MAG.

XXXIV.

From all her lanes and alleys fair Dundee
   Has sent her happy citizens away;
They come with mickle jolliment and glee,   275
   Crossing in clumsy boat their shallow Tay;
Their heads are bonneted most fair to see,
   And of the tartan is their back's array:
From Perth, Dunkel, from Brechin, Forfar, Glams,
Roll down the sweaty crowds with wearied legs and hams.   280

XXXV.

And from the Mearn-shire, and from Aberdeen,
  Where knit by many a wench is many a stocking,
From Banff and Murray, where of old were seen
  The witches by the chief so fain to go king,
Descend in neckless coats brush'd smooth and clean,   285
  And eke with long pipes in their mouths a-smoking,
The northern people, boisterous and rough,
Bearing both chin and nose bedaub'd with spilth of snuff.

XXXVI.

Comes next from Ross-shire and from Sutherland
  The horny-knuckled kilted Highlandman: 290
From where upon the rocky Caithness strand
  Breaks the long wave that at the pole began,
And where Lochfyne from her prolific sand
  Her herrings gives to feed each bord'ring clan,
Arrive the brogue-shod men of gen'rous eye,   295
Plaided, and breechless all, with Esau's hairy thigh.

XXXVII.

They come not now to fire the Lowland stacks
  Or foray on the banks of Fortha's firth;
Claymore, and broad-sword, and Lochaber-ax,
  Are left to rust above the smoky hearth;   300
Their only arms are bagpipes now and sacks;
  Their teeth are set most desp'rately for mirth;
And, at their broad and sturdy backs, are hung
Great wallets cramm'd with cheese and bannocks, and cold tongue.

XXXVIII.

Nor staid away the islanders, that lie   305
  To buffet of th' Atlantic surge expos'd;
From Jura, Arran, Barra, Uist, and Skye,
  Piping they come, unshav'd, unbreech'd, unhos'd;
And from that isle, whose abbey, structur'd high,
  Within its precincts holds dead kings enclos'd,   310
Where St Columba oft is seen to waddle
Gown'd round with flaming fire upon the spire astraddle.

XXXIX.

Next from the far-fam'd ancient town of Ayr,
  (Sweet Ayr! with crops of ruddy damsels blest,
That, shooting up, and waxing fat and fair,   315
  Shine on thy braes, the lilies of the west;)
And from Dumfries, and from Kilmarnock (where
  Are night-caps made, the cheapest and the best,)
Blithely they ride on ass and mule, with sacks
In lieu of saddles plac'd upon their asses' backs.   320

Close at their heels, bestriding well-trapp'd nag,
    Or humbly riding asses' backbone bare,
Come Glasgow's merchants, each with money-bag,
    To purchase Dutch lintseed at ANSTER FAIR;
Sagacious fellows all, who well may brag   325
    Of virtuous industry and talents rare,
Th' accomplish'd men o' the counting-room confest,
And fit to crack a joke, or argue with the best.

Nor keep their homes the borderers that stay,
    Where purls the Jed, and Esk, and little Liddel,   330
Men, that can rarely on the bagpipe play,
    And wake th' unsober spirit of the fiddle;
Avow'd free-booters that have many a day
    Stol'n sheep and cow, yet never own'd they did ill;
Great rogues, for sure that wight is but a rogue,   335
That blots the eighth command from Moses' decalogue.

And some of them in sloop of tarry side
    Come from North-Berwick harbour sailing out;
Others, abhorent of the sick'ning tide,
    Have ta'en the road by Stirling brig about,   340
And eastward now from long Kirkcaldy ride,
    Slugging on their slow-gaited asses stout,
While, dangling, at their backs are bagpipes hung,
And, dangling, hangs a tale on ev'ry rhimer's tongue.

Amid them rides, on lofty ass sublime,   345
    With cadger-like sobriety of canter,
In purple lustihood of youthful prime,
    Great in his future glory, ROB the RANTER;
(I give the man what name in little time
    He shall acquire from pipe and drone and chanter;)   350
He comes apparell'd like a trim bridegroom,
Fiery and flush'd with hope, and like a god in bloom.

No paltry vagrant piper-carle is he,
    Whose base-brib'd drone whiffs out it's wind for hire,
Who, having stroll'd all day for penny fee,   355
    Couches at night with oxen in the byre;
ROB is a border laird of good degree,
    A many-acred, clever, jolly squire,
One born and shap'd to shine and make a figure,
And bless'd with supple limbs to jump with wondrous vigour.   360

XLV.

His waggish face, that speaks a soul jocose,
   Seems t' have been cast i' the mould of fun and glee,
And on the bridge of his well-arched nose
   Sits Laughter plum'd, and white-wing'd Jollity;
His manly chest a breadth heroic shows;   365
   Bold is his gesture, dignified and free;
Ev'n as he smites with lash his ass's hip,
'Tis with a seemly grace he whirls his glitt'ring whip.

XLVI.

His coat is of the flashy Lincoln green,
   With silver buttons of the prettiest mould;   370
Each buttonhole and skirt and hem is seen
   Sparkishly edg'd with lace of yellow gold;
His breeches of the velvet smooth and clean,
   Are very fair and goodly to behold;
So on he rides, and let him e'en ride on,   375
We shall again meet ROB, to-morrow at the loan;

XLVII.

But mark his ass ere off he ride; – some say,
   He got him from a pilgrim lady fair,
Who, landing once on Joppa's wave-worn quay,
   Had bought him of Armenian merchant there,   380
And prest his padded pack, and rode away
   To snuff devotion in with Syria's air;
Then brought him home in hold of stout Levanter,[7]
All for the great good luck of honest ROB the RANTER.

XLVIII.

Along Fife's western roads, behold, how hie   385
   The travel-sweltry crowds to ANSTER loan,
Shaded, o'erhead, with clouds of dust that fly
   Tarnishing heav'n with darkness not its own;
And scarcely can the Muse's lynx-sharp eye
   Scan, through the dusty nuisance upward blown,   390
The ruddy plaids, black hats, and bonnets blue,
Of those that rush below, a motley-vestur'd crew!

XLIX.

Nor only was the land with crowds opprest,
   That trample forward to th' expected fair;
The harass'd ocean had no peace or rest,   395
   So many keels her barmy bosom tear;
For, into view, now sailing from the west,
   With streamers idling in the bluish air,
Appear the painted pleasure-boats unleaky,
Charg'd with a precious freight, the good folk of Auld Reekie.   400

L.

They come, the cream and flow'r of all the Scots,
    The children of politeness, science, wit,
Exulting in their bench'd and gaudy boats,
    Wherein some joking and some puking sit;
Proudly the pageantry of carvels floats,   405
    As if the salt sea frisk'd to carry it;
The gales vie emulous their sails to wag,
And dally as in love with each long gilded flag.

LI.

Upon the benches seated, I descry
    Her gentry; knights, and lairds, and long-nail'd fops;   410
Her advocates and signet-writers sly;
    Her gen'rous merchants, faithful to their shops;
Her lean-cheek'd tetchy critics, who, O fy!
    Hard-retching, spue upon the sails and ropes;
Her lovely ladies, with their lips like rubies;   415
Her fiddlers, fuddlers, fools, bards, blockheads, blackguards, boobies.

LII.

And red-prow'd fisher-boats afar are spy'd
    In south-east, tilting o'er the jasper main,
Whose wing-like oars, dispread on either side,
    Now swoop on sea, now rise in sky again;   420
They come not now, with herring-nets supply'd,
    Or barbed lines to twitch the haddock train,
But with the townsfolk of Dunbar are laden,
Who burn to see the FAIR, man, stripling, wife and maiden.

LVIII.

And many a Dane, with ringlets long and red,   425
    And many a starv'd Norwegian, lank and brown,
(For over seas the fame of MAG had spread
    Afar from Scandinavian town to town,)
Maugre the risk of drowning, and the dread
    Of *krakens*, isles of flesh of droll renown,   430
Have dar'd to cross the ocean, and now steer
Their long outlandish skiffs direct on ANSTER pier.

LIV.

Forward they scud; and soon each pleasure-barge,
    And fisher-boats, and skiffs so slim and lax,
On shore their various passengers discharge,   435
    Some hungry, queasy some and white as flax;
Lightly they bound upon the beach's verge,
    Glad to unbend their stiffen'd houghs and backs;
But who is that, O Muse, with lofty brow
That from his lacker'd boat is just forth-stepping now?   440

LV.

Thou fool! (for I have ne'er since Bavius' days
  Had such a dolt to dictate to as thou)
Dost thou not know, by that eye's kingly rays,
  And by the arch of that celestial brow,
And by the grace his ev'ry step displays,   445
  And by the crowds that round him duck and bow,
That that is good king James, the merriest Monarch
That ever sceptre sway'd since Noah steer'd his own ark?

LVI.

For, as he in his house of Holyrood,
  Of late was keeping jovially his court,   450
The gipsey Fame beside his window stood,
  And hollow'd in his ear fair MAG's report;
The Monarch laugh'd, for to his gamesome mood
  Accorded well th' anticipated sport;
So here he comes with lord and lady near,   455
Stepping with regal stride up ANSTER's eastern pier.

LVII.

But mark you, boy, how in a loyal ring
  (As does obedient subjects well become)
Fife's hospitable lairds salute their king,
  And kiss his little finger or his thumb;   460
That done, their liege lord they escorting bring
  To ANSTER House,⁸ that he may eat a crumb;
Where in the stucco'd hall they sit and dine,
And into tenfold joy bedrench their blood with wine.

LVIII.

Some with the ladies in the chambers ply   465
  Their bounding elasticity of heel,
Evolving, as they trip it whirlingly,
  The merry mazes of th' implicit reel;
'Tween roof and floor, they fling, they flirt, they fly,
  Their garments swimming round them as they wheel;   470
The rafters creak beneath the dance's clatter;
Tremble the solid walls with feet that shake and patter.

LIX.

Some (wiser they,) resolv'd on drinking-bout,
  The wines of good Sir John englut amain;
Their glasses soon are fill'd and soon drunk out,   475
  And soon are bumper'd to the brim again;
Certes, that laird is but a foolish lout,
  That does not fuddle now with might and main,
For gen'rous is their host, and, by my sooth,
Was never better wine apply'd to Scottish mouth.   480

28

With might and main they fuddle and carouse;
  Each glass augments their thirst, and keens their wit;
They swill, they swig, they take a hearty rouse,
  Cheering their flesh with Bacchus' benefit,
Till, by and bye, the windows of the house   485
  Go dizzily whirling round them where they sit;
And had you seen the sport, and heard the laughing,
You'd thought that all Jove's gods in ANSTER House sat quaffing.

Not such a wassail, fam'd for social glee,
  In Shushan's gardens long ago was held,   490
When Ahasuerus, by a blithe decree,
  His turban'd satraps to the bouse compell'd,
And bagg'd their Persian paunches with a sea
  Of wine, that from his carved gold they swill'd,
Whilst overhead was stretch'd (a gorgeous show)   495
Blue blankets, silver-starr'd, a heav'n of callico!

Nor less is the disport and joy without,
  In ANSTER town and loan, through all the throng;
'Tis but one vast tumultuous jovial rout,
  Tumult of laughing and of gabbling strong;   500
Thousands and tens of thousands reel about,
  With joyous uproar blustering along;
Elbows push boringly on sides with pain,
Wives hustling come on wives, and men come slap on men.

There lacks no sport: tumblers, in wondrous pranks,   505
  High-stag'd, display their limbs' agility,
And now, they, mountant from the scaffold's planks,
  Kick with their whirling heels the clouds on high,
And now like cat, upon their dextrous shanks,
  They light, and of new monsters cheat the sky;   510
Whilst motley Merry-Andrew, with his jokes,
Wide through th' incorp'rate mob the bursting laugh provokes.

Others upon the green, in open air,
  Enact the best of Davie Lindsay's plays;
While ballad-singing women do not spare   515
  Their throats to give good utt'rance to their lays,
And many a leather-lung'd co-chanting pair
  Of wood-legg'd sailors, children's laugh and gaze,
Lift to the courts of Jove their voices loud,
Y-hymning their mishaps to please the heedless crowd.   520

29

LXV.

Meanwhile the sun, fatigued, (as well he may,)
  With shining on a night till seven o'clock,
Beams on each chimney-head a farewell ray,
  Illuming into golden shaft its smoke,
And now in sea, far west from Oronsay, 525
  Is dipp'd his chariot-wheel's refulgent spoke,
And now a section of his face appears,
And, diving, now he ducks clean down o'er head and ears.

LXVI.

Anon uprises, with blithe bagpipe's sound,
  And shriller din of flying fiddlestick, 530
On the green loan and meadow-crofts around,
  A town of tents, with blankets roofed quick;
A thousand stakes are rooted in the ground;
  A thousand hammers clank and clatter thick;
A thousand fiddles squeak and squeal it yare; 535
A thousand stormy drones out-gasp in groans their air.

LXVII.

And such a turbulence of gen'ral mirth
  Rises from ANSTER loan upon the sky,
That from his throne Jove starts, and down on earth,
  Looks, wond'ring what may be the jollity; 540
He roots his eye on shores of Forthan firth,
  And smerks, as knowing well the market nigh,
And bids his gods and goddesses look down,
To mark the rage of joy that maddens ANSTER town.

LXVIII.

From Cellardyke to wind-swept Pittenweem, 545
  And from Balhouffie to Kilrennymill,
Vaulted with blankets crofts and meadows seem,
  So many tents the grassy spaces fill;
Meantime the moon, yet leaning on the stream,
  With fluid silver bathes the welkin chill, 550
That now Earth's half-ball, on the side of night,
Swims in an argent sea of beautiful moonlight.

LXIX.

Then to his bed full many a man retires,
  On plume, or chaff, or straw, to get a nap,
In houses, tents, in haylofts, stables, byres, 555
  And or without, or with, a warm night-cap;
Yet sleep not all; for by the social fires
  Sit many, cuddling round their toddy-sap,
And ever and anon they eat a lunch,
And rinse the mouthfuls down with flav'rous whisky punch. 560

LXX.

Some, shuffling paper nothings, keenly read
  The Devil's maxims in his painted books,
Till the old serpent in each heart and head
  Spits canker, and with wormwood sours their looks:
Some o'er the chess-board's chequer'd champain lead   565
  Their inch-tall bishops, kings and queens, and rooks;
Some force, t' inclose the Tod, the wooden Lamb on;
Some shake the pelting dice upon the broad backgammon.

LXXI.

Others of travell'd elegance polite
  With mingling music MAGGIE's house surround,   570
And serenade her all the live-long night,
  With song and lyre, and flutes' inchanting sound,
Chiming and hymning into fond delight
  The heavy night-air that o'ershades the ground;
While she, right pensive, in her chamber-nook   575
Sits pond'ring on th' advice of little Tommy Puck.

NOTES

1 The harr is the name given by the fishermen to that gentle breeze, which generally blows from the east in a fine spring or summer afternoon.

2 Anster Lintseed Market (as it is called) is on the 11th of April, or on one of the six days immediately succeeding.

3 The Student wishing to understand this Ladder may consult Plato. Conviv. tom. iii. page 211. of Serrani's Edit.

4 A Crails capon is a dried haddoc.

5 Boarhills.

6 Leslie.

7 Ship trading to and from the Levant, so called by seamen.

8 Anster House was demolished in 1811.

ANSTER FAIR

CANTO III

ARGUMENT

The morning of Anster Fair rises beautifully. The crowd, awakened by the ringing of all the bells of the neighbourhood, rush out to the loan, the scene of their amusements; whither, also, rides forth Maggie Lauder attended by the king and his nobility. The beauty of her person described. She and the monarch sit down upon a little hillock or knoll on the southern extremity of the loan. After several very loud congratulations from the mob, the king's herald commands the competitors intending to venture in the ass-race to step forward, and at the same time promises, in the king's name, to the conqueror two hundred acres of land to go along with the fair prize. The suitors appear, with their asses, in great numbers, among whom is Rob the Ranter. After a short address from the king, the Race signal is given, and they start off with great impetuosity. They are all, however, soon outstripped by the Ranter, whose ass, having turned the northern limit of the race, overthrows in his southern course his sluggish brethren that meet and oppose him. Their riders are thrown off in great confusion, and retreat, covered with shame and the slime of rotten eggs hurled at them by the rabble. Rob gains the starting-line and is saluted victor.

I.

I wish I had a cottage snug and neat
    Upon the top of many-fountain'd Ide,
That I might thence in holy fervour greet
    The bright-gown'd Morning tripping up her side;
And when the low Sun's glory-buskin'd feet   5
    Walk on the blue wave of th' Aegean tide,
O, I would kneel me down, and worship there
The God who garnish'd out a world so bright and fair!

II.

The saffron-elbow'd Morning up the slope
    Of heav'n canaries in her jewell'd shoes,   10
And throws o'er Kelly-law's sheep-nibbled top
    Her golden apron dripping kindly dews,
And never, since she first began to hop
    Up Heav'n's blue causeway, of her beams profuse,
Shone there a dawn so glorious and so gay,   15
As shines the merry dawn of ANSTER Market-day.

III.

Round through the vast circumference of sky
    One speck of small cloud cannot eye behold,
Save in the East some fleeces bright of die,
    That stripe the hem of heav'n with woolly gold,   20
Whereon are happy angels wont to lie
    Lolling, in amaranthine flow'rs enroll'd,
That they may spy the precious light of God
Flung from the blessed East o'er the fair Earth abroad.

IV.

The fair Earth laughs through all her boundless range,   25
    Heaving her green hills high to greet the beam;
City and village, steeple, cot and grange,
    Gilt as with Nature's purest leaf-gold seem;
The heaths and upland muirs, and fallows, change
    Their barren brown into a ruddy gleam,   30
And, on ten thousand dew-bent leaves and sprays,
Twinkle ten thousand suns and fling their petty rays.

V.

Up from their nests and fields of tender corn
    Right merrily the little sky-larks spring,
And on their dew-bedabbled pinions born,   35
    Mount to the heav'n's blue key-stone flickering;
They turn their plume-soft bosoms to the morn,
    And hail the genial light and cheerly sing;
Echo the gladsome hills and valleys round,
As half the bells of Fife ring loud and swell the sound.   40

VI.

For, when the first up-sloping ray was flung
  On ANSTER steeple's swallow-harb'ring top,
It's bell and all the bells around were rung
  Sonorous, jangling loud without a stop,
For toilingly each bitter beadle swung,   45
  Ev'n till he smok'd with sweat, his greasy rope,
And almost broke his bell-wheel, ush'ring in
The morn of ANSTER FAIR with tinkle-tankling din.

VII.

And, from our steeple's pinnacle out-spread,
  The town's long colours flare and flap on high,   50
Whose anchor, blazon'd fair in green and red,
  Curls pliant to each breeze that whistles by;
Whilst, on the boltsprit, stern, and topmast-head
  Of brig and sloop that in the harbour lie,
Streams the red gaudery of flags in air,   55
All to salute and grace the morn of ANSTER FAIR.

VIII.

Forthwith from house and cellar, tent and byre,
  Rous'd by the clink of bells that jingle on,
Uncabin'd, rush the multitude like fire,
  Furious and squeezing forward to the loan;[1]   60
The son, impatient, leaves his snail-slow sire;
  The daughter leaves her mam to trot alone;
So madly leap they, man, wife, girl, and boy,
As if the senseless earth they kick'd for very joy.

IX.

And such the noise of feet that trampling pass,   65
  And tongues that roar and rap from jaw to jaw,
As if ten thousand chariots, wheel'd with brass,
  Came hurling down the sides of Largo-law;
And such the number of the people was,
  As when in day of Autumn, chill and raw,   70
His small clouds Eurus sends, a vap'ry train,
Streaming in scatter'd rack, exhaustless, from the main.

X.

For who like arrant slugs can keep their heads
  In contact with their pillows now unstirr'd?
Grandfathers leave their all-year-rumpled beds,   75
  With moth-eat breeches now their loins to gird,
And, drawn abroad on tumbrils and on sleds,
  Chat off their years and sing like vernal bird;
Men, whom cold agues into leanness freeze,
Imblanketed walk out, and snuff the kindly breeze.   80

XI.

And flea-bit wives, on whose old arms and cheeks
  The spoiler Time hath driv'n his furrowing plough,
Whose cold dry bones have all the winter weeks
  Hung, shiv'ring o'er their chimney's peat-fed glow,
Now warm and flexible and lithe as leeks,   85
  Wabbingly walk to see the joyous show;
What wonder? when each brick and pavement-stone
Wish'd it had feet that day to walk to ANSTER Loan.

XII.

Upon a little dappled nag, whose mane
  Seem'd to have robb'd the steeds of Phaeton,   90
Whose bit and pad, and fairly-fashion'd rein,
  With silvery adornments richly shone,
Came MAGGIE LAUDER forth, enwheel'd with train
  Of knights and lairds around her trotting on;
At James' right hand she rode, a beauteous bride,   95
That well deserv'd to go by haughtest Monarch's side.

XIII.

Her form was as the Morning's blithesome star
  That, capp'd with lustrous coronet of beams,
Rides up the dawning orient in her car
  New-wash'd, and doubly fulgent from the streams;   100
The Chaldee shepherd eyes her light afar,
  And on his knees adores her as she gleams:
So shone the stately form of MAGGIE LAUDER,
And so th' admiring crowds pay homage and applaud her.

XIV.

Each little step her trampling palfrey took   105
  Shak'd her majestic person into grace,
And, as at times, his glossy sides she strook
  Endearingly with whip's green silken lace,
(The prancer seem'd to court such kind rebuke
  Loit'ring with wilful tardiness of pace)   110
By Jove, the very waving of her arm
Had pow'r a brutish lout t' unbrutify and charm!

XV.

Her face was as the summer cloud, whereon
  The dawning sun delights to rest his rays;
Compar'd with it, old Sharon's vale, o'ergrown   115
  With flaunting roses had resign'd its praise;
For why? Her face with Heav'n's own roses shone,
  Mocking the morn, and witching men to gaze,
And he that gaz'd with cold unsmitten soul,
That blockhead's heart was ice thrice bak'd beneath the pole. 120

XVI.

Her locks, apparent tufts of wiry gold,
  Lay on her lily temples, fairly dangling,
And on each hair, so harmless to behold,
  A lover's soul hung mercilessly strangling;
The piping silly zephyrs vied t' infold   125
  The tresses in their arms so slim and tangling,
And thrid in sport these lover-noosing snares,
And play'd at hide-and-seek amid the golden hairs.

XVII.

Her eye was as an honour'd palace, where
  A choir of lightsome graces frisk and dance;   130
What object drew her gaze, how mean so e'er,
  Got dignity and honour from the glance;
Wo to the man on whom she unaware
  Did the dear witch'ry of her eye elance!
'Twas such a thrilling, killing, keen, regard –   135
May Heav'n from such a look preserve each tender bard.

XVIII.

Beneath it's shading tucker heav'd a breast
  Fashion'd to take with ravishment mankind,
For never did the flimsy Chian vest
  Hide such a bosom in its gauze of wind;   140
Ev'n a pure angel, looking had confest
  A sinless transport passing o'er his mind,
For, in the nicest turning-loom of Jove,
Turn'd were these charming hills t' inspire a holy love.

XIX.

So on she rode in virgin majesty,   145
  Charming the thin dead air to kiss her lips,
And with the light and grandeur of her eye
  Shaming the proud sun into dim eclipse,
While, round her presence clust'ring far and nigh,
  On horseback some, with silver spurs and whips,   150
And some afoot with shoes of dazzling buckles,
Attended knights, and lairds, and clowns with horny knuckles.

XX.

Not with such crowd surrounded nor so fair
  In form, rode forth Semiramis of old,
On chariot where she sat in iv'ry chair,   155
  Beneath a sky of carbuncle and gold,
When to Euphrates' banks to take the air,
  Or her new rising brickwalls to behold,
Abroad she drove, whilst round her wheels were pour'd
Satrap, and turban'd squire, and pursy Chaldee lord.   160

XXI.

Soon to the Loan came MAG, and from her pad
  Dismounting with a queen-like dignity,
(So from his buoyant cloud, man's heart to glad,
  Lights a bright angel on a hill-top high,)
On a small mound, with turfy greenness clad   165
  She lit, and walk'd enchantment on the eye;
Then on two chairs, that on it's top stood ready,
Down sat the good King James, and ANSTER's bonny lady.

XXII.

Their chairs were finely carv'd, and overlaid
  With the thin lustre of adorning gold,   170
And o'er their heads a canopy was spread
  Of arras, flower'd with figures manifold,
Supported by four boys, of silver made,
  Whose glittr'ing hands the vault of cloth uphold;
On each side sat or stood, to view the sport,   175
Stout lord, and lady fair, the flow'r of Scotland's court.

XXIII.

On their gilt chairs they scarce had time to sit,
  When uprose, sudden, from th' applauding mob,
A shout enough to startle hell, and split
  The roundness of the granite-ribbed globe;   180
The mews of May's steep islet, terror-smit,
  Clang'd correspondent in a shrill hubbub,
And had the moon then hung above the main,
Crack'd had that horrid shout her spotted orb in twain.

XXIV.

Thrice did their shouting make a little pause,   185
  That so their lungs might draw recruiting air,
Thrice did the stormy tumult of applause
  Shake the Fife woods and fright the foxes there;
Sky rattled, and Kilbrachmont's crows and daws,
  Alarm'd, sung hoarsely o'er their callow care: 190
O never, sure, in Fife's town-girdled shire,
Was heard, before or since, a shout so loud and dire.

XXV.

Nor ceas'd th' acclaim when ceas'd the sound of voice,
  For fiddlesticks, in myriads, bick'ring fast,
Shriek'd on their shrunken guts a twangling noise;   195
  And pipe, and drone, with whistle, and with blast,
Consorted, humm'd and shrill'd, and swell'd the joys
  With furious harmony too high to last;
And such a hum of pipe and drone was there,[2]
As if on earth men pip'd, and devils dron'd in air.   200

37

XXVI.

Thus did the crowd with fiddle, lungs and drone,
   Congratulate fair MAGGIE and their King,
Till, at the last, wide-spreading round the loan,
   They form'd of huge circumference a ring,
Inclosing green space, bare of bush and stone,   205
   Where might the asses run, and suitors spring;
Upon its southmost end, high chair'd were seen
The monarch and the dame, and overlook'd the green.

XXVII.

Anon the king's stout trumpet blew aloud,
   Silence imposing on the rabble's roar;   210
Silent as summer sky stood all the crowd;
   Each bag was strangled and could snort no more;
(So sinks the roaring of the foamy flood,
   When Neptune's clarion twangs from shore to shore,)
Then through his trump he bawl'd with such a stress,   215
One might have known his words a mile beyond Crawness.

XXVIII.

Ho! hark ye, merry mortals! hark ye, ho!
   The king now speaks, nor what he speaks is vain;
This day's amount of bus'ness well ye know,
   So what ye know I will not tell again: 220
He hopes your asses are more swift than doe;
   He hopes your sacks are strong as iron chain;
He hopes your bags and pipes are swoln and screw'd;
He hopes your rhime-cramm'd brains are in a famous mood.

XXIX.

For, verily, in ANSTER's beauteous dame   225
   Awaits the victor no despis'd reward;
Sith well she merits that the starry frame
   Should drop Apollo on that grassy sward,
That so he might by clever jumping claim
   A fairer Daphne than whom once he marr'd;   230
So fair is MAG: yet, not her charms alone,
A present from the King shall be the victor's own:

XXX.

For as a dow'r, along with MAGGIE's hand,
   The monarch shall the conqueror present
With ten score acres of the royal land,   235
   All good of soil, and of the highest rent;
Near where Dunfermline's palace-turrets stand,
   They stretch, array'd in wheat, their green extent:
With such a gift the king shall crown to-day
The gen'rous toils of him who bears the prize away.   240

38

XXXI.

And he, prize-blest, shall enter MAGGIE's door,
  Who shall in *all* the trials victor be;
Or, if there hap no victor in the *four*,
  He who shall shine and conquer in the *three*;
But, should sly fortune give to two or more,   245
  An equal chance in equal victory,
'Tis MAG's of these to choose the dearest beau; –
So bring your asses in, bring in your asses, ho!

XXXII.

Scarce from his clam'rous brass the words were blown,
  When from the globe of people issued out   250
Asses in dozens, and in scores, that shone
  In purple some, and some in plainer clout,
With many a wag astraddle plac'd thereon,
  Green-coated knight, and laird, and clumsy lout,
That one and all came burning with ambition,   255
To try their asses' speed in awkward competition.

XXXIII.

And some sat wielding silver-headed whips,
  Whisking their asses' ears with silken thong;
Some thrash'd and thwack'd their sturdy hairy hips
  With knotted cudgels ponderous and strong;   260
And some had spurs whose every rowel dips
  Amid their ribs an inch of iron long;
And some had bridles gay and bits of gold,
And some had hempen reins most shabby to behold.

XXXIV.

Amid them enter'd, on the listed space,   265
  Great ROB (the RANTER was his after name,)
With Fun's broad ensign hoisted in his face,
  And aug'ring to himself immortal fame;
And aye, upon the hillock's loftier place,
  Where sat, his destin'd spouse, the blooming dame,   270
A glance he flung, regardless of the reins,
And felt the rapid love glide tingling through his veins.

XXXV.

She, too, upon the bord'rer's manly size
  With prepossessing favour fix'd her sight,
For woman's sharp and well-observing eyes   275
  Soon single out the seemliest, stateliest wight;
And, oh! (she to herself thus silent sighs)
  Were't but the will of Puck the dapper sprite,
I could – La! what a grace of form divine –
I could, in sooth, submit to lose my name in thine!   280

Forward they rode, to where the King and MAG
　O'erlook'd, superior, from the southern mound,
When, from his brute alighting every wag
　His person hunch'd into a bow profound,
And almost kiss'd his shoes' bedusted tag,　285
　Grazing with nose most loyally the ground,
As earthward crook'd they their corporeal frames
Into obeisance due, before the gracious James.

XXXVII.

Rise, rise, my lads, the jovial monarch said,
　Here is not now the fitting place to ply　290
The courtier's and the dancing-master's trade,
　Nuzzling the nasty ground obsequiously;
Up, up – put hat and bonnet upon head –
　The chilling dew still drizzles from the sky;
Up – tuck your coats succinct around your bellies;　295
Mount, mount your asses' backs like clever vaulting fellows.

XXXVIII.

And see, that, when the race's sign is given,
　Each rider whirl his whip with swingeing might,
Or toss his whizzing cudgel up to heav'n,
　That with more goodly bang it down may light;　300
And let the spur's blood-thirsty teeth be driven
　Through hide and hair by either heel aright,
For 'tis a beast most sluggish, sour, and slow; –
Be mounting then, my hearts, and range ye in a row:

XXXIX.

And look ye northwards – note yon mastlike pole　305
　Tassel'd with ribbons and betrimm'd with clout,
Yon – mark it – is the race-ground's northern goal,
　Where you must turn your asses' heads about,
And jerk them southward, till with gladsome soul
　You reach that spot whence now you're setting out;　310
And he that reaches first, shall loud be shouted
The happy happy man – I'll say no more about it.

XL.

This said, they like the glimpse of lightning quick,
　Upvaulted on their backbones asinine,
And marshal'd, by the force of spur and stick,　315
　The long-ear'd lubbards in an even line:
Then sat, awaiting that momentous nick
　When James's herald should y-twang the sign:
Each whip was rear'd aloft in act to crack,
Each cudgel hung in sky surcharg'd with stormy thwack.　320

XLI.

Frisk'd with impatient flutter every heart
   As the brisk anxious blood began to jump;
Each human ear prick'd up its fleshiest part,
   To catch the earliest notice of the trump;
When hark! with blast that spoke the sign to start,   325
   The brass-ton'd clarion gave the air a thump,
Whoop – off they go – halloo – they shoot – they fly –
They spur – they whip – they crack – they bawl – they curse – they cry. –

XLII.

A hundred whips, high toss'd in ether, sung
   Tempestuous, flirting up and down like fire;   330
'Tween sky and earth as many cudgels swung
   Their gnarled lengths in formidable gyre,
And, hissing, from their farther ends down flung
   A storm of wooden bangs and anguish dire;
Woe to the beastly ribs, and sculls, and backs,   335
Foredoom'd to bear the weight of such unwieldy cracks!

XLIII.

Woe to the beastly bowels, doom'd alas!
   To bear the spur's sharp steely agony;
For through the sore-gall'd hides of every ass
   Squirts the vext blood in gush of scarlet die,   340
While, as they slug along the hoof-crush'd grass,
   Rises a bray so horrid and so high,
As if all Bashan's bulls, with fat o'ergrown,
Had bellow'd on the green of ANSTER's frighted loan.

XLIV.

Who can in silly pithless words paint well   345
   The pithy feats of that laborious race?
Who can the cudgellings and whippings tell,
   The hurry, emulation, joy, disgrace?
'Twould take for tongue the clapper of a bell,
   To speak the total wonders of the chace;   350
'Twould need a set of sturdy brassy lungs,
To tell the mangled whips, and shatter'd sticks and rungs.

XLV.

Each rider pushes on to be the first,
   Nor has he now an eye to look behind;
One ass trots smartly on, though like to burst   355
   With bounding blood, and scantiness of wind;
Another, by his master bann'd and curs'd,
   Goes backward through perversity of mind,
Inching along in motion retrograde,
Contrarious to the course which Scotland's monarch bade.   360

XLVI.

A third obdurate stands and cudgel-proof,
  And stedfast as th' unchisel'd rock of flint,
Regardless though the heaven's high marble roof
  Should fall upon his scull with mortal dint,
Or though, conspiring Earth, beneath his hoof,   365
  Should sprout up coal with fiery flashes in't,
Whilst on his back his griev'd and waspish master,
The stubborner he stands, still bangs and bans the faster.

XLVII.

Meantime, the rabblement, with fav'ring shout,
  And clapping hand set up so loud a din,   370
As almost with stark terrour frighted out
  Each ass's soul from his partic'lar skin;
Rattled the bursts of laughter round about;
  Grinn'd every phiz with mirth's peculiar grin;
As through the loan they saw the cuddies awkward   375
Bustling some straight, some thwart, some forward, and some
XLVIII.   backward.

As when the clouds, by gusty whirlwind riven,
  And whipp'd into confusion pitchy-black,
Detach'd, fly diverse round the cope of heaven,
  Reeling and jostling in uncertain rack,   380
And some are northward, some are southward driven,
  With storm embroiling all the zodiac,
Till the clash'd clouds send out the fiery flash,
And peals with awful roll the long loud thunder crash.

XLIX.

Just in such foul confusion and alarm   385
  Jostle the cuddies with rebellious mind,
And reek with sweat their bowels grow so warm,
  And loudly bray before, and belch behind:
But who is yon, the foremost of the swarm,
  That scampers fleetly as the rain-raw wind?   390
'Tis ROBERT SCOT, if I can trust my eyne;
I know the bord'rer well, by his long coat of green.

L.

See how his bright whip, brandish'd round his head,
  Flickers like streamer in the northern skies;
See how his ass on earth with nimble tread   395
  Half-flying rides, in air half-riding flies,
As if a pair of ostrich wings, out-spread,
  To help him on, had sprouted from his thighs:
Well scamper'd, ROB – well whipt – well spurr'd – my boy;
O haste ye, ROBERT, haste – rush – gallop to thy joy!   400

42

The pole is gain'd; his ass's head he turns
    Southward, to tread the trodden ground again;
Sparkles like flint the cuddy's hoof and burns,
    Seeming to leave a smoke upon the plain;
His bitted mouth the foam impatient churns;   405
    Sweeps his broad tail behind him like a train:
Speed, cuddy, speed – O, slacken not thy pace;
Ten minutes more like this, and thou shalt gain the race!

He comes careering on the sounding loan,
    With pace unslacken'd hasting to the knoll,   410
And, as he meets with those that hobble on
    With northward heads to gain the ribbon'd pole,
Ev'n by his forceful fury are o'erthrown
    His long-ear'd brethren in confusion droll;
For as their sides, he passing, slightly grazes,   415
By that collision shock'd, down roll the founder'd asses.

Heels over head they tumble; ass on ass
    They dash, and twenty times roll o'er and o'er,
Lubberly wallowing along the grass,
    In beastly ruin and with beastly roar;   420
While their vext riders in poor plight, alas!
    Flung from their saddles three long ells and more,
Bruis'd and commingling, with their cuddies sprawl,
And curse th'impetuous brute whose conflict caus'd their fall.

With hats upon their heads they down did light,   425
    Withouten hats disgracefully they rose;
Clean were their faces ere they fell and bright,
    But dirty-fac'd they got up on their toes;
Strong were their sinews ere they fell and tight,
    Hip-shot they stood up, sprain'd with many woes;   430
Blithe were their aspects ere the ground they took,
Grim louring rose they up, with crabbed ghastful look.

And, to augment their sorrow and their shame,
    A hail abhorr'd of nauseous rotten eggs,
In rascal volleys from the rabble came   435
    Opprobrious, on their bellies, heads and legs,
Smearing with slime that ill their clothes became,
    Whereby they stunk like wash-polluted pigs,
For in each white curs'd shell a juice was found,
Foul as the dribbling pus of Philoctetes' wound.   440

LVI.

Ah! then with grievous limp along the ground,
　They sought their hats that had so flown away,
And some were, cuff'd and much disaster'd, found,
　And haply some not found unto this day:
Meanwhile, with vast and undiminish'd bound,　　　　　　445
　Sheer through the bestial wreck and disarray,
The brute of Mesopotam hurries on,
And in his madding speed devours the trembling loan.

LVII.

Speed, cuddy, speed – one short, short minute more,
　And finish'd is thy toil and won the race–　　　　　　450
Now – one half minute and thy toils are o'er –
　His toils are o'er and he has gain'd the base!
He shakes his tail the conscious conqueror;
　Joy peeps through his stupidity of face;
He seems to wait the monarch's approbation,　　　　　　455
As quiver his long ears with self-congratulation.

LVIII.

Straight from the stirrup ROB dislodg'd his feet,
　And, flinging from his grasp away the rein,
Off sprung, and louting in obeisance meet
　Did lowly duty to his king again:　　　　　　　　　460
His king with salutation kind did greet
　Him the victorious champion of the plain,
And bade him rise, and up the hillock skip,
That he the royal hand might kiss with favour'd lip:

LIX.

Whereat, obedient to the high command,　　　　　　　465
　Great ROBERT SCOT, upbolting from the ground,
Rush'd up, in majesty of gesture grand,
　To where the monarch sat upon the mound,
And kiss'd the hard back of his hairy hand,
　Respectfully, as fits a monarch crown'd;　　　　　　470
But with a keener ecstacy he kiss'd
The dearer tend'rer back of MAGGIE's downy fist.

LX.

Then took the trumpeter his clarion good,
　And, in a sharp and violent exclaim,
Out from the brass among the multitude　　　　　　　475
　Afar sent conqu'ring ROB's illustrious name;
Which heard, an outcry of applause ensued,
　That shook the dank dew from the starry frame;
Great ROBERT's name was halloo'd through the mob,
And Echo blabb'd to heav'n the name of mighty ROB.　　480

But, unapplauded, and in piteous case,
  The laggers on their vanquish'd asses slow,
Shame-stung, with scurvy length of rueful face,
  Ride sneaking off to save them further woe;
For, cramm'd with slime and stench and vile disgrace,   485
  Th' abominable shells fly moe and moe,
Till slink the men amid the press of folk,
Secure from shame and slime and egg's unwholesome yolk.

NOTES

1 Anster loan must, in those days, have been of great extent; at present it's limits are
   contracted almost to the breadth of the highway.
2 Such a yell was there,
   As if men fought upon the earth,
   And fiends in upper air.   SCOTT's Marmion.

ANSTER FAIR

CANTO IV

ARGUMENT

The herald again sounds his trumpet, ordering the sack-racers to appear on the ground. They come out in great numbers each wagging his bag. They are put into their sacks by some of King James' soldiers, and are ranged in a line ready to jump at the signal. At the first leap many fall down; some proceed a little way, till by degrees, all except two fall prostrate and wallowing on the green. Their great uneasiness described when in that grovelling situation. Of the two jumpers who still persevere in the race one is Rob the Ranter; the other happens to be a waggish Edinburgh Gentleman who had craftily provided for himself a half-rotten sack, that in the course of jumping, he might thrust out one of his legs to support and assist him in his dangerous race. They both arrive at the starting-line together, but by the voice of king and crowd, the victory is adjudged to Rob. The people then eat a luncheon; after which the pipers are summoned forth to try their skill at piping. They surround the knoll, and all at once commence, disorderly, a fierce and unruly music; in a moment, however, their bagpipes are consumed by a miraculous globe, or ball of fire from heaven. Rob the Ranter's bagpipe being the only one spared, he ascends the eminence, and plays the tune since well known by the name of Maggie Lauder. It's amazing influence on the mob, in exciting them all to dance, from one end of the loan to the other.

I.

O that my noddle were a seething kettle,
  Frothing with bombast o'er the Muses' fire!
O that my wit were sharper than a nettle!
  O that with shrill swans' guts were strung my lyre!
So should I rant and sing with such a mettle,   5
  That each old wife in Fife's full-peopled shire
Should, Maenad-like, spring from her spinning-wheel,
And frolic round her bard and wince a tott'ring reel!

IA.

[THERE are who say, (the devil pinch them for it!)
  That I am but a silly poetaster,   10
A trencher-licker in Apollo's court,
  A sorry boy, an arrant paper-waster;
The louts! I'll make them mend their bad report,
  Or on their mouths will clap a pitchy plaster;
Ye blockheads, read my ass-race, and avow it,   15
That I'm Homeric stuff – ay, every inch a poet.]¹

II.

Again the herald at the king's desire,
  His tube of metal to his mouth apply'd,
And, with a roysting brazen clangour dire,
  Round to the heaving mass of rabble cry'd,   20
Inviting every blade of fun and fire,
  That wish'd to jump in hempen bondage ty'd,
Forthwith to start forth from the people's ring,
And fetch his sack in hand, and stand before the king.

III.

No sooner in the sky his words were blown   25
  When, through the multitude's compacted press
Wedging their bodies, push to th' open loan
  Th' audacious men of boasted springiness;
Some, Sampson-thigh'd, and large and big of bone,
  Brawn-burden'd, six feet high or little less,   30
Some, lean, flesh-wither'd, stinted, oatmeal things,
Yet hardy tough and smart, with heels like steely springs.

IV.

Nor were the offer'd candidates a few;
  In hundreds forth they issue, mad with zeal
To try, in feats which haply some shall rue,   35
  Their perilous alacrity of heel:
Each mortal brings his sack wherein to mew
  As in a pliant prison, strong as steel,
His guiltless corse, and clog his nat'ral gait
With cumberance of cloth, embarrassing and strait.   40

47

V.

And in their hands they hold to view on high
  Vain-gloriously, their bags of sturdy thread,
And toss and wave them in th' affronted sky,
  Like honour-winning trophies o'er their head,
Assuming merit that they dare defy   45
  The dangers of a race so droll and dread:
Ah, boast not, sirs, for premature's the brag;
'Tis time in troth to boast when off you put the bag!

VI.

Onward they hasten'd, clamorous and loud,
  To where the monarch sat upon the knoll,   50
And, having to his presence humbly bow'd,
  And bare'd of reverential hat their poll,
Their dirty sacks they wagg'd, erect and proud,
  Impatient, in their fiery fit of soul,
And pertly shak'd, ev'n in the monarch's eyes,   55
A cloud of meal and flour that whirling round them flies.

VII.

But as the good king saw them thus prepar'd
  To have their persons scabbarded in cloth,
He order'd twenty soldiers of his guard,
  All swashing fellows and of biggest growth,   60
To step upon the green loan's listed sward,
  That they may lend assistance, nothing lothe,
To plunge into their pliant sheaths, neck-deep,
Th' ambitious men that dare to try such vent'rous leap.

VIII.

They stepp'd obedient down, and in a trice   65
  Put on the suitors' comical array;
Each sack gap'd wide its monstrous orifice,
  To swallow to the neck it's living prey;
And, as a swineherd puts in poke a grice
  To carry from it's sty some little way,   70
So did the soldiers plunge the men, within
Their yawning gloomy gulfs ev'n to the neck and chin.

IX.

As when of yore the Roman forum, split
  By earthquake, yawn'd a black tremendous hole,
Voracious, deep'ning still, though flung in it   75
  Were stones and trees with all their branches whole,
Till, in a noble patriotic fit,
  The younker Curtius of devoted soul
Down headlong yarely gallop'd, horse and all,
And dash'd his gallant bones to atoms by the fall.   80

48

X.

So fearlessly these men of fair Scotland
    (Though not to death) down plung'd into their sacks,
Entoiling into impotence to stand
    Their feet, and mobbling legs and sides and backs,
Till tightly drawn was every twisted band   85
    And knotted firmly round their valiant necks,
That, in their rival rage to jump forthright,
They might not struggle off their case of sackcloth tight.

XI.

Nor, when their bodies were accoutred well,
    Upon their cumber'd feet stood all upright,   90
But some, unpractis'd or uncautious, fell
    Sousing with lumpish undefended weight,
And roll'd upon the turf full many an ell,
    Incapable of uprise, sad in plight;
Till, rais'd again, with those that keep their feet,   95
Join'd in a line they stand each in his winding-sheet.

XII.

O 'twas an awkward and ridic'lous show,
    To see a long, sack-muffled line of men,
With hatless heads all peeping in a row,
    Forth from the long smocks that their limbs contain,   100
For in the wide abyss of cloth below
    Their legs are swallow'd, and their stout arms twain;
From chin to toe one shapeless lump they stand,
In clumsy uniform, without leg, arm, or hand,

XIII.

And such their odd appearance was, and show   105
    Of human carcases in sackcloth dight,
As when the trav'ler, when he haps to go
    Down to Grand Cairo in the Turk's despite,
Sees in her chamber'd catacombs below
    Full many a mummy horribly upright,   110
A grisly row of grimly-garnish'd dead,
That seem to pout and scowl and shake the brainless head.

XIV.

So queer and so grotesque to view they stood,
    All ready at the trump's expected sound,
To take a spring of monstrous altitude,   115
    And scour with majesty of hop the ground:
Yet not so soon the starting-blast ensued;
    For, as they stand intent upon the bound,
The hum'rous monarch, eyeing their array,
Gave them his good advice before they rush'd away.   120

XV

O friends! since now your loins are girt, he cry'd,
　For journey perilous and full of toil,
Behoves it you right cautiously to guide
　Your ticklish steps along such vexing soil;
For sorry is the road, and well supply'd　　　　　　　　　125
　With stumps and stumbling-blocks and pits of guile,
And snares, and latent traps with earth bestown,
To catch you by the heels, and bring you groaning down.

XVI.

And woe betide, if unaware you hap
　Your body's well-adjusted poise to lose,　　　　　　　130
For bloody bump and sorrowful sore slap
　Await your falling temple, brow, and nose;
And, when once down and fetter'd in a trap,
　Hard task 'twill be to extricate your toes:
So, lads, if you regard your nose's weal,　　　　　　　135
Pray pick out stable steps, and tread with wary heel.

XVII.

And he that longest time without a fall
　Shall urge his sad perplexity of way,
And leave behind his fellow-trav'llers all
　Growling for help and grovelling on the clay,　　　　140
He, for his laudable exertions, shall
　Be sung the second victor of the day:
And so God speed you, sirs! – The monarch spoke,
And on the surging air the trumpet's signal broke.

XVIII.

As when a thunderclap, preluding nigh　　　　　　　　145
　A storm, growls on the frontiers of the west,
Ere yet the cloud, slow toiling up the sky,
　Hath in it's mass the mid-day sun supprest,
Alarm'd, the timid doves that basking lie
　Upon their cot's slope sunny roof at rest,　　　　　150
At once up-flutter in a sudden fray,
And poise th' unsteady wing, and squir in air away.

XIX.

So started, as the herald gave the blast,
　At once the suitors in their sacks away,
With gallant up-spring, notable and vast,　　　　　　155
　A neck-endang'ring violent assay;
The solid earth, as up to sky they past,
　Push'd back, seem'd to retire a little way;
And, as they up-flew furious from the ground,
The gash'd and wounded air whizz'd audibly a sound.　160

50

XX.

As when on summer eve a soaking rain
    Hath after drought bedrench'd the tender grass,
If chance, in pleasant walk along the plain,
    Brushing with foot the pearl-hung blades you pass,
A troop of frogs oft leaps from field of grain,   165
    Marshall'd in line, a foul unseemly race,
They halt a space, then vaulting up they fly,
As if they long'd to sit on Iris' bow on high.

XXI.

So leap'd the men, half-sepulchred in sack,
    Up-swinging, with their shapes be-monstring sky,   170
And cours'd in air a semicircle track,
    Like to the feath'ry-footed Mercury;
Till, spent their impetus, with sounding thwack
    Greeted their heels the green ground sturdily;
And some, descending, kept their balance well,   175
Unbalanc'd some came down, and boisterously fell.

XXII.

The greeted earth beneath the heavy thwacks
    Of feet that centripetal down alight,
Of tingling elbows, bruised loins and backs,
    Shakes passive, yet indignant of the weight;   180
For, o'er her bosom, in their plaguy sacks,
    Cumbrously roll (a mortifying sight)
Wreck'd burgher, knight and laird, and clown pell-mell,
Prostrate, in grievance hard, too terrible to tell.

XXIII.

And aye they struggle at an effort strong   185
    To re-instate their feet upon the plain,
Half-elbowing, half-kneeing sore and long
    Abortively, with bitter sweat and pain,
Till, half uprais'd, they to their forehead's wrong
    Go with a buffet rapping down again,   190
And sprawl and flounce and wallow on their backs,
Crying aloud for help t'uncord their dolorous sacks.

XXIV.

Not in severer anguish of distress
    The fabled giant under Etna lies,
Though rocks and tree-proud promontories press   195
    With vengeance fitting Jove his ruffian size;
Wallowing supine beneath the mountain's stress,
    Half-broil'd with brimstone ever hot, he fries,
And, as he turns his vasty carcase o'er,
Out-belches molten rocks and groans a hideous roar.   200

XXV.

In such vexatious plight the mortals lie
  That founder'd on the threshold of the race,
Where let us leave them, and lift up our eye
  To those that keep their feet and hop apace:
Gramercy! how they bounce it lustily,   205
  Maugre their misery of woven case!
How with their luggage scour they o'er the loan,
And toil, and moil, and strain, and sweat, and lumber on.

XXVI.

Strange thing it is that men so penn'd in clout,
  So wound with swaddling-clothes should trip it so;   210
See how with spring incomparably stout,
  Spurning the nasty earth, they upward go,
As if they wish'd t'unsocket and knock out
  With poll the candles that i' the night-sky glow!
See, how, attain'd the zenith of their leap,   215
Earthward they sink again with long-descending sweep.

XXVII.

They halt not still; again aloft they hop,
  As if they tread the rainbow's gilded bend,
Again upon the quaking turf they drop,
  Lighting majestic on their proper end;   220
I ween, they do not make a moment's stop;
  O who may now his precious time mispend?
'Tis bustling all and swelt'ring – but behold!
Swop! there a jumper falls, aflat upon the mould;

XXVIII.

How can his gyved arms be forward thrust   225
  To break the downsway of his fall just now?
Ah, 'tis his tender nose, alone that must
  In loving kindness save from bump his brow;
His soft nose, to its site and duty just,
  Is martyr'd to its loyalty, I trow,   230
For, flatten'd into anguish by the clod,
It weeps – see how it weeps – warm trickling tears of blood!

XXIX.

He bleeds, and from his nostrils' double sluice
  Redly bedews the sod of ANSTER loan,
Till, in a puddle of his own heart's juice,   235
  He welt'ring writhes with lamentable moan,
And sends his sack in curses to the deuce,
  Banning the hour when first he put it on:
Meanwhile, o'erlabour'd in their hobbling pother,
Douse, drops a second down, and whap! there sinks another!   240

XXX.

Wearied, half-bursten with their hot turmoil,
   Their lungs like Vulcan's bellows panting strong,
Pow'rless to stand, or prosecute their toil,
   Successively they souse and roll along,
Till, round and round, the carcase-cumber'd soil   245
   Is strewn with havock of the jumping throng,
That make a vain endeavour off to shuffle
The cruel sackcloth coil that does their persons muffle.

XXXI.

All in despair have sunk, save yonder two
   That still their perpendic'lar posture keep,   250
The only remnant of the jumping crew,
   That urge their emulous persisting leap;
Oddspittkins! how with poise exactly true
   Clean forward to the ribbon'd pole they sweep;
I cannot say that one is 'fore the other,   255
So equal side by side they plod near one another:

XXXII.

The pole is gain'd, and to the glorious sun
   They turn their sweaty faces round again;
With inextinguishable rage to run,
   Southward unflagging and unquell'd they strain.   260
What? – Is not yonder face, where young-ey'd Fun
   And Laughter seem enthron'd to hold their reign,
One seen before – ev'n R O B the bord'rer's phiz! –
Aye, now I ken it well, by'r lakin it is his!

XXXIII.

Haste, haste ye, R O B, half-hop, half-run, half fly,   260
   Wriggle and wrestle in thy bag's despite;
So! shoot like cannon-bullet to the sky;
   So! – stably down upon thy soles alight;
Up, up, again, and fling it gallantly! –
   Well-flung, my R O B, thou art a clever wight;   270
'Sblood, now thy rival is a step before,
String, string thy sinews up, and jump three yards and more!

XXXIV.

'Tis done – but who is he that at thy side
   Thy rival vigorously marches so?
Declare, O Muse, since thou art eagle-ey'd,
   And thine it is, ev'n at a glance, to know   275
Each son of mortal man, though mumm'd and ty'd
   In long disguising sack from chin to toe!
He, boy, that marches in such clumsy state,
Is old Edina's child, a waggish Advocate;   280

53

XXXV.

For he too has, for MAGGIE LAUDER, dar'd
  To prove the mettle of his heels and shin,
A jolly wight, who trickishly prepar'd
  A treach'rous sack to scarf his body in,
A sack whose bottom was with damp impair'd   285
  Fusty, half-rotten, mouldy, frail,and thin,
That he, unseen, might in the race's pother,
Thrust out one helpful leg, and keep incag'd its brother.

XXXVI.

And seest thou not his right leg peeping out,
  Enfranchis'd, trait'rously to help his gait,   290
Whilst th' other, still imprison'd in its clout,
  Tardily follows its more active mate?
I see it well – 'tis treachery, no doubt;
  Beshrew thee now, thou crafty Advocate!
Unfair, unfair! 'tis quite unfair, I say,   295
Thus with illicit leg to prop thy perilous way!

XXXVII.

Half-free, half-clogg'd, he steals his quick advance,
  Nearing at each unlicens'd step the base,
While honest ROBERT plies the hardier dance
  Most faithful to his sack and to the race;   300
Now for it, ROB – another jump – but once –
  And overjump'd is all th' allotted space; –
By Jove, they both have reach'd the base together,
Gain'd is the starting-line, yet gain'd the race hath neither!

XXXVIII.

At once they bend, each man his body's frame   305
  Into a bow before the king and MAG;
At once they ope their lips to double-claim
  The race's palm, (for now Auld Reekie's wag
As snail draws in its horn, had, fy for shame!
  Drawn his dishonest leg into his bag;)   310
At once they plead the merits of their running,
Good ROB with proofs of force, the wag with quips and punning.

XXXIX.

Me lists not now to variegate my song
  With all his sophistry and quip and pun;
O 'twould be tiresome, profitless and long,   315
  To quote his futile arguments air spun,
His oratoric tricks that dress the wrong
  In garb of right, his gybes of naughty fun,
Quiddits and quillits that may well confound one,
And make a *rotten sack* appear *a goodly sound one!*   320

XL.

But ROBERT to the people's eyes appeal'd,
  And to the eyes of royal James, and MAG,
Who saw his rival's foot too plain reveal'd,
  And impudently peering from its bag;
He said 'twas roguish thus to come a-field   325
  With such a paltry hypocritic rag;
The very hole, through which his foot was thrust,
Gap'd evidence to prove his claim was quite unjust.

XLI.

Long was the plea, and longer it had been,
  Had not the populace begun aloud   330
T' express with clamour their resentment keen
  At him who quibbled in his rotten shroud;
A thousand hands, uplifted high, were seen
  Over the hats and bonnets of the crowd,
With paly hens' eggs that their fingers clench,   335
To hurl upon his sack conviction, slime, and stench.

XLII.

Which, when he saw all white upheld to view,
  Ready to rattle shame about his ears,
He, straightway, the perplexing claim withdrew,
  Urg'd to resign by his judicious fears,   340
For had he but one minute stay'd or two,
  He, for his subtilties, and quirks, and jeers,
Had reap'd a poor and pitiful reward,
And smell'd from head to foot – but not with Syrian nard.

XLIII.

The monarch, then, well pleas'd that thus the mob   345
  Had settled with prejudging voice the case,
Orders his trumpeter to blazon ROB
  Again the winner of the second race:
The fellow blew each cheek into a globe,
  And puff'd into deformity his face,   350
As to the top of heaven's empyreal frame
He, in a storm of breath, sent up the conqu'ror's name.

XLIV.

His name the rabble took; from tongue to tongue
  Bandy'd it flew like fiery-winged shot,
That the blue atmosphere around them rung   355
  With the blabb'd honours of great ROBERT SCOT;
Nor when they thus his triumph stoutly sung,
  Were the race-founder'd gentlemen forgot,
That in their trammels still a-flound'ring lay,
And, had they not been rais'd, had lain there to this day.   360

XLV.

But soon up-rear'd they were; the lads, that late
  Had help'd their uncouth livery to don,
Now step upon the green compassionate,
  To free them from the house of dole and moan;
The cords, that on their necks were knotted straight,   365
  Are loos'd, and as they lie extended prone,
Of their long scabbards are discas'd the men,
And stand upon their feet, unclogg'd, and free agen.

XLVI.

They take no time, (such shame the vanquish'd stung)
  Each to snatch up his bag and bring it off;   370
Away they start and plunge amid the throng,
  Glad their embarrassment of cloth to doff;
(So shoots the serpent to the brake along,
  And leaves to rot his cast despised slough;)
Deep in the throng with elbows sharp they bore,   375
And fear contemptuous laugh and hateful egg no more.

XLVII.

But now the sun, in mid-day's gorgeous state,
  Tow'rs on the summit of the lucid sky,
And human stomachs that were cramm'd of late,
  Now empty, send their silent dinner-cry,   380
Demanding something wherewithal to sate
  Their hunger, bread and beer, or penny-pie:
The crowd, obedient to the belly's call,
Begin to munch, and eat, and nibble one and all.

XLVIII.

Some from their pockets, or their wallets, drew   385
  Lumps of the roasted flesh of calf or lamb;
Some ply their teeth-arm'd grinding jaws to chew
  The tougher slices of the thirsty ham;
Others with bits of green cheese nice and new
  Ev'n to the throat their clownish bellies cram,   390
While horns of ale, from many a barrel fill'd,
Foam white with frothy rage, and soon are swigg'd and swill'd.

XLIX.

James, too, and MAG, and all the courtly train
  Of lords and ladies round them not a few,
With sugar'd biscuits sooth'd their stomachs' pain,   395
  For courtly stomachs must be humour'd too;
And, from their throats to wash the dusty stain
  That they had breath'd when from the sacks it flew,
A glass of wine they slipp'd within their clay,
And, if they swallow'd twain, the wiser folk were they.   400

L.

Nor ceas'd the business of the day meanwhile;
   For as the monarch chew'd his sav'ry cake,
The man, whose lungs sustain the trumpet's toil,
   Made haste again his noisy tube to take,
And with a cry, which, heard full many a mile,   405
   Caus'd the young crows on Airdrie's trees to quake,
He bade the suitor-pipers to draw nigh,
That they might, round the knoll, their powers of piping try.

LI.

Which when the rabble heard, with sudden sound
   They broke their circle's huge circumference,   410
And, crushing forward to the southern mound,
   They push'd their many-headed shoal immense,
Diffusing to an equal depth around
   Their mass of bodies wedg'd compact and dense,
That, standing nigher, they might better hear   415
The pipers squeaking loud to charm Miss MAGGIE's ear.

LII.

And soon the pipers, shouldering along
   Through the close mob their squeez'd uneasy way,
Stood at the hillock's foot, an eager throng,
   Each asking license from the king to play;   420
For with a tempest, turbulent and strong,
   Labour'd their bags impatient of delay,
Heaving their bloated globes outrageously,
As if in pangs to give their contents to the sky.

LIII.

And every bag, thus full and tempest-ripe,   425
   Beneath its arm lay ready to be prest,
And, on the holes of each fair-polish'd pipe,
   Each piper's fingers long and white were plac'd;
Fiercely they burn'd in jealous rivalship;
   Each madding piper scoff'd at all the rest,   430
And fleer'd and toss'd contemptuously his head,
As if his skill alone deserv'd fair MAGGIE's bed.

LIV.

Nor could they wait, so piping-mad they were,
   Till James gave each man orders to begin,
But in a moment they displode their air   435
   In one tumultuous and unlicens'd din;
Out-flies, in storm of simultaneous blare,
   The whizzing wind comprest their bags within,
And, whiffling through the wooden tubes so small,
Growls gladness to be freed from such confining thrall.   440

LV.

Then rose, in burst of hideous symphony,
  Of pibrochs and of tunes one mingled roar;
Discordantly the pipes squeal'd sharp and high,
  The drones alone in solemn concord snore;
Five hundred fingers, twinkling funnily,   445
  Play twiddling up and down on hole and bore
Now passage to the shrilly wind denying,
And now a little rais'd to let it out a-sighing.

LVI.

Then rung the rocks and caves of Billyness,
  Reverberating back that concert's sound,   450
And half the lurking Echoes that possess
  The glens and hollows of the Fifan ground,
Their shadowy voices strain'd into excess
  Of out-cry, loud huzzaing round and round
To all the Dryads of Pitkirie wood,   455
That now they round their trees should dance in frisky mood.

LVII.

As when the sportsman with report of gun
  Alarms the sea-fowl of the Isle of May,
Ten thousand mews and gulls that shade the sun
  Come flapping down in terrible dismay,   460
And with a wild and barb'rous concert stun
  His ears, and scream, and shriek, and wheel away;
Scarce can the boatman hear his plashing oar;
Yell caves and eyries all, and rings each Maian shore.

LVIII.

Just so around the knoll did pipe and drone   465
  Whistle and hum a discord strange to hear,
Tort'ring with violence of shriek and groan
  Kingly, and courtly, and plebeian ear;
And still the men had humm'd and whistled on,
  Ev'n till each bag had burst its bloated sphere,   470
Had not the king, uprising, wav'd his hand,
And check'd the boist'rous din of such unmanner'd band.

LIX.

On one side of his face a laugh was seen,
  On t'other side a half-form'd frown lay hid;
He frown'd, because they petulantly keen,   475
  Set up their piping forward and unbid;
He laugh'd, for who could have controul'd his mien,
  Hearing such crash of pibrochs as he did?
He bade them orderly the strife begin,
And play each man the tune wherewith the fair he'd win.   480

Whereat the pipers ceas'd their idle toil
  Of windy music wild and deafening,
And made too late (what they forgot e'erwhile)
  A general bow to MAGGIE and their king;
But, as they vail'd their bare heads tow'rd the soil,   485
  O then there happ'd a strange portentous thing,
Which had not good my Muse confirm'd for true,
Myself had not believ'd, far less have told to you.

For lo! whilst all their bodies yet were bent,
  Breaks from the spotless blue of eastern sky   490
A globe of fire, (miraculous ostent!)
  Bursten from some celestial cleft on high;
And thrice in circle round the firmament
  Trail'd its long light the gleamy prodigy,
Till on the ring of pipers down it came,   495
And set their pipes and drones and chanters in a flame.

'Twas quick and sudden as th' electrick shock;
  One moment lighted and consum'd them all;
As is the green hair of the tufted oak
  Scath'd into blackness by the fulmin'd ball,   500
Or, as spark-kindled, into fire and smoke,
  Flashes and fumes the nitrous grain so small,
So were their bagpipes, in a twink, like tinder
Fir'd underneath their arms and burn'd into a cinder.

Yet so innocuous was the sky-fall'n flame   505
  That, save their twangling instruments alone,
Unsing'd their other gear remain'd the same,
  Ev'n to the nap that stuck their coats upon;
Nor did they feel it's heat when down it came
  On errand to destroy pipe, bag and drone,   510
But stood in blank surprise, when to the ground
Dropt down in ashes black their furniture of sound.

Crest-fall'n they stood, confounded and distrest,
  And fix'd upon the turf their stupid look,
Conscious that Heav'n forbade them to contest   515
  By such a burning token of rebuke:
The rabble, too, it's great alarm confest,
  For every face the ruddy blood forsook,
As with their white, uprolling, ghastly eyes
They spy'd the streaky light wheel whizzing from the skies.   520

LXV.

And still they to that spot of orient heav'n,
   Whence burst the shining globe, look up aghast,
Expecting when th' empyreal pavement riven
   A second splendour to the earth should cast;
But when they saw no repetition given,   525
   Chang'd from alarm to noisy joy at last,
They set up such a mix'd tremendous shout,
As made the girdling heav'ns to bellow round about.

LXVI.

And such a crack and peal of laughter rose,
   When the poor pipers bagpipe-less they saw,   530
As when a flock of inky-feather'd crows,
   On winter morning when the skies are raw,
Come from their woods in long and sooty rows,
   And over ANSTER through their hoarse throats caw;
The sleepy old-wives, on their warm chaff-beds,   535
Up from their bolsters rear, afear'd, their flannel'd heads.

LXVII.

Then did th' affronted pipers slink away,
   With faces fix'd on earth for very shame,
For not one remnant of those pipes had they
   Wherewith they late so arrogantly came,   540
But in a black and ashy ruin lay
   Their glory moulder'd by the scathing flame;
Yet in their hearts they curs'd (and what the wonder?)
That fire to which their pipes so quick were giv'n a plunder.

LXVIII.

And scarce they off had slunk, when with a bound   545
   Great ROBERT SCOT sprung forth before the king,
For he alone, when all the pipers round
   Stood rang'd into their fire-devoted ring,
Had kept snug distance from the fated ground,
   As if forewarn'd of that portentous thing;   550
He stood and laugh'd, as underneath his arm
He held his bagpipe safe, unscath'd with fiery harm.

LXIX.

His hollow drone, with mouth wide-gaping, lay
   Over his shoulder pointing to the sky,
Ready to spue it's breath and puff away   555
   The lazy silver clouds that sit on high;
His bag swell'd madly to begin the play,
   And with its bowel-wind groan'd inwardly;
Not higher heav'd the wind-bags which of yore
Ulysses got from him who rul'd th' Æolian shore.   560

LXX.

He thus the king with reverence bespoke;
    My liege, since Heav'n with bagpipe-levell'd fire
Hath turn'd my brethren's gear to dust and smoke,
    And testify'd too glaringly it's ire,
It fits me now, as yet my bagpipe's poke   565
    Remains unsing'd and every pipe entire,
To play my tune – O king, with your good will –
And to the royal ear to prove my piping-skill.

LXXI.

Nodded his liege assent, and straightway bade
    Him stand a-top o' th' hillock at his side;   570
A-top he stood; and first a bow he made
    To all the crowd that shouted far and wide,
Then, like a piper dext'rous at his trade,
    His pipes to play adjusted and apply'd;
Each finger rested on its proper bore;   575
His arm appear'd half-rais'd to wake the bag's uproar.

LXXII.

A space he silent stood, and cast his eye
    In meditation upwards to the pole,
As if he pray'd some fairy pow'r in sky
    To guide his fingers right o'er bore and hole,   580
Then pressing down his arm he gracefully
    Awak'd the merry bagpipe's slumb'ring soul,
And pip'd and blew and play'd so sweet a tune
As might have well unspher'd the reeling midnight moon.

LXXIII.

His ev'ry finger, to its place assign'd,   585
    Mov'd quiv'ring like the leaf of aspen tree,
Now shutting up the skittish squeaking wind,
    Now op'ning to the music passage free;
His cheeks, with windy puffs therein confin'd,
    Were swoln into a red rotundity,   590
As from his lungs into the bag was blown
Supply of needful air to feed the growling drone.

LXXIV.

And such a potent tune did never greet
    The drum of human ear with lively strain,
So merry, that from dancing on his feet   595
    No man undeaf could stockishly refrain,
So loud, 'twas heard a dozen miles complete,
    Making old Echo pipe and hum again,
So sweet, that all the birds in air that fly,
Charm'd into new delight, come sailing through the sky.   600

LXXV.

Crow, sparrow, linnet, hawk, and white-wing'd dove,
  Wheel in aërial jigg o'er ANSTER loan;
The sea-mews from each Maian cleft and cove
  O'er the deep sea come pinion-wafted on;
The light-detesting bats now flap above,   605
  Scaring the sun with wings to day unknown,
Round Robert's head they dance, they cry, they sing,
And shear the subtil sky with broad and playful wing.

LXXVI.

And eke the mermaids that in ocean swim,
  Drawn by that music from their shelly caves,   610
Peep now unbashful from the salt-sea brim,
  And flounce and plash exulting in the waves;
They spread at large the white and floating limb,
  That Neptune amorously clips and laves,
And kem with combs of pearl and coral fair   615
Their long sleek oozy locks of green redundant hair.

LXXVII.

Nor was it's influence less on human ear;
  First from their gilded chairs up-start at once
The royal James and MAGGIE seated near,
  Enthusiastic both and mad to dance;   620
Her hand he snatch'd and look'd a merry leer,
  Then caper'd high in wild extravagance,
And on the grassy summit of the knoll,
Wagg'd each monarchial leg in galliard strange and droll.

LXXVIII.

As when a sun-beam, from the waving face   625
  Of well-fill'd waterpail reflected bright,
Varies upon the chamber-walls it's place,
  And, quiv'ring, tries to cheat and foil the sight;
So quick did MAGGIE, with a nimble grace,
  Skip patt'ring to and fro, alert and light,   630
And, with her noble colleague in the reel,
Sublimely toss'd her arms, and shook the glancing heel.

LXXIX.

The lords and ladies, next, who sat or stood,
  Near to the piper and the king around,
Smitten with that contagious dancing mood,   635
  'Gan hand in hand in high lavolt to bound,
And jigg'd it on as featly as they cou'd,
  Circling in sheeny rows the rising ground,
Each sworded lord a lady's soft palm griping,
And to his mettle rous'd at such unwonted piping.   640

62

LXXX.

Then did th' infectious hopping-mania seize
  The circles of the crowd that stood more near,
Till, round and round, far spreading by degrees,
  It madden'd all the loan to kick and rear;
Men, women, children, lilt and ramp, and squeeze,   645
  Such fascination takes the gen'ral ear!
Ev'n babes, that at their mothers' bosoms hung,
Their little willing limbs fantastically flung.

LXXXI.

And hoar-hair'd men and wives, whose marrow Age
  Hath from their hollow bones suck'd out and drunk,   650
Canary in unconscionable rage,
  Nor feel their sinews wither'd now and shrunk;
Pellmell in random couples they engage,
  And boisterously wag their bodies' trunk,
Till from their heated skin the sweat out-squirts,   655
And soaks with clammy dew their goodly Holland shirts.

LXXXII.

And cripples from beneath their shoulders fling
  Their despicable crutches far away,
Then, yok'd with those of stouter limbs, up-spring
  In hobbling merriment, uncouthly gay;   660
And some on one leg stand y-gamboling;
  For why? The other short and frail had they;
Some, whose both legs distorted were and weak,
Dance on their poor knee-pans in mad prepost'rous freak.

LXXXIII.

So on they trip, king, MAGGIE, knight, and earl,   665
  Green-coated courtier, satin-snooded dame,
Old men and maidens, man, wife, boy, and girl,
  The stiff, the supple, bandylegg'd, and lame,
All suck'd and rapt into the dance's whirl,
  Inevitably witch'd within the same;   670
Whilst ROB, far-seen, o'erlooks the huddling loan,
Rejoicing in his pipes, and squeals serenely on.

LXXXIV.

But such a whirling and a din there was,
  Of bodies and of feet that heel'd the ground,
As when the Maelstrom in his craggy jaws   675
  Engluts the Norway waves with hideous sound;
In vain the black sea-monster plies his paws
  'Gainst the strong eddy that impels him round;
Work'd into barm, the torrent surges roar,
And fret their frothy wrath and reel from shore to shore.   680

LXXXV.

So reel the mob, and with their feet up-cast
　From the tramp'd soil a dry and dusty cloud,
That shades the huddling hurly-burly vast
　From the warm sun as with an earthy shroud;
Else, had the warm sun spy'd them wriggling fast,　　　685
　He sure had laugh'd at such bewitched crowd,
For never, since heaven's baldric first he trod,
Tripp'd was such country dance beneath his fiery road.

LXXXVI.

Then was the shepherd, that on Largo-law
　Sat idly whistling to his feeding flock,　　　690
Dismay'd, when looking southeastward he saw
　The dusty cloud more black than furnace-smoke;
He lean'd his ear, and catch'd with trembling awe
　The dance's sounds that th' ambient ether broke;
He bless'd himself, and cry'd, By sweet St John!　　　695
The devil hath got a job in ANSTER's dirty loan.

LXXXVII.

At length the mighty piper, honest ROB,
　His wonder-working melody gave o'er,
When on a sudden all the flouncing mob
　Their high commotion ceas'd and toss'd no more;　　　700
Trunk, arm, and leg, forgot to shake and bob,
　That bobb'd and shak'd so parlously before;
On ground, fatigu'd, the panting dancers fall,
Wond'ring what witch's craft had thus embroil'd them all.

LXXXVIII.

And some cry'd out, that o'er the piper's head　　　705
　They had observ'd a little female fay,
Clad in green gown, and purple-striped plaid,
　That fed his wind-bag, aidant of the play;
Some, impotent to speak and almost dead
　With jumping, as on earth they sat or lay　　　710
Wip'd from their brows with napkin, plaid or gown,
The globes of shining sweat that ooze and trickle down.

LXXXIX.

Nor less with jigg o'erlabour'd and o'erwrought,
　Down on their chairs dropt MAGGIE and the king,
Amaz'd what supernat'ral spell had caught　　　715
　And forc'd their heels into such frolicing;
And much was MAG astonish'd when she thought
　(As sure it was an odd perplexing thing)
That ROBERT's tune was to her ear the same
As what Tom Puck late play'd, when from her pot he came.　　　720

64

XC.

But from that hour the monarch and the mob
    Gave MAGGIE LAUDER's name to ROBERT's tune,
And so shall it be call'd while o'er the globe
    Travels the waneing and the crescent moon:
And from that hour the puissant piper ROB,   725
    Whose bagpipe wak'd so hot a rigadoon,
From his well-manag'd bag and drone and chanter,
Obtain'd the glorious name of Mighty ROB the RANTER.

NOTE
1 [Editorial note: see Notes.]

ANSTER FAIR

CANTO V

ARGUMENT

Rob the Ranter, snatching the trumpet from the king's herald, rouses the people, now prostrate from the fatigue of dancing, to hear his tale; the tenour of which is as follows: – Miss Susan Scott, a young heiress, beautiful, but of a sour, unamiable, and avaricious disposition, lives at Thirdpart, under the guardianship of her uncle, the famous magician, Sir Michael Scott. Her wealth and beauty attract many suitors; of these she prefers Charles Melvil, the Laird of Cairnbee, who, by gratifying her covetous inclination with costly presents, obtained from her a promise of marriage. One fine evening, as they walked in Thirdpart avenue, mutually entertained with amorous colloquy, they are interrupted by the attack of a bull from a neighbouring park. Melvil interposes to save his sweetheart, and holds the animal by the horns till she has time to escape. On letting go his hold, however, his face is injured by a blow from the horn. He goes home, and is for several weeks confined to his chamber by the wound. During this interval, he learns that Miss Susan had broken the promise made to him, and was about to be married to the Laird of Newark. Enraged at her deceit, he goes straightway to Thirdpart to upbraid the jilt. He meets with an uncivil reception both from her and her uncle. As he takes a walk in the avenue, in meditation of vengeance, he is accosted by Puck, the fairy, who, hopping from a brake, advises him by what method to punish Sir Michael and his niece. He follows his advice, and on the day when Susan weds Newark, he, in the presence of the whole bridal company, works some strange and shameful transformations on the persons of the wizard and his ward.

I.

O FOR that pond'rous broomstick whereon rode
  Grim Betty Laing,[1] hors'd daringly sublime!
So should I fly above the solar road
  To where the Muses sit on high and chime;
Eigh! I should kiss them in their bright abode,   5
  And from their lips suck Poetry and Rhime;
Till Jove (if such my boldness should displease him)
Cry, Fy, thou naughty boy! pack off and mount thy besom.

II.

It needed not that with a third exclaim
  King JAMES's trumpeter aloud should cry   10
Through his long alchemy the famous name
  Of him who, piping, got the victory;
For, sooth to tell, man, boy, and girl, and dame
  Him the great Prince of pipers testify,
Not with huzzas and jabbering of tongues,   15
But with hard-puffing breasts and dance-o'erweary'd lungs.

III.

And truly had the crier will'd to shout
  The doughty piper's name through polish'd trump,
His breath had not suffic'd to twang it out,
  So did the poor man's lights puff, pant and jump: 20
Wherefore to rest them from that dancing-bout,
  A while they sat or lay on back or rump,
Gulping with open mouths and nostrils wide
The pure refreshing waves of Jove's aerial tide.

IV.

But, unfatigued, upon the hillock's crown   25
  Stood ROB, as if his lungs had spent no breath,
And look'd with conscious exultation down
  Upon the dance's havock wide beneath,
Laughing to see th' encumber'd plain bestrown
  With people whirl'd and wriggled nigh to death;   30
Erelong he thus addrest, with reverent air,
The king that, breathless yet, sat puffing in his chair.

V.

My liege! though well I now with triple claim
  The guerdon of my threefold toils may ask,
As independent of success i' the game   35
  Of jingling words, the ballad-maker's task,
Yet, as I too, with honourable aim
  Have tapp'd Apollo's rhime-o'er-flowing cask,
Allow me, good my king! to ope my budget,
And tell my witty tale that you and MAG may judge it.   40

VI.

Whereto his breathless king made slow reply;
  (He drew a gulp of air each word between),
Great – Piper! – Mighty – ROB! – Belov'd – of sky!
  O prov'd – too well thy – piping-craft – has been;
Witness my lungs – that play so puff – ingly,   45
  And witness yonder – laughter-moving scene!
I'm pinch'd for wind – Ha, ha! – scarce breath I draw –
Pardi! – a sight like yon my kingship never saw!

VII.

Woes me! how sweating in prostration vast,
  Men, wives, boys, maidens, lie in dust bestrown,   50
Gaping for respiration, gasping fast,
  Half my liege subjects wreck'd on ANSTER loan!
'Twill need, methinks, a hideous trumpet-blast
  To rouse them from thus grov'lling basely prone;
For such effort my man's lungs yet are frail;   55
So, ROB, take thou his trump and rouse them for thy tale.

VIII.

He spake, and at the hint the Ranter took
  The throated metal from the herald's hand,
And blew a rousing clangour, wherewith shook
  Green sea, and azure sky and cloddy land: 60
Up-sprung as from a trance with startled look
  The prostrate people, and erected stand,
Turning their faces to the knap of ground,
Whence burst upon their ears the loud assaulting sound.

IX.

Then, crowding nearer in a vasty shoal,   65
  They press their sum of carcases more close,
Till crush'd and cramm'd and straiten'd round the knoll,
  They rear and poise their bodies on their toes:
So were they pack'd and mortis'd, that the whole
  Seem'd but one lump incorp'rate to compose;   70
One mass of human trunks unmov'd they show,
Topp'd with ten thousand heads all moving to and fro.

X.

And from the tongues of all those heads there rose
  A confus'd murmur through the multitude,
As when the merry gale of summer blows   75
  Upon the tall tops of a stately wood,
And rocks the long consociated boughs
  Rustling amid the leaves a discord rude;
High perch'd aloft the cuckoo rides unseen,
Embower'd with plenteous shades, and tufts of nodding green.   80

XI.

Then wav'd the R ANTER round and round his hand,
  Commanding them to still their hubbub loud;
All in a moment, still and noiseless stand
  The widely-circumfus'd and heaving crowd,
As if upon their gums at R O B's command   85
  Were pinn'd those tongues that jabber'd late so proud,
Tow'rds him, as to their centre, every ear
Inclines it's mazy hole, th' expected tale to hear.

XII.

But when the R ANTER from his height beheld
  The silent world of heads diffus'd below,   90
With all their ears agape, his visage swell'd
  And burn'd with honest Laughter's ruddy glow;
For who had not from Gravity rebell'd,
  Girt with infinitude of noddles so?
He soon into composure starch'd his phiz,   95
And op'd his fluent mouth, and told his tale – which is –

XIII.

Where Thirdpart-house upon the level plain
  Rears up its sooty chimneys high in air,
There liv'd of old, in Alexander's reign,
  Miss Susan Scot, a lady young and fair,   100
Who, as cold death her parents both had ta'en,
  Sole child, their coffers and their fields did heir,
Their fields that wav'd with Ceres' green array,
Their coffers, gorg'd with gold, where Mammon prison'd lay.

XIV.

Her form was beauteous as the budding Spring,   105
  Shap'd by the mother of almighty Love;
Her soul was but a sorry paltry thing,
  As e'er was quicken'd by the breath of Jove:
Her person might have pleas'd a crowned king,
  Or shone a Dryad in her Thirdpart grove;   110
Her soul, her silly soul, alas, to tell!
Was as a rotten egg inclos'd in golden shell.

XV.

All day she, sitting at her window, cast
  O'er her estate a proud and greedy eye,
Now measuring her fields how broad, how vast,   115
  How valuably rich they sunning lie,
Now summing up the bolls that in the blast
  Wave yet unshorn, obnoxious to the sky,
And counting avariciously what more
Of gold th' unsickled crop would add unto her store.   120

XVI.

But when the grim and hooded Night let fall
   O'er Thirdpart's smoky roofs her ugly shade,
She hasten'd from her candle-lighten'd hall
   To where her darling coffer'd god was laid,
And freeing him with key from box's thrall,   125
   On floor the gaudy deity display'd,
And with a miser's fumbling palm'd each toy,
And kiss'd bare Mammon's limbs and laugh'd in silly joy.

XVII.

With her resided that fam'd wizard old,
   Her uncle and her guardian, Michael Scot,   130
Who there, in Satan's arts malignly bold,
   His books of dev'lish efficacy wrote;
And, lackey'd round (tremendous to be told!)
   With demons hung with tails like shaggy goat,
Employ'd their ministrations damn'd, to ring   135
Madrid's resounding bells, and fright the Spanish king.

XVIII.

Fit guardian he for such a peevish ward:
   He check'd not her perversity of soul,
But, hell's pernicious logic studying hard,
   Gave up the lady to her own controul;   140
Thus fost'ring, by his foolish disregard,
   The cank'ring vice that o'er her spirit stole:
Captious and proud she was, and fond of strife,
The pertest prettiest jade of all the girls of Fife.

XIX.

Yet not the less her beauty's wafted fame   145
   A mob of suitors to her mansion drew;
Her face had charms to lure them and inflame,
   Her dow'r had mickle fascination too:
On cap'ring steeds from all the county came
   Fife's sparkish lairds, all resolute to woo   150
And win, with courtship's sly assiduous art,
Fair Susan's worthy dow'r, and pettish worthless heart.

XX.

So num'rous were her lovers that, in troth,
   I scarce by name can reckon up them all;
Ardross and Largo, gallant fellows both,   155
   Pitcorthie, and Rankeilor, and Newhall,
And Newark with his coat of scarlet cloth,
   And short Stravithy, and Rathillet tall,
And proud Balcomie with his tassel'd hat,
And Gibliston the lean, and Sauchop round and fat.   160

XXI.

All these, and many more love-pining men,
    She flouted from her chamber scornfully;
To one alone she us'd not such disdain,
    The goodly Charly Melvil of Carnbee;
For he, the singly cunning of the train,   165
    Enforc'd with costly gifts his am'rous plea,
And brib'd her dull affections icy-cold,
With jewel'd gairish rings and knacks of labour'd gold.

XXII.

For ev'ry time he snatch'd her downy fist
    With its soft warmth to paddle and to play,   170
He hung a bracelet on her iv'ry wrist,
    A golden bracelet like a sunbeam gay;
And, when her lip he rapturously kist,
    (A kiss she ne'er refused for such a pay,)
He dropt upon her white neck from his hand   175
A tangled chain of gold worth many a rood of land.

XXIII.

Till, of his trinkets so profuse he grew,
    That soon exhausted was his purse's store,
And half his lands were in a month or two
    Mortgag'd for money to procure her more;   180
Yet ne'er could he prevail on froward Sue,
    Though ne'er he ceas'd t'importune and implore,
T' appoint the long-retarded marriage-day,
And cure his love, and give her promis'd hand away.

XXIV.

One summer eve as in delightful walk,   185
    I landed, they past down Thirdpart's avenue,
And, in a lightsome interchange of talk,
    Whine'd out their loves, as lovers use to do,
Whilst ev'ry hairy bush upon its stalk
    Nodded for joy around them where it grew,   190
Charles took advantage of the lovely hour,
Again t' impress his suit with tongue's glib wordy power.

XXV.

O my sweet Susan! sweet my Susan, O! –
    (Here beat the poor laird his afflicted breast,)
Cast round thine eye, that eye that witches so,   195
    On God's wide world in beauty's garment drest,
On yonder many-listed clouds that glow
    Heav'n's tapst'ry curtaining the blazing west,
On yonder setting rays up-shot on high,
Like tiny wires of gold aslant the gorgeous sky;   200

71

XXVI.

Look how the bushy top of ev'ry tree
  Is mantled o'er with Evening's borrow'd sheen,
And seems to wag and wave more boastfully
  To the sweet breeze its leafy wig of green;
Each herb, and flow'r, and whin, and bush, we see,   205
  Laughs, jocund in creation's richest scene,
While earth reflects on heav'n, and heav'n on earth,
Of God's created things the beauty and the mirth:

XXVII.

All these are passing lovely to the view,
  But lovelier, tenfold lovelier are to me,   210
Thy form and countenance, my bonny Sue!
  Creation's beauties all are summ'd in thee;
Thine eye out-lustres heav'n's most lucid blue;
  Thy cheek out-blooms earth's bloomiest flow'r and tree;
And Evening's gaudy clouds, that paint the air,   215
Are fripp'ry to the locks of thy long golden hair!

XXVIII.

Then hey! my sweeting, when shall come the day
  Ordain'd to give me such transcendent charms?
Still must I pine and fret at thy delay,
  Capriciously forbidden from thy arms?   220
And like a pair of bellows puff away
  My sighs, and swelter in hot Cupid's harms? –
For heav'n's sake, Susan, on my case have pity,
And fix our wedding-day, my chick, my dear, my pretty!

XXIX.

This said, he, gazing on her saucy eye,   225
  Forestalls the angry answer of her tongue;
When hark! a sound of rushing, wildly high,
  Is heard the trees adjoining from among,
As if a whirlwind, bursting from the sky,
  Their tops on one another sore had swung;   230
And lo! out-springs in maddest pitch of wrath
Pitcorthie's biggest bull upon their peaceful path.

XXX.

Fly, fly, my love! the gen'rous Melvil said,
  And interpos'd to meet the monster's shock,
For fiercely rush'd he on th' endanger'd maid,   235
  Mad at the glaring of her scarlet frock;
Fly, fly, my love! – she turn'd about and fled,
  With face through terrour pale and white as smoke,
And left her laird, at danger of his scull,
To wrestle for his life and parry with the bull.   240

The bull's long horns he grip'd, and tow'rd the ground
  Press'd down with might his hugy head robust,
Whilst, madder thus defrauded of his wound,
  The brawny brute his bulk still forward thrust,
And, riving with his heels the soil around,   245
  Bespatter'd heav'n with turf, and sod, and dust,
And bellow'd till each tree around him shook,
And Echo bellow'd back from her aerial nook.

XXXII

At last th' intrepid lover, guessing well
  That now far off from harm his Sue was sped,   250
Ungrip'd the horns, that, white and terrible,
  From brow their long and curling menace spread;
But scarce his grasp was loos'd, when (sad to tell!)
  Th' advantag'd brute toss'd churlishly his head,
And with one horn, that suddenly uprose,   255
Demolish'd and tore off the gallant Melvil's nose.

Clean by the roots uptorn was Melvil's nose,
  Leaving its place deform and foul with blood;
Yet stood he not to reap some heavier blows,
  And catch in napkin the red rushing flood;   260
But, quite regardless of his face's woes,
  He, hurrying down the alley of the wood,
Fled as if life were hung upon his heels,
Nor in his sweaty haste his nose's torment feels.

XXXIV

Thus by the mettle of his heels he bore   265
  His life in safety from the brute away,
And left behind, his wound's unsightly gore
  To all the wild-cats of the grove a prey;
Homeward, in dumpish mood, afflicted sore,
  He took with lamentation loud his way,   270
Wailing his piteous bitterness of case,
His nasal honours crush'd, and ghastly havock'd face.

Six weeks he kept his mansion at Carnbee,
  Waiting his nose's re-establishment;
In vain; repair'd, alas! it could not be,   275
  Too sore that horn the cartilage had shent;
Fife's surgeons crowding came, for love of fee,
  With plaisters and with saws of loathsome scent;
In vain; what could or saw or surgeon do?
Gone was the good old nose, and who could rear a new?   280

XXXVI.

Meanwhile he ceas'd not twice a week, to send
  Sweet cards to her, who did his thoughts employ,
Memorials dear, which as he sat and penn'd,
  Perch'd laughing on his quill Love's mighty boy,
And on the paper from its inky end
  Distill'd delight, and tenderness, and joy;
His cards he sent, but (O, the sin and shame!)
From wicked shameless Sue there ne'er an answer came.

XXXVII.

Nor could her cruel silence be explain'd,
  Till Fame blew up the tidings to his house,
That she, for whom his nose was marr'd and pain'd,
  To whom so long he had addrest his vows,
Had, for another, now his love disdain'd,
  Urg'd by her uncle Newark to espouse,
That publish'd were their bans, that now was fixt
The wedding to be held on Monday forenoon next.

XXXVIII.

Then was the heart of injur'd Melvil rent
  With bitter passion at a slight so base;
That moment up he started with intent
  To go and chide th' apostate to her face:
Forth from his house in surly chafe he went
  Apparell'd in his coat of golden lace,
And eastward took his way alone and sad,
Half cursing, in his heart, a maid so base and bad.

XXXIX.

But when the little boys and girls survey'd
  His lack-nose visage as he travell'd by,
Some to their mothers' houses ran, afraid,
  To tell them what a face had met their eye;
Some with their fingers pointed, undismay'd,
  Giggling and blithe at his deformity,
Ev'n ploughmen, at the road-edge, paus'd from toil,
And held their sturdy sides, and loudly laugh'd a while.

XL.

Yet onward held the hapless laird his gait,
  Regardless of their mockery and scorn;
His sole vexation was the girl ingrate,
  In whose defence his beauty had been shorn:
He soon attain'd the ample hall, where sate
  In morning dishabille the fair forsworn,
And, ent'ring boldly in his angry mood,
With grimly-flatten'd face before her frowning stood.

285

290

295

300

305

310

315

320

74

XLI

Fy, Horror! who art thou, she scoffing said,
　　That with defeature horrible to see
Dar'st thus into my room advance thy stride
　　To fright my lapdog and to sicken me?
Go, hie thee homeward, thou deform, and hide　　　　325
　　That aspect in the dingles of Carnbee;
There with thy rabbits burrow thee, till sprout
Forth from between thy cheeks a beautifying snout.

This said, th' insulting creature from her chair,
　　Red with resentment, on a sudden springs,　　　　320
And bolting forward with a saucy air,
　　Her shapely person from the chamber flings,
Leaving her honest laird confounded there,
　　Heart-anguish'd by vexation's sharpest stings,
That he may vent his anger and his fume　　　　335
On the fair carved chairs that decorate her room.

XLIII

He got no long time to displode and vent
　　On the fair chairs his bosom-choking ire;
For, from his closet by Miss Susan sent,
　　Sir Michael rush'd, the sorcerer stout and dire,　　　　340
With staff in hand to rattle chastisement
　　Upon the ribs and backbone of the squire;
He beat him from the house with magic stick,
And added surly words and rude discourteous kick.

Poor Melvil! griev'd and mortify'd and dampt,　　　　345
　　His back he turn'd upon the uncivil door,
And, musing vengeance, down the alley trampt,
　　As boil'd his heart with indignation o'er;
He bit his lip, and curs'd the soil and stampt,
　　Chafing his wrath with imprecation more;　　　　350
For what man, so misus'd, could have forborne
To ban Sir Michael Scot, and Sue the fair forsworn?

XLV

So down the avenue he banning past,
　　Scarce conscious whither in his fret he went,
Till Twilight tenanted the sky at last,　　　　355
　　Pavilioning o'er earth her sable tent,
And the round moon, up-wheeling from the vast
　　Of sea, in pomp of clouds magnificent,
Embellish'd with her sober silvery shine
The leaves and barky trunks of Thirdpart's fir and pine.　　　　360

XLVI.

Alas! was e'er like me poor lover crost!
　(He thus aloud deplor'd his wretched case)
So fool'd, abus'd and cocker'd to my cost,
　So beaten into sorrow and disgrace!
Was't not enough that for the jade I lost
　The rising honours of my ruin'd face,
But, like a hedge-born beggar tatters-hung,
Thus from her hated gate I must be switch'd and flung?

365

XLVII.

May vengeance seize thee, thou foul wizard churl,
　For basting me at such an irksome rate!
May Satan gripe thee by the heel and hurl
　Thy carcase whizzing through Hell's hottest gate!
And as for thee thou proud ingrateful girl,
　Whose baseness to my grief I know too late,
May some good pow'r, the injur'd lover's friend,
On thy perfidious head a wing'd requital send!

370

375

XLVIII.

His pray'r he thus ejaculating spake,
　Nor knew that some good pow'r was nigh to hear,
For in the middle of a flow'ry brake,
　That white with moonshine spread it's thicket near,
Lay Tommy Puck the gentle fay awake,
　And Mrs Puck his gentle lady dear,
Basking and lolling in the lunar ray,
And tumbling up and down in brisk fantastic play.

380

XLIX.

Quoth frisky Tommy to his elfin wife;
　Didst thou not hear the gentleman, my chuck?
'Tis young Carnbee – the sweetest laird of Fife,
　Whom sour Sir Michael with his cane has struck:
What think ye? – By Titania's precious life!
　Fits it not now the tender-hearted Puck
T' assist an injur'd lover, and to plot
A scheme of nice revenge on Sue and Michael Scot?

385

390

L.

O yes, my dear! his fairy consort said,
　Go forth, and to the man address thy talk;
This heard, he from his bushy arbour's shade
　Flung out his minim stature on the walk,
And stood in dwarfish finery array'd,
　Gaudy as summer-bean's bloom-cover'd stalk;
He doff'd his hat and made a bow profound,
And thus bespoke the laird in words of pleasing sound.

395

400

76

LI.

Marvel not, Melvil, that before thy feet
  I plant me thus in fearless attitude,
For I have heard within my close retreat
  What thou hast utter'd in thy fretful mood,
And well I know thy truth how with deceit 405
  Repaid, thy faith with base ingratitude;
Good soul! I pity thee with all my heart,
And therefore from my bush to thy assistance start:

LII.

For much it grieves Tom Puck's too feeling breast,
  That one so good, so liberal and true, 410
Should thus become a laughter and a jest,
  Mock'd, jilted, beaten into black and blue:
I like to help whom Malice has opprest,
  And prompt a lover generous as you;
So with attention list what I propose 415
To baffle and avenge and laugh to scorn your foes.

LIII.

On Monday next th' appointed wedding day
  For perjur'd Sue her Newark to espouse,
When her long hall with feasting shall be gay,
  And smoke with meats, with riot, and with bouse, 420
From thy paternal mansion haste away
  At height of noon to Thirdpart's bustling house,
That thou, by time of dinner may be there,
Prepar'd to climb the steps of her detested stair.

LIV.

And when th' exulting bridegroom and his bride, 425
  Surrounded with their festive spousal train,
Are seated at their tables long and wide,
  Wielding their noisy forks and knives amain,
Then burst into the hall with dauntless stride,
  Through menials, greasy cooks and servingmen, 430
Nor speak a word though in thy way they stand,
But dash the scroyls aside with swing of boist'rous hand.

LV.

Surprise, be sure, shall seize the feasters all
  At such a bold intruder on their treat;
Their forks, half-lifted to their mouths, shall fall 435
  Down on their plates, unlighten'd of their meat;
Yet speak not still, but, casting round the hall
  An eye whose every glance is fire and threat,
Thou in a corner of the room shalt see
Sir Michael's magic staff, the same that basted thee. 440

LVI.

Snatch up that magic energetic stick,
   And, in thy clench'd hand wielding it with might,
On Michael's white bald pate discharge thou quick
   A pelt enough to stun the wizard wight;
Strange consequence shall follow from that lick;   445
   Yet be not thou amaz'd or struck with fright,
But springing to the table's upper end,
Let on his niece's nose an easier pat descend.

LVII.

I will not now unfold what odd event
   From either stroke will suddenly ensue;   450
Enough to know, that plenteous punishment
   Shall light on grim Sir Michael and on Sue:
Go – by your nose's cure, be confident
   That Tommy Puck aright thus counsels you:
This said, he, from a vial silver-bright,   455
Pour'd out upon his palm a powder small and white;

LVIII.

And to his mouth up-lifting it, he blows
   The magic dust on Melvil's blemish'd face,
When (such its power) behold another nose
   Sprouts out upon the scarr'd and skinless place,   460
And to th' astonished moon, fair-jutting, shows
   It's supplemental elegance and grace:
Which done, he, shining like a bright glow-worm
Plung'd deep amid the brake his puny pretty form.

LIX.

Amaze had taken Melvil, when appear'd   465
   Erect before his steps the pigmy fay,
Yet not with less attention had he hear'd
   What courteous Tommy did so kindly say:
That heart, late vex'd and tortur'd, now was cheer'd,
   And merrily beat in Hope's delightful play;   470
Homeward he jogg'd from Thirdpart's haunted shade,
Proud of his novel nose, and Tommy's tender'd aid.

LX.

Arrived the day when saucy Sue should wed
   Young Newark vap'ring in his scarlet coat,
From his paternal mansion Melvil sped   475
   To Thirdpart house t' atchieve his ready plot:
'Twas dinner-time; the tables all were spread
   With luscious sirloins reeking richly hot,
Gravies and pies and steaming soups of hare,
And roasted hen and goose, and titbits nice and rare.   480

LXI.

Sue at the table's place of honour sat
    Dealing the warm broth from its vessel out,
Whilst, slashing with his knife through lean and fat,
    Carv'd at the lower end Sir Michael stout;
'Twas nought but mirth, and junketing and chat,   485
    And handing wings and legs of fowl about,
And noise of silver spoons, and clank and clatter
Of busy forks and knives, of porringer and platter.

LXII.

Squire Melvil heard without the dinner's din;
    Nor tarry'd; but with brisk and boist'rous bound,   490
Jump'd up the stairs, and rudely rushing in
    Dash'd down whom standing in his way he found;
Menials and apron'd cooks of greasy chin,
    Fist-founder'd, went a-rapping to the ground,
With all their loads of sauces, meats, and plates,   495
In ruin fat and rich hurl'd on their pitiful pates.

LXIII.

Astonish'd were the feasters when they view'd
    Such bold intruder stand before their eyes;
The morsels in their mouths that lay half-chewed,
    Could not be swallow'd through their great surprise,   500
Their half-rais'd forks, bestuck with gobbets good,
    Dropt, as if impotent more high to rise;
Each on his neighbour cast a meaning stare,
As if he dumbly ask'd, What does Squire Melvil there?

LXIV.

'Twas for a moment silent in the hall,   505
    As if pale Death the chapless and the grim,
Had taken by the throat and choak'd them all
    With his long, fleshless, scraggy, fingers slim;
Till, throwing round his glance from wall to wall,
    The Squire discern'd the staff with tassel trim,   510
Sir Michael's staff with head of silver white,
Wherewith he was enjoin'd it's owner's poll to smite.

LXV.

He flew, he grasp'd it by its silver rind,
    And to the ceiling swinging it on high,
Brought down on Michael's pate, as quick as wind,   515
    A pelt that whizz'd and rattled horribly;
Sounded his bald scull with the stroke unkind,
    Re-echoing in each lore-fill'd cavity,
When, O the wonder, on his high arm-chair,
Chang'd was the churlish knight that instant to a hare!   520

His dainty head with learning so replete,
  Collaps'd, grew round, and little, and long-ear'd;
His arms, that yet were stretch'd to carve the meat,
  Quite shrunken into two fore-legs appear'd;
His brawny thighs turn'd hind-legs on his seat   525
  Whereon his metamorphos'd form was rear'd;
And, to complete the quadruped, out-sprouted
A short tail from his rump, with plenteous hair about it.

LXVII.
He sat not long, so transmew'd, on his chair,
  But, lighting on the carpet-cover'd floor,   530
Scudded as swift as lightning down the stair
  On his four bestial legs to gain the door;
Hollo! cry'd boy and groom, A hare! a hare!
  As flew he from the house their eyes before;
Hollo! let loose on Puss the fleet grey-hound!   535
Was bawl'd in Thirdpart's court from one to t'other round.

LXVIII.
Unkennel'd in a twink was fleet grey-hound,
  And after Puss commenced the keen pursuit;
O'er plough'd, o'er sown, o'er green, o'er fallow ground,
  With lev'ret craft, and wile of weary foot,   540
With skip and scud and ditch-o'erleaping bound,
  The wizard ran in guise of hairy brute,
While snuffing out with sapient nose his track,
Came yelling at his heels all Thirdpart's clam'rous pack.

LXIX.
Eastward they scour'd, out-scampering the gale,   545
  Long-winded dog and pursy panting hare,
Till, taking refuge in the streets of Crail,
  Sir Michael plung'd him in a *jawhole* there,
And left, without, his foes with wagging tail
  Worrying the sky with bark of loud despair,   550
As he, secure, was fain to slink and cuddle
Encav'd beneath the street within his miry puddle.

LXX.
There let us leave the knight to cuddle fain,
  And long-tongu'd dog to volley out his yell,
And turn we to the banquet-hall again,   555
  Where Michael's metamorphosis befel:
No sooner saw the squire that not in vain
  The staff had lighted, but succeeded well,
Than, bounding up to where jilt Susan sat,
On her fair nose's bridge he brought a gentle pat.   560

LXXI.

A second miracle ensues, for lo!
　　That nose, her countenance's pride and grace,
Grows out and shoots and lengthens at the blow,
　　Ridiculously sprouting from her face,
And aye it swells and beetles moe and moe,　　　　　　565
　　Tap'ring to such a length it's queer disgrace
That dips it's point at last amid the broth,
That near her lies in dish upon the table-cloth.

LXXII.

Nor did her aspect only suffer shame;
　　For, in proportion as extends her nose,　　　　　　570
Her shoulders, late so beautiful of frame,
　　Into a hump up-heaving, hugely rose,
Most mountainous and gross, as ill became
　　Fair bride array'd in sumptuous wedding clothes,
Her very gown was burst and riven through,　　　　　575
With the large fleshy swell, so monstrous big it grew!

LXIII.

Then shook the room with laughter's frequent crack,
　　As saw the guests each droll excrescence rise;
One pointed to her still-upheaving back,
　　One to her nose's still-enlarging size;　　　　　　580
Ha! ha! from every squire's throat loudly brake,
　　Te-hee! each lady chuckles and replies;
Heav'ns, what a hideous nose! cried every dame;
Heav'ns, what a hideous hump! did every laird exclaim.[2]

LXXIV.

Such was the punishment which silly Sue　　　　　　585
　　From her resentful much-wrong'd lover bore,
And so was sour Sir Michael punish'd too,
　　For caneing honest Melvil from her door;
Wherefore, as now the work of vengeance due
　　Was finish'd, Charlie left her chamber-floor,　　　590
And turn'd his face, rejoicing, towards home,
Mutt'ring his grateful thanks to little elfin Tom.

NOTES

1　The famous witch of Pittenweem. See *Satan's Invisible World Discovered*.
1　It may here be not improper to remark, that Wieland gives to one of his Fairy Tales
　　a catastrophe somewhat similar, if I recollect right, to the above.

ANSTER FAIR

Canto VI

ARGUMENT

The people having loudly testified their approbation of Robert's
Story, the monarch joins the hands of Maggie and the conqueror,
ordering his trumpeter, to publish with clang of trump, the marriage.
As evening now falls down, the multitude break up and disperse. The
king and his nobility attend the bride and bridegroom to the house of
Maggie, where they sit down, till supper be prepared. In the mean-
time, the town is ringing with joy – Bonfires burn – Ale and porter
flow from their hogheads – While the young and supple dance in the
loan. The company in the house of Maggie then sit down to supper;
immediately after which the bridegroom rises, and relates, how he was
incited to come forward, as a candidate to the fair, by a female fairy,
who, on an evening as he sat in his own house at supper, rose splen-
didly from his pepper-box, and having encouraged him with promise
of her assistance in the games, desired him to carry with him that box
wherein she was by spell confined, and set it on the table of
Maggie. He produces it accordingly: it leaps to the middle of the
table, and is there joined by the pot, whence Puck arose heretofore.
The two fairies instantly appear from their separate cells, and fall on
one another's necks in embrace. Puck then tells the company,
wherefore, and by what wizard, they had been thus shut up in such
ignominious prisons. Having finished his narration, he seizes the
hand of Mrs Puck and flies away with her through the window. The
company, after drinking a few glasses, retire from table.

I.

Gay-hearted I began my playful theme,
  But with a heavy heart I end my song;
For I am sick of life's delirious dream,
  Sick of this world and all its weight of wrong;
Ev'n now, when I again attempt to stream   5
  My merry verse, as I was wont, along,
'Tween ev'ry sportive thought, there now and then
Flows a sad serious tear upon my playful pen.

II.

Scarce had the victor ceas'd his hindmost clause,
  When from th' immensity of folk afar,   10
Rose such a hideous shout of loud applause,
  As ever stunn'd with outcry sun or star;
Each tongue grew riotous within its jaws,
  Clacking an acclamation popular;
Hands, high o'erhead uplifted, round and round   15
Struck plausive palm on palm, and clapt a rattling sound.

III.

And twice ten thousand hats, aloft upthrown
  In black ascension, blot heaven's blue serene,
O'ercanopying ANSTER's crowded loan
  With crown and rim as with a dusky screen,   20
And bonnets broad, and caps of sharp'ning cone
  Whirling 'twixt earth and firmament are seen,
And lasses cowls, and hoods, uptost on high,
Encroach with tawdry clout upon the clouds of sky.

IV.

As when a troop of locusts, famine-pin'd,   25
  From Edom's unblest monster-breeding womb,
Sail on the hot wings of the southern wind
  Wriggling aloft their sky-hung mass of gloom;
And where El Sham's clear golden riv'lets wind
  Through her gay gardens distributing bloom,   30
They light, and spread their devastation round,
Bepainting black as pitch the green luxuriant ground.

V.

Just such a darkness mounts into the sky
  Of hat, and hood, of bonnet, and of cap,
So thick, that those who swing them up on high   35
  Below i' the shade are heard to shout and clap,
For still the folk applaud it lustily,
  And pain their tingling palms with noisy rap,
Expressing thus, with deaf'ning acclamation,
Of ROBERT's merry tale, their hearty approbation.   40

VI.

Nor sits the monarch idle to th' acclaim;
   But, rising up majestic from his chair,
With kingly praise augments the victor's fame,
   And, clapping, grinds between his palms the air:
Then seizes he the fingers of the dame,   45
   And gently raising from her seat the fair,
He, as the sign and seal of marriage-band,
Slips into ROBERT's grasp his MAGGIE's tender hand.

VII.

He bade his choir of trumpeters apply
   To mouth their hollow instruments of sound,   50
And, in an unison of clangour high,
   Publish the marriage to the world around;
The fellows blew it to the peak of sky,
   And sky sent down again the loud rebound;
Earth did to Heav'ns high top the news up-throw,   55
And Heav'n re-bruited back th' alarum down below.

VIII.

But now the beam-hair'd coursers of the sun,
   Y-smoking with their fiery hot fatigue,
Their task of charioting had pranc'd and run,
   And hurled in sea their hissing golden gig;   60
Their unshorn driver had but just begun
   Beyond the Isle of Bute the wave to swig;
And, twinkling o'er Auld Reekie's smoke afar,
Peep'd through Heav'ns mantle blue the modest evening star.

IX.

And soon the moon in hood of silver drest,   65
   All glistering and gladsome as may be,
Forth from her glorious casement in the east
   Look'd laughing down upon both land and sea;
And on the bosom of the dark'ning west
   Her pearly radiance shot rejoicingly: 70
Also the heads of all that fill the loan
Wax'd yellow with the rays that on them streaming shone.

X.

Wherefore as now the damp nocturnal air
   Began to dribble down its chilly dew,
And as of all the business of the fair,   75
   Nought now remain'd upon the green to do,
The herald, from beside the monarch's chair,
   Abroad the signal of dispersion blew,
That the wide multitude, dispread around,
Should now break up its mass, and leave the nighted ground.   80

XI.

Which heard, the congregated folk upbroke
　With loud disruption their diffusion vast,
And, split and shoaling off in many a flock,
　With homeward squeeze they turbulently past;
Beneath their feet the pillar'd Earth did rock,　　　　　　85
　As up to Jove a dusty cloud they cast,
That blear'd the bright eyes of Night's glimm'ring queen,
And chok'd the brilliant stars and dimm'd their twinkling sheen.

XII.

And such the clutter was, when shoal from shoal
　With violent impulse was torn and riven,　　　　　　90
As when the vaulting ice that floors the pole,
　Touch'd by the fiery shafts of warming Heaven,
Splits into fractur'd isles that crash and roll
　Diverse, athwart the molten ocean driven;
The Greenland boatman hears the noise afar,　　　　　　95
And blesses for its heat day's winter-routing star.

XIII.

So loudly rush'd from ANSTER's cumber'd loan
　The burthenous and bustling multitude,
Kicking th' o'ertrampled earth they trod upon
　With saucy heel in their impetuous mood;　　　　　　100
Some to their tents of blanket jump'd anon
　That on the fields and crofts adjoining stood;
Some to their booths and houses in the town
Hie hot with huddling haste and hop and hurry down.

XIV.

Meanwhile, the king, as now sufficient space　　　　　　105
　Was for his passage clear'd about the mound,
Descended from his lofty honour'd place,
　Where sat he mid his gallant courtiers round:
Close at his right hand, downward walk'd with grace,
　The well-earn'd prize, bright MAGGIE the renown'd,　110
While the great victor at his other side
Attended blithe and brisk, exulting in his bride.

XV.

On their brave nags their persons up they swing,
　And to the borough gently jogging ride,
Hemm'd thick around with an illustrious ring　　　　　　115
　Of gay court-ladies trooping side by side,
And lords, whose coats with gold lace spangled, fling
　Back on th' abashed moon her beamy pride,
And jolly knights, and booted esquires stout,
And burghers, clowns, and boys, a noisy rabble-rout.　　120

XVI.

As downward to the town they tramp and trot,
  The mingled peals of gratulation rise;
For, on their catlings, fiddlesticks, I wot,
  Bicker'd and skipt in funny furious wise,
And trumpet rear'd again its solemn note   125
Sonorously, assailant on the skies,
Full loudly lifting in a jocund tune,
The name of RANTER ROB up to the man i' th' moon.

XVII.

And sounding cymbals clink and ring sublime,
  Clash'd overhead in lofty unison;   130
And fife and flute in merry whistle chime,
  Soothing the lulled ear with dulcet tone;
While aye, the bass-drum at his proper time,
  Swallows the music with his sudden groan;
Till drum, flute, cymbal, trumpet, all, are drown'd   135
In shouts that pealing rise from the mad mob around.

XVIII.

Thus rode the train, as if in triumph down,
  Exulting, through the night's moon-gilded shade,
Till, reaching MAGGIE's quarter of the town,
  Stops at her house the splendid cavalcade;   140
(For be it now, my good co-townsmen! known
  That in th' East-green's best house fair MAGGIE stay'd,
Near where St Ayle's small lodge in modern day
Admits to mystic rites her bousy masons gay.)

XIX.

At MAGGIE's door they stopp'd; when, lighting there,   145
  The bridegroom brisk, and jolly-minded king,
And showy nobleman, and lady fair,
  From pad and saddle on the causey spring,
And, passing in due order up her stair,
  The good landlady to her chamber bring,   150
A pomp of rare attendance brave and bright,
With sweetly-biting jest, and joke of dear delight.

XX.

In her torch-brighten'd chamber down they sate
  Upon her chairs, jocundly one and all,
And exercise their tongues in social prate,   155
  Till MAGGIE's cooks and James's seneschal
May well prepare and range each supper-plate
  On her long table in her dining-hall:
There let us leave awhile, king, lord, and lady,
And saunter through the town till supper's fare be ready.   160

XXI.

Heav'ns! how from street to street the people reel,
    As if they knew not where to rush for joy!
How rocks the causey with incessant heel
    Of hurrying man, and wife, and maid, and boy!
From lane and wynd the sounds of gladness peal,   165
    Hitting the stars with clamorous annoy;
As all the houses' walls and roofs are bright
With bonfire's yellow glow and candles' gentler light.

XXII.

For in each window's every pane is seen,
    Stuck into fitly-fashion'd wood or clay,   170
A tallow candle flinging forth it's sheen,
    T' augment th' illumination's grand display!
How flame the houses with a lustre keen,
    In emulation of the sun-bright day!
Ev'n the poor old-wife's backroom-window glows,   175
Gilding the good green kail that underneath it grows:

XXIII.

While in each street and lane both broad and strait,
    And at the Cross and up along the loan,
Their spiry curls huge bonfires elevate,
    Cracking with heat the ground and causey stone;   180
For ev'ry bonfire was a cart-load great
    Of Dysart coal that redly flash'd and shone,
Emblazing with its tongues of flame so bright
The dusk and smutty brow of star-bestudded night.

XXIV.

And, gawntress'd round each ruddy fire about,   185
    Hogsheads of porter and of cheery ale
Forth from their little gurgling bung-holes spout
    Their genial streams in tankard, pot, and pail:
O 'twas a wild notorious guzzling-bout!
    That night no throat was narrow or was frail,   190
But, in long draughts delicious, swallow'd down
The barley's mantling cream and bev'rage stout and brown.

XXV.

(Not from thy brew-house's well-barrel'd store,
    O Roger! comes a drink of stronger proof,
Though foams thy hearty ale the tankard o'er,   195
    And sends its cork a-thund'ring to the roof:)
Ev'n ancient men, whose hairs were thin and hoar,
    Then staid not from the fuddle's fun aloof,
But drank till every head was giddy turning,
And to their reeling eyes their fires in sky seem'd burning.   200

XXVI.
Yet not, beside each coal-fed splendour drank
  The younkers with their sweet-hearts blithe and boon;
They on the loan in many a lusty rank
  Twist the long reel beneath the lightsome moon,
Or thrid the country-dance's maze and crank,   205
  Tossing and twinkling their nigh-bursten shoon,
Whilst, ever and anon, or ere she wist,
Smack by her partner dear each bonny lass was kiss'd.

XXVII.
Such out of doors was the disport and bouse;
  But higher was the pitch of joy within;   210
That night was ANSTER's every barn and house
  Converted into tippling-shop, and inn;
Garrets and bed-rooms reek with hot carouse,
  And steaming punch of whisky and of gin;
The kitchen fires are crowded round and round   215
With rings of lively lads that swig their bowls profound.

XXVIII.
Hey! how their glasses jingle merrily!
  How rings the table with their revel-roar!
How, as they toast their MAG with three times three,
  Sounds with loud heel the vex'd tormented floor!   220
They sing, they clap, they laugh with honest glee;
  Were never seen such merry men heretofore!
Thro' window glass and stony wall bursts out
Abroad on night's dull ear the wassail's frequent shout.

XXIX.
But now in MAGGIE's tap'stry-decked hall   225
  Serv'd is the sumptuous marriage-supper up,
And clean neat-handed cook and seneschal
  Hath set each mess, and dish, and plate, and cup;
So down in seemly order sit they all,
  With stomachs stiff and resolute to sup,   230
And set their griding forks and knives to work
On turkey, goose, and hen, cold veal, and cheek of pork.

XXX.
Behoves it not my bardship to relate
  What various viands burden'd MAGGIE's board;
What lay on this, and what on t' other plate,   235
  What lady first was help'd, and by what lord,
What mess the king and what the others ate:
  That would be tedious trifling, 'pon my word;
I will not do't – tho' I could tell, in sooth,
How oft each fork was rais'd to every munching mouth.   240

XXXI.

Suffice it, good my townsmen, that ye know
  That there fastidious teeth found pleasant food,
That all the cates that kingly banquets show
  Were spread before them, fragrant, rich, and good;
And that, tho' some ate less and some ate moe,   245
  Each ate as much, be certain, as he cou'd;
Till, tir'd at last of piddling with their gums,
They eas'd of knife and fork their fingers and their thumbs.

XXXII.

But when the sound of teeth had ceas'd i' the hall,
  And fork and knife lay idle on their plate,   250
And guest and hostess, backward leaning all,
  Their picktooths now were plying, saturate,
Up from his seat arose the bridegroom tall,
  Where to his blooming spouse oppos'd he sate,
And, e'er the table-cloth was ta'en away,   255
He turn'd him to the king, and thus addrest his say.

XXXIII.

Think not, my liege, that Fortune or that Chance
  To-day hath made me in my conquest blest,
Impelling me by casual circumstance
  To jump without a warrant like the rest;   260
'Twas not alone with Heav'ns high sufferance,
  I put my jumping-prowess to the test;
'Twas by its order I in sack was bound;
'Twas with its favour too, that I my bride have found.

XXXIV.

Nor deem that some dumb beldam, Satan's tool,   265
  Or wily witch, or second-sighted seer,
Hath, oracling, decceiv'd me like a fool,
  To think I to supernal Pow'r am dear;
No, monarch; by the cowl of old St Rule!
  I heard the order with no proxy ear,   270
And with my own true eye unfalsify'd,
I ev'n upon my chair the goodly vision spy'd:

XXXV.

For, on an evening in December last
  ('Twas just the evening of that day whereon
The stout-lung'd criers through the Border past,   275
  Proclaiming what should hap in ANSTER loan),
As down to supper's sober cool repast
  I sat me in my dining-room alone,
Musing upon the late heard news so odd
Blown from the trump of fame and crier's throat abroad.   280

89

XXXVI.

I happen'd in my fingers up to take
  The pepper-box where lurk'd my spicy stores,
And held it o'er my plate intent to shake
  The fragrant atoms from its little bores,
When, as my hand inverted it, there brake   285
  Out from the tin lid's perforated pores,
A stream of beauteous smoke, that like a mist
Curl'd its delicious wreaths around my shaded fist.

XXXVII.

Astonish'd at the prodigy, I threw
  The steaming box upon the table-cloth,   290
When, more with miracle t' amaze my view,
  It frisk'd and trotted mid the plates, i' troth,
And ceas'd not from its num'rous holes to spue
  Its incense white as flakes of ocean froth,
Up-sending to the ceiling of the room   295
Its supernat'ral flux of pure and fragrant fume.

XXXVIII.

I sat and gaz'd – not long; when, strange to say,
  Forth from that reeky pillar's paly base
Started at once a little female fay
  Giggling and blithely laughing in my face: 300
Her height was as the lily that in May
  Lifts to the sun her head's envermeil'd grace;
Her beauty as the rays of various glow
That glorify the length of Heav'n's sea-drinking bow.

XXXIX.

The gown in which her elf-ship was array'd   305
  Like to the peacock's painted feather shin'd,
And on the tablecloth redundant spread
  Its lustrous train for half a foot behind;
Over her breast her purple-striped plaid
  Lay floating loose and thin as woven wind;   310
And gorgeous was her head-dress as the hue
Of Iris-flow'r that spreads her velvet petals blue.

XL.

Deck'd was her neck's circumference with row
  Of di'monds strung on thread in costly band,
Small pearly berries that are wont to grow   315
  Upon the bushes of old Fairyland;
And in each di'mond's orb so fair in show
  My candle's image burning seem'd to stand
That her white slender neck was all in gleam
Doubly impearled thus with Light's reflected beam.   320

And pendent from her neck by golden thread
   A little dangling silver lute I saw,
Of fashion rare, and quaintly polished,
   Not thicker than a pipe of oaten straw:
She laugh'd and nodded courteously her head,   325
   Belike to clear away my doubt and awe,
For, sooth to say, I was not unafear'd
When from my pepper-box good lady fay appear'd.

She dropt a curtsy, reverently low,
   And thus bespoke in clear and mellow voice;   330
('Twas sweeter than the chiming winds that blow
   Upon th' Æolian harp a whiffled noise;)
Excuse me, good your worship! that I so
   With my quaint presence mar your supper's joys;
I have some little matter to impart;   335
'Twill not detain you long – Nay, Robert – do not start:

Compose thee, squire, and calmly give thine ear
   To what shall from my gentle mouth proceed,
For mickle shall it profit thee to hear
   And prize aright the value of my rede;   340
And be assur'd thy person, ROB, is dear
   To the slim creatures of the fairy breed,
That thus I peer from out my box of spice,
To tender, for thy weal, my uncompell'd advice:

XLIV

Hast thou not heard the wond'rous news to-day   345
   Through all the marches of the Border blown,
Of sports, and games, and celebrations gay,
   Promulgate to be held in ANSTER loan,
And that a maid the victor's toils shall pay,
   A maid, whose beauty is excell'd by none?   350
Thou hast – and I surpris'd thee deep in muse
A-pond'ring on th' import of such amazing news:

Go, when o'er Cockraw peeps Light's golden horn,
   And seek a supple ass whereon to ride;
Go, seek a long sack, sturdy and untorn,   355
   Wherein to jump with drolly-trammel'd stride;
Go, seek a bagpipe whose wind-pouch unworn
   May well the wrath of prison'd breath abide;
Go, set thy brain to work like vat of ale,
And skim thou off for MAG some smart ingenious tale.   360

XLVI.

And know, when at the loan is try'd thy skill,
   Thy ass I'll nettle on with spur unseen;
Into thy bones and sinews I'll instil
   Great vigour to o'erjump the quaking green;
Thy bagpipe's pouch with tempest I will fill,   365
   Lending thy tune a witchery not mean;
And from thy study-rack'd perplexed brains
A merry tale I'll squeeze, the help-mate of thy pains.

XLVII.

So shalt thou, squire, in Scotland's view be crown'd
   Upon the spot with victory and fame,   370
And ride a happy bridegroom from the ground,
   Elate and glorying in thy peerless dame:
Yet when thy toil's transcendant prize is found,
   And marriage-revelries thy joy proclaim,
I charge thee, as my aid shall make thee blest,   375
Forget not what I now, as to my box, request:

XLVIII.

This box – this pepper box – this homely shrine
   Wherein confin'd by wizard spell I stay,
Must be transported in a pouch of thine,
   When thou to ANSTER loan dost take thy way;   380
And when thou down to marriage feast and wine
   Shalt sit, in MAGGIE's hall, a bridegroom gay,
Then from thy pocket draw it in a trice,
And on the table-cloth lay down the box of spice.

XLIX.

Ask not the purport of my odd behest;   385
   'Twill be unriddled in the proper place;
'Tis thine t' effect the task, and leave the rest
   To Madam Puck's good complaisance and grace:
Here Madam Puck her piping voice supprest,
   And, with a sweet smile on her lily face,   390
Rear'd up the small lute in her lily fist
And with her rose-red lip its furbish'd silver kiss'd.

L.

She play'd a tune so delicate and sweet,
   So overpow'ring with it's ravishment,
That sit I could no longer on my seat,   395
   But up and cap'ring o'er my chamber went,
As if within the soles of both my feet
   A store of frisky Mercury was pent;
(And, by the bye, 'twas just the tune with which
My bagpipe did today your reeling loan bewitch.)   400

LI

At length she ceas'd, and in a stroke o' th' eye
  Delv'd down within her jail of tin again,
And in her stead left curling bonnily
  A smoke whose odour ravish'd nose and brain –
No more, my gracious liege – what need have I   405
  Longer to talk where talking would be vain? –
Behold – what Mrs Puck commanded me –
'Tis but a sorry thing – the pepper-box – d'ye see?

Thus speaking, from the pocket of his coat,
  Wherein he had convey'd it to our town,   410
The goblin-haunted pepper-box he brought,
  And, laughing, set it on the table down;
Great laughter crackled in the monarch's throat,
  As on the cloth he saw the tin y-thrown;
And giggling guest 'gan fling his jeers and jokes   415
Upon the paltry frame of Rob's poor pepper-box.

LIII

But soon was chang'd their blithe to fearful mood,
  When strait, afore each half-mistrusting eye,
The bawbling box of pepper where it stood
  Began again to dance spontaneously,   420
And fidg'd and frisk'd, in strange inquietude,
  Among the plates that thickly-ranged lie,
Directing to the table's middle part
Its motion by the side of broken pie and tart.

Yet to a greater pitch their wonder grew,   425
  When at the table's other end they spy
Fair MAGGIE's mustard-pot commencing too
  To gambol and to fidge in sympathy;
(The self-same pot whence burst to MAGGIE's view
  Of late Tom Puck with brightly-breeched thigh;)   430
As would a hen leap on a fire-hot griddle,
So leap'd the mustard-pot toward the table's middle.

LV

Short while they flirted, pepper-box and pot,
  Most laughable, yet fearful to be view'd,
Till, meeting on the table's midmost spot,   435
  Stock-still th' ignoble bouncing vessels stood,
And from their little cells, where lay the hot
  Ground pepper, and the biting mustard good,
Were in a moment seen at once to break
Two parallel white shafts of silv'ry spouting reek: 440

LVI.

Ascending curl'd, not long, each sep'rate fume,
  Up-throwing to the roof it's preciousness,
When with a fire-flash that emblaz'd the room,
  Burst from the hollow mustard-pot's recess
Good Tommy Puck, the fay of roseate bloom,   445
  Clad in his custom'd gaudery of dress
And, with a second gleam of flashy light,
Sprung from the spicy box good Madam Puck to sight:

LVII.

With faces to each other turn'd they rise,
  Scarce sunder'd by a finger's length of space,   450
And, in an instant as they recognise
  With glimpse of quick eye each the other's face,
They fall, as if o'ercome with sweet surprise,
  On one another's necks in close embrace,
Like friends that, having long liv'd far apart,   455
Meet and relieve in tears the joy-o'er-burden'd heart.

LVIII.

Astonishment his whitely ensign shows
  On each spectator's visage at the sight;
Courtier and king, that sat to table close,
  Slily push'd back their chairs, confounded quite: 460
The ladies hid their faces in their clothes,
  Or underneath the table slunk for fright;
Save MAG and ROB, who laugh'd to see once more,
The tricksy kindly ouphes that hail'd them heretofore.

LIX.

A while the pair of pigmies on the spot   465
  Lock'd their fantastic persons jole to jole,
And, as two doves of plumy-varnish'd throat
  Sit billing in their dove-cot's nested hole,
Their liquid wee lips twitter'd kisses hot
  In fond commutuality of soul;   470
It was a treat to see how sweetheart-like
Their fiery fairy mouths the dear collision strike!

LX.

At length, as rapture's first excess was past,
  They disentangle their endear'd embrace,
And, tow'rd the king and guests that sat aghast,   475
  Turn'd round each minim prettyness of face;
Dame Puck, to MAG and those beside her placed,
  Let fall a curtsy with a courtly grace;
Tom, fronting James, took hat from off his brow,
And curv'd his goblin back into a goodly bow.   480

LXI.

A glance upon the company he shot,
  And smil'd on M AG that sat at head o' the board,
Then from his silly dulcet-piping throat
  Sweet utterance of word-clad breath he pour'd;
O monarch! let amazement seize thee not;   485
  Be of good cheer, each dame and noble lord!
Ungown your timid faces, all ye fair!
Draw ye to table close, each gentleman your chair!

LXII.

For do not think that in us twain you spy
  Two spirits of the perter wicked sort,   490
That, buzzing on bad errand through the sky,
  In pranks of molestation take their sport,
Confounding old-wives' churns, and slipping sly
  Their stools from underneath them to their hurt,
Or chucking young sweet maids below the chin,   495
That so they bite the tongue their tender mouths within.

LXIII.

Of kindlier hearts are Tommy and his spouse,
  Aidant to some, benevolent to all,
For oft we sweep the thrifty matron's house
  With besom quaint, invisible, and small,   500
Oft from her cheese and butter chase the mouse
  Preyless, into the cavern of his wall,
And oft her churn-staff gripe that in a twink
The waves of bubbling cream to buttery masses sink.

LXIV.

But chiefly of young lovers true and kind,   505
  The patrons and the guardians good are we,
Linking each mutual and harmonious mind
  In silver cord of dear complacency;
But when the vows, that should restrain and bind,
  Broke to another's misery we see,   510
'Tis ours to take the injur'd lover's part,
And on the perjur'd head deal out th' avenging smart.

LXV.

Witness what vengeance hit Miss Susan Scot
  Whose back and visage, for her breach of troth,
Obtain'd a penal and opprobrious blot,   515
  Swoln out to counterpoise each other's growth;
And, though, for our suggestion of that plot
  To punish her and her sour guardian both,
My wife and I hath suffer'd hard and long,
Yet, by my monarch's beard! 'twas right t' avenge the wrong: 520

95

LXVI.

O we have suffer'd much! – that wizard foul
  (Beshrew his meagre vile malicious ghost!)
No sooner scap'd from Crail's vile sewer-hole,
  And took again the shape that he had lost,
Than, with his long-tail'd demons black as coal   525
  That whiz to serve him from Hell's every coast,
Consulting in his study, soon he learn'd
Who prompted Charles to wreak the vengeance justly earn'd.

LXVII.

Then churn'd the sorc'rer's mouth the surly foam;
  He clench'd his fist and swore by Beelzebub   530
He forthwith should o'er half the country roam,
  Beating each thicket with his oaken club,
To find out dapper intermeddling Tom
  In his inhabited and secret shrub,
And heel him forth reluctant to the day,   535
And for his pranks chastise upon his breech the fay.

LXVIII.

His hat he put on his craft-crammed head;
  He grip'd his hugy gnarled staff in hand,
And down his study-stair with sounding tread
  Came spitting smoke like newly-lighted brand;   540
Forth from the gate he in a hurry sped,
  To beat the total bushes of the land,
Cursing at every step the harmless breed
Of elfs that aid the wrong'd in grievous time of need.

LXIX.

Need it be told? Alas! too soon he found   545
  The bush, where with my dame I sleeping lay;
Too soon his cudgel, thrashing round and round,
  Graz'd our slim bodies in it's dang'rous play,
And, had not Ob'ron sav'd us both from wound,
  Our brains had fairly been dash'd out that day;   550
We woke; we shriek'd; his rugged hand he stretch'd
And from our leafy bed us by the heels he fetch'd.

LXX.

His long-nail'd hairy fingers, grasping tight
  Our waists, uprear'd us to his bearded chin,
And held us there in melancholy plight   555
  Wriggling our innocent frail members thin;
He spat upon our faces with despite,
  Glooming his phiz into a joyful grin;
Then, lowering down, he plung'd us ere we wot
Each int' a sep'rate pouch of his great clumsy coat.   560

LXXI.

There lay we button'd in, and closely pent
   In a dark dungeon of detested cloth,
As, tracing back his steps, he homeward went,
   And to his chamber bore us dangling both;
He drew us forth, the wicked churl, intent   565
   On base revenge, malevolent and wroth,
And with unseemly usage treated each,
And slapp'd with scurvy palm my little harmless breech.

LXXII.

Then did he in his wickedness begin
   To practise his detestable device;   570
He took a paltry pepper-box of tin,
   And hoisting up my consort in a trice,
He push'd her weeping ladyship within
   Clean through the lid amid the pungent spice;
(For fairy shapes can be contracted so   575
As through a needle's eye right easily to go;)

LXXIII.

He push'd her shrieking down into the cell,
   With cruel taunt, and mocking devilish,
And mutter'd o'er her a confining spell
   Of Hell's abhorr'd and uncouth gibberish;   580
Lie there, Dame Puck! he cried, and bed thee well
   In the snug durance of thy penal dish;
There be a tenant till the day shall come
Ordain'd t' enfranchise thee from thy ignoble tomb!

LXXIV.

A sorry mustard-pot then took the knight,   585
   And, 'tween his fingers lifting me sublime,
He push'd and plung'd me, yelling with affright,
   Amid the mustard's yellow sloughy slime;
And, *Lie thou there, he cry'd, thou meddling sprite!*
   And do the proper penance for thy crime;   590
There be a tenant till the day shall come
Ordain'd t' enfranchise thee from thy ignoble tomb!

LXXV.

Nor meet Tom Puck and Madam Puck agen,
   Until the fairest maid of Scottish land
Shall to the supp'lest of all Scotland's men,   595
Charm'd by his jumping, give her bed and hand:
This said, he mumbled o'er me in my den
   His damned spell too hard to understand,
Of virtue to impound and cage me there,
Ev'n till the day fore-doom'd to let me loose to air.   600

LXXVI.

And further, he, to sunder us the more,
  And interpose large space between us twain,
To Melrose Abbey journeying, with him bore
  The spicy jail, where lay my spouse in pain,
And gave it to the monks skill'd deep in lore,   605
  That in their charge it might for years remain,
To grace the abbey-table, and supply
Their kail on feasting-days with pepper hot and dry.

LXXVII.

And there, methinks, for ages it has been;
  Till, as roll'd onward Time's fulfilling round,   610
By the wise care of our fair fairy-queen
  To ROB the RANTER's house the way it found,
Where, from her box upstarting to his eyne,
  (The spell that moment lost its power t' impound,)
My wife bade Scotland's supplest man prepare,   615
All for her weal and his, to jump at ANSTER FAIR.

LXXVIII.

For me – when first that stern felonious knight
  Had dungeon'd me in penal-pot so fast,
My jail he did commit that very night
  To Pittenweem's fat monks of belly vast,   620
That from its small profundity they might
  Supply with mustard every rich repast,
And in the abbey-pantry guard the cell,
Where I, alas! was doom'd for many an age to dwell.

LXXIX.

And there I dwelt in dolesome house of clay,   625
  Far sunder'd from my wife in sad divorce;
Till onward drew the freedom-giving day,
  Fix'd and appointed in Time's fatal course,
When Oberon, the silver-scepter'd fay,
  That rules his phantom-tribes with gentle force,   630
My mustard-pot by secret means convey'd
To MAGGIE's house – the house of Scotland's fairest maid.

LXXX.

Here as one night upon her supper-board
  Imbogg'd amid my biting mire I lay,
My king a moment broke the spell abhorr'd   635
  That kept me pent and pester'd night and day;
I rose, I loos'd my tongue to mortal word,
  Commanding her to publish sans delay
The merry games effectual to decide
What supplest-sinew'd Scot should gain her for his bride.   640

LXXXI.

Abroad the games were blown o'er Scottish ground,
  And hurry'd thousands in to ANSTER FAIR:
The work is done: the supplest man is found;
  He sits the bridegroom and the landlord there;
The fairest maid of all the realm around   645
  Sits yonder, star-like shining on her chair;
The happiest couple they of all beside;
God bless you richly both, fair bridegroom and fair bride!

LXXXII.

Nor think, my wedded dears! that you alone
  By ANSTER's gamesome FAIR are render'd blest;   650
We too, that have so long with mutual moan
  In torment and divorcement liv'd distrest,
Meet now again, (great thanks to Oberon!)
  Re-wedded, re-possessing, re-possess'd,
A pair of happy fays conjoin'd for ever,   655
Whom henceforth wizard's hate shall have no might to sever.

LXXXIII.

And now, O king! we must, forsooth, away
  To taste the sweets of new-found liberty,
To ride astraddle on the lunar ray
  In airy gallop to the top of sky,   660
And lave our limber limbs and plash and play
  Amid the milk that dims the galaxy:
Farewell! – may joys be rain'd on each of you!
Adieu, thou bridegroom sweet! thou bonny bride, adieu!

LXXXIV.

This having said, he on his shiny hair   665
  Did gracefully his silver'd hat replace,
And, seizing by the hand his lady fair,
  A while look'd smerking, winking, in her face;
Then, swift as spark from fire, or beam from star,
  That unsubstantial, slim, frail, fairy-brace,   670
From table heaving off their phantasms small,
Sheer through the window flew of MAGGIE's dining-hall.

LXXXV.

Sheer through the window fleetly flew the twain,
  Mocking the eye that try'd to follow them,
Yet, strange to add! nor wood nor glassy pane   675
  Was injur'd of the fay-pierc'd window frame!
Amazement ran in ev'ry beating vein
  Of bride, and groom, and king, and lord, and dame,
As they beheld the coupled goblins fly
Through window-shut and glass, abroad into the sky.   680

99

LXXXVI.

Recover'd quickly from their short surprise,
  They drew to table nearer each his chair;
A bumper fill, the sportive monarch cries,
  To Tom and Lady Puck the elfin pair!
Landlord and guest his brimming glass supplies   685
  From bottle with the dainty vine-blood rare;
Clean to the dregs their glasses drink they all,
As "Tom and Mrs Puck" sound echoing through the hall.

LXXXVII.

Thus they the social happy minutes spend
  In wine, and chat, and harmless revelry,   690
Till slow began the round moon to descend
  Down the starr'd ladder of the western sky,
And sleep, that toil-worn man's frail frame must mend,
  His spunge's balsam wrung on human eye;
From table, then, withdrew to sleeping room,   695
Courtier, and king, and dame, and bride, and glad bridegroom.

END OF ANSTER FAIR

PAPISTRY STORM'D;

OR, THE

DINGIN' DOWN O' THE CATHEDRAL.

ANE POEM, IN SAX SANGS

MEMORIAE

DAVIDIS LYNDSAEI, POETAE FIFENSIS
CELEBERRIMI,

HOCCE POEMA, QUANTULUMCUNQUE SIT,
PRAE AMORE OBSERVANTIAQUE NOSTRA,

DEDICATUR.

A PROŒMIUM
(*In the Southron Idiome.*)

It is a daring thing, now-a-days, to write a long poem in Scottish. Yet that language, the richest, perhaps, and most flexible for humorous purposes, of any dialect of modern Europe, – that in which our accomplished and facetious Stewarts once deigned to sport their wit, and to pen their lively lays, – which was once honourably sounded from our pulpits, at our tribunals, and in the halls of our nobility, – deserves to be recalled now and then, if possible, to the ears and recollections of this our anglicised and prim generation, that they may know in what terms their forefathers spoke, and jested, and laughed.

The author has borrowed the style and manner and diversified strophes of Sir David Lindsay. He may be considered the Chaucer of Scotland; and in his writings, and in those of Dunbar, appear, more than in those of any other of our vernacular poets, the facetious strength, fluency, and vivacity of our native speech.

The Demolition, which is the theme of these verses, is of some interest in the history of Fife. Hardly has it ever been much applauded; it has been palliated rather as an extraordinary achievement of popular excitement, as an ebullition of ultra-protestantism, condemned or at least disclaimed by the principal leaders. It may therefore be deemed *fair game* for a humourist, who intermeddles not with principles, – these are too deeply seated, too sacred for his light and playful touch, – but who has a right to appropriate to himself acts of popular violence or extravagance as a proper subject for facetious narration or animadversion. Knox himself has set a good example of this sort of humour against his adversaries. His ludicrous relations of Popish disasters, distresses, and discomfitures, show much dexterity in their kind, and prove him to have been a man not only of sound head, but, had he chosen to indulge it, of excellent jocularity.

For the introduction of one or two allegorical personages, the Author has to plead the example of the poets of Southern Europe, who scruple not, in their serious as well as ludicrous poems, to employ such actors, and to mix up their shadowy and symbolical names in the same stanzas with those that are real and historical.

PAPISTRY STORM'D

Sang First

ARGUMENT

The Muse, invokit for this wark,
  Screeds aff her dainty dittie;
How folk begoud to gowl and bark
  Contrair the Roman city;
And how Dan Momus stirr'd a clark
  Of stalwart saul and witty;
And how wi' dreams a chieftain stark
  Was fir'd withouten pity.

I sing the steir, strabush, and strife,
Whan, bickerin' frae the towns o' Fife,
Great bangs of bodies, thick and rife,
  Gaed to Sanct Androis town,
And, wi' John Calvin i' their heads,   5
And hammers i' their hands and spades,
Enrag'd at idols, mass, and beads,
  Dang the Cathedral down:
I wat the bruilzie then was dour,
Wi' sticks, and stanes, and bluidy clour,   10
Ere Papists unto Calvin's power
  Gaif up their strangest places;
And fearfu' the stramash and stour,
Whan pinnacle cam doun and tow'r,
And Virgin Maries in a shower   15
  Fell flat and smash't their faces;
The capper roofs, that dazzlit heaven,
Were frae their rafters rent and riven;
The marble altars dash't and driven;
  The cods wi' velvet laces,   20
The siller ewers and candlesticks,
The purple stole and gowden pyx,

And tunakyls and dalmatyks,
   Cam tumblin' frae their cases;
The Devil stood bumbaz'd to see   25
The bonny cosy byke, whair he
Had cuddlit monie a centurie,
   Ripp't up wi' sic disgraces!

O Muse, that frae Parnassus' crown,
Cam in thy multi-spanglet shoon,   30
Lampin' alang in joyeus glee
Frae jaw to jaw athort the sea,
To meet the Chian king o' sang,
That in his cave the lee day lang,
Sat culyieing thee beside the shore   35
Whairon th' Aegean's jappers roar;
There sat he, on lone bink reclin'd,
Deep musin' in his mightie mind,
Some famous argument to find;
Thou at his elbuck stood unseen,   40
And wi' thy glamour glaik'd his een,
   Bewitchin' them to joy;
Than, than, by him was brightlie seen
The bitter collieshangie keen
   That wrocht the Greeks annoy;   45
Ilk bluidy brulziement and battle
Wi' swords, and stanes, and chariots' brattle,
That never blindit nor did sattle,
Till erthlins wi' a dunderin' rattle
   Tummlet the tow'rs o' Troy;   50
O come down frae thy cloud on hie,
Whair thou art singin' merrilie,
And wi' thy wings owrshadow me,
   And fan my spreit to joy;
And up thy magic lantern hold,   55
That in its lookin'-glass o' gold,
My glaikit ee may well behold
   The Papists and their faes comminglit
In monie a fecht and tulzie-mulzie,
Herryin' o' kirks, and image-spulzie,   60
   Whairwi' nae ear as yet hath tinglet;
Thou kenn'st it a'; for thou wert there,
Pitch't on the steeple's tap in air,
Markin' the faces, everilk one,
O' them by wham the wark was done,   65
And notin' down within thy book
Ilk motion, gesture, speik, and look,

Aiblins to use on future time,
And blazon them abraid in rhime:
Till, underneath thy feet, I trow,   70
Dinnelin' *Deaf Meg* and *Crookit Mou* ¹
Begoud wi' ane terrifick blatter
At the great steeple's found to batter,
   Garrin' the stanes to dance;
The steeple rock't at ilka swack;   75
Thou saw'st the comin' crash and wrack;
And flafft thy wings, and in a crack
   Flew frae th' unsicker stance!

Say, first, what set the folks a-fire,
And made them wraithly to conspire,   80
Contrair Cathedral, monk, and spire?
The Cardinal's bluid (now rest his saul!)
Lay clotter't on the castill-wall,
And bauld Johne Knox, now grown the baulder,
That Beaton lay in's kist the caulder,   85
Past like a lion round the land,
And wi' the wangyle in his hand,
And wechtie Calvin in his wallet,
Was as it were an iron mallet
To break the Man o' Sin to flinders,   90
And hurl the *mass* amang the cinders;
He preachit east, he preachit wast;
His voice was as the whirlwind's blast,
   That aftentimes, in days o' simmer,
Comes swirlin' sudden frae the sea,   95
And swoops the hay-cocks aff the lea,
   And tirls the kirks, and strips the timmer;
The vera steeples round about
Rebellow'd to his nobill shout,
And rang wi' texts baith in and out;   100
The dows and daws that there aboundit,
As if affrichtit and confoundit,
Out-whirr'd and whitter't at the sound o't;
The bells and bartisans reboundit;
Strang pupits flew about in blads,   105
Breakin' the hearers' pows wi' dads;
Men, women, kirtled girls, and lads,
Were fir'd and furiated in squads;
Sae wud and wicket was their wraith
Gainst Papish trash and idol-graith,   110
   The patter'd prayers and beads,
They scarce could sattle on the benches,

But cock't their fists in fearfu' clenches,
And slappit furiouslie their henches,
   And shook their angrie heads.   115
Ae man bang't upwarts frae his place,
And toss'd his nieve, withouten grace,
Richt i' the Virgin Mary's face.
Anither wicht was mair uncivil:
He brak St Ayle owr by the neevil,   120
And bann'd baith pieces to the deevil.
Some say, – maybe 'twas but a clatter, –
That the town's piper, wi' a blatter,
Whummlet and skail't the halie water;
Be't true, be't fause, it's little matter: 125
Had Bellarmine been sittin' cockin
In Anster kirk, he'd gat a yokin'
Yon day, that wou'd hae cow'd his croakin',
And garr'd his head hing like a doken:
The vera dead men's mooler't banes,   130
   That i' the kirk-ayle lay at rest,
Amaist caught life aneath their stanes,
   And bowtit up amang the rest
To smash the stany saints, whilk they
Had worship't on a former day   135
Whan tabernaclin' i' their clay!

But hoolie, Muse! reprime your haste;
   Descrybe mair gently a' the matter;
Ye needna rin as ye were chas'd,
   And blast and blaw wi' sic a blatter!   140

Now, had the Sun's meridian chair
Been heiz'd up heicher i' the air,
The fiery Bull, that, e'en and morn,
Keeps ever buttin' at Orion,
Had toss'd Apollo up in scorn   145
Aff frae his star-betippet horn,
   And up the zodiack sent him flyin';
The Twins, where up they stand on heicht,
Stretch'd out their arms, aye glitterand bricht,
   And caught him mid a show'r o' beams,   150
That halflins blindet wi' their sheen,
As down they fell intil his een,
   The gentle Castor wi' their gleams:
And merry May, fram whare she lay
   In Abyssinia's gardens sleepin',   155
Wak'd by the Hours frae bonnie bowers,

Up Titan's peth comes lampin', leapin';
And ever as she gaes a-trippin',
Her fingers in her basket dippin',
Pick witch-bells out, dear daffodillies, 160
Kingcups and spinks, and livelie lilies,
And sparple them in frisky mirth
Ow'r the great waist o' mither Yerth.
Auld mither Yerth, now sick o' frost,
 Unwrinkles a' her cauldrife face, 165
And shines abraid thro' ilka coast,
 And breirds and beautifies apace:
'Mid sic joyeusitie, I wot,
Th' east neuk o' Fife was nae forgot:
The aits and barley there were springin', 170
The lavricks i' the lift were singin',
The leas wi' ploughmen's lilts were ringin';
Auld grandshers at their doors sat beikin,
While younksters, by the sea-side streikin',
Gaed paidlin' in without a breik on; 175
E'en senseless kye did rowt wi' glee;
The sillie fishes i' the sea
Lap frae their element in play
To kiss the gowden gleam o' day.
Nae marvel then, that, to his mither, 180
 Cried Piper-Jock, "May I be licket,
Gin there has been sic guid spring-weather
 Syn' Cardinal Beaton's craig was sticket!"
Sic was the season, siccan wedder,
 Whan Maister Knox and Maister Rough, 185
Twa cronies link't in love thegidder,
 Merrilie march'd frae Edinbrogh,
To hunt the Roman beast in Fife,
And ettle fiercely at his life
Wi' Calvin's lang sharp-nebbit knife. 190
The tane atween Kinghorn and Crail
 Eastlins frae town to town gaed preachin';
The tither, nae less brym in zeal,
 In landwart parochins gaed stretchin';
Kirkcaldy Papists, iron-heartit, 195
Now wi' their stany idols partit;
The Gallowtown was clean convertit;
The Dysart heughmen left their places
O' darkness now, and wash'd their faces,
Ardent for homilies and graces. 200
The Upper Largo and the Nether
Deem'd Papistry now but a blether;

Weems cried out, *"Hang it in a tether."*
The sinfu' bodies o' the Elie
Were spain'd frae image-worship hailly;   205
St Monan's fishermen, brain-wud,
Flang their auld dead stock-saint o' wood
Aff their puir pier intil the flood;
Mad Pittenweem waged deadly weir
Wi' their fat capon-lined prior;   210
(Need little wonder be o' that;
They were his lean, and he sae fat!)
Wast Anster town was clean uprisen;
East Anster burghers, monie a dozen,
Were fraithin' at the mou', and fizzin'   215
    At beads and halie water;
Cauld Cellardyke had ta'en the gee;
Her boats, deil ane was now at sea,
Haddocks and skate were let abee
    For mair important matter;   220
Crail town was up wi' gashin' gabs;
Wabsters, throu' zeal, forgat their wabs;
Tailors' fierce mou's gaif bitter stabs;
And brewsters' tongues, wi' dads and dabs,
    Rome's skelpie-limmer thumpet;   225
Clerk Diston ca'd the Paip an ass;
And the strang craig o' Baillie Glass,
Through ilka street as he did pass,
Against our Ladie and the mass
    Gaed rairin' like a trumpet.   230

While thus in town and royal bough
    The burghers' tongues were set a-birrin',
Nae less, inflam't by Maister Rough,
    The lairds in landwart pairts were stirrin':
Kilbrachmont Ramsay raise in anger,   235
The laird o' Grange could thole nae langer;
Stout Fisher-Willie swore, gin he
    Drew but anither drave o' fish up,
He'd sooner fling them back i' the sea
    Than gi'e ae teind-skate to the bishop: 240
Balcaskie's tongue rapp't out a rippet
'Gainst shaven-crowns sae trigly clippit,
And Cordelier, round cap, and tippet:
Ane beggin' freir he frae his wicket
Wi' terrible fierce birr he kicket;   245
He gave his lunzie sic a lounder
As did the sillie man dumfounder,

And dang him flatlins like ane flounder.
Sour Sipsie showl'd a saucy mou'
Whan onie idol met his view;   250
He bann'd thir Virgins made o' stane;
He'd never kneel again to ane.
But Barns, a laird o' gentler breedin',
Held at his Latin Bible readin',
Pickin' out pithfu' texts and strang,   255
Wharewi' Crail's gaukit priest he dang
Garrin' him ride John Calvin's stang.
Carnbee, though sober, grave, and douce,
Turnin' tongue-ferdy now and crouse,
Gaed stormin' round frae house to house,   260
Blasphemin' with a glorious din
The king-corruptin' bawd o' sin;
Pitcorthie, though his wife yet wavers,
    His faith confessit manfullie:
"Sorrow gin Paip was boil'd to taivers,   265
    And I'd a platefu' o' the bree!"

While thus the furious folk o' Fife
At Paip and idol in their strife,
    Were murgeonin' and mockin',
Lo! on Olympus' taps preclair   270
The goddess o' men-blessin' lear,
Owr-archit by a rainbow bricht,
That, ow'r her dribblet blobs o' licht,
    Sat workin' at her stockin';
For she had task'd hersel, perfay,   275
To work before a certain day
    A pair o' stockins to her daddy,
And there, upon the mountain's tap,
Her clew o' worsit in her lap,
    Sat Wisdom's winsome lady: 280
The wyres were gowden, braw to see,
Wharewi' her fingers prettilie
    Did niddle i' their play;
As hitch on hitch succeedin' fast,
Aff frae the gowden points were cast,   285
And, sattlin' on the dazzlin' hose,
Heigher and heigher still arose,
    In texture rich and gay:
Sae was she busy, whan, by chance,
Stravaigin throu' the sky, her glance   290
Saw far ayont the hills o' France
    The folk o' Fife in stirr;

Her lairds on kirk-reform intent,
Her burghers on the bruilzie bent,
Clerk Diston wud at painted saint,   295
And Barns, at's Latin Testament,
    Fast readin' wi' a birr:
She saw, and joyeus at the view,
Down on the yird she drave and threw
Stockin', and wire, and worsit-clew,   300
    And to her feet upsprang;
"What! maun I see yon bairns o' mine,"
She cry'd, "sae bown on deeds divine,
And I na help their weak ingyne
    Wi' my suggestions strang?   305
Mine be the wark!" And, as she said,
    She weeglit her wing-wavin' shoon,
And frae Olympus' gowany head
    Aff-flew like fairy frae the moon.

There is within the warld somewhair   310
    (I ken it, though I downa tell)
A hollow, happie place, where Care,
That hunts poor mortals late and air,
    Hath never yet been kent to dwell.
For why? Fun at the door-stane stands,   315
And slaps him back wi' baith his hands.
That temple's flures and wa's are lined
Wi' leifsum pictures a' kinkind;
Ilk comic scene of ilka age,
Glean'd out of ilka sayar's page,   320
Frae him wha sang how mouse and frog
Waged bluidy bruilzie i' their bog,
Garrin' its rashies shake and shog,
Down to that later baird wha tauld,
How, for ane useless bucket auld,   325
The Lombard hosts ilk ither maul'd:²
A' thae, ensculptur'd bricht and braw,
Garnish'd ilk bonnie marble wa';
Great gaulfs o' lauchter aye resound
In ilka corner round and round,   330
Like rorie-buckies, i' their din,
Loud soundin' as the sea comes in:
Syk is the nature o' that grot
To echoe sae, e'en should there not
Be gaupin body on the spot;   335
Around the altar prance and pace
Globe-cheekit Fun, whase fatty face

Bonnily blumes wi' glad grimace,
And Comus, his renownit brither,
(Twin-bairns o' Revelry their mither,)   340
Ticklin' to frenzy ane anither;
As priests and as attendants, they
Wait on and serve baith nicht and day,
    Enravishin' Dan Momus' nose
Wi' fumes frae comedie and play,   345
Ballad, and mime, and roundelay,
    The marrow o' sweet verse and prose,
Whairwi' that altar aye is fed,
Makin' wi' smeik his naistrills gled: –
Aloft the godkin sits in pride,   350
    Exultin' in the jokes o' men,
And thro' his mask, that jimp can hide
The glee that on his cheeks doth ride,
    Blinks waggish glances now and then,
And flytes upon his priests sae jolly   355
For heaviness and melancholy;
The friskier for the flytin', they
Gaffaw and smirkle in their play.
'Mid sic like daffery and glaikin',
Baith god and priest were merry-makin',   360
Whan, hark! upon the gowden door,
Tirl! comes a rap, as seld' before;
    Sir Fun uplifts the sneck,
And, lo! the goddess in her glore
    Gaes in and mak's her beck;   365
Dan Momus look't bombas't a wee
Her learnit ladyship to see;
Quo' she, – "All hail, sweet son o' Nox!
Father o' daffin, jaips, and jokes! –
    O, be na put in fricht,   370
That thus I bang upon thine een
Sae sudden, wi' confoundin' sheen,
    Down fram Olympus heicht;
I hae a sma' demand to make,
Whilk, for mine and my deddy's sake,   375
I houp thou'lt think na scorn to take
    Some fashery to do richt."
Quo' he, – "Speik out your will mair clear;
Mass! I am glad to see you here;
You've been a stranger monie a year;   380
    Ye're welcome to my sicht."
Quo' she, – "I maunna tarry lang;
Fife's merry bodies now are thrang

III

Berappin' wi' their tongues, ding-dang,
Sir Paip and a' his rotten gang; 385
    Their cause is your's and mine,
And it is Learning's; thairfore come
And let us at the bawd o' Rome.
Her bordel-house maun down be plucket,
Her huge Augean stable muckit, 390
    Ere Lear shoot up and shine:
Gang you then to auld Caryl town,
(An ancient brogh o' some renown,
    Near to the neis o' Fife,)
There catch and cleik her cunnin' clark, 395
And in his bosom clap a spark,
Enflamin' him for this guid wark
    O' kirk-rapyne and strife;
While I sall aff to Anster town,
And raise a chieftain o' renown, 400
Makin' him fiery-wud and bown
    To seek the harlot's life.
Gude Fisher-Willie is his name,
For lollardie o' meikle fame,
Wha sits within his house o' Dreil 405
Blasphemin' with a valiant zeal
Twa ne'er-do-weels, the Paip and deil,
    Wi' gleeks at Guise and Mary;
He and the clerk, twin-heroes baith,
At our suggest, shall no be laith 410
    (Bein' wally wichts and wary)
To raise the mob, for 'sault and scaith,
And sailzie kirk wi' weir and wraith,
    And make a fierie-farie."

This said, Dan Momus wasna slaw, 415
By lauchter, his assent to shaw;
He nicker't sic a lang gaffaw
The cavern rang frae wa' to wa':
    Anon, he, in a blink,
Tucks up his pyrnit tunic bra, 420
And, whirrin' throu' the key-hole sma',
Down, down the heav'n's star-studdit ha'
Gaes whizzin' like a fiery ba',
    Mair quick than man can think:
He lichts, preceese at aucht o'clock, 425
On Crail's auld steeple's weathercock;
Tip-taes upon its capper crown
    He stands, and casts his een about

Round the hale houses o' the town,
  To spy the noble not'ry out.   430

Now sae it chanc'd, that, on that nicht,
Girt wi' a groupe o' gossips bricht,
Clerk Diston, thron'd and seatit richt,
  In Luckie Kay's was sittin':
A burde afore him, braid and lang,   435
Whare stoups and jinglin' glasses thrang,
Wi' helter-skelter cling-and-clang,
  Gaed flyckerin' and flittin';
The flotter't table maist was steepit,
Wi' claret-dubs that drapt and dreepit,   440
As the mad bottles never sleepit,
But firstlins ae cork, then the ither,
Hetly they chasit ane anither,
In bousy Bacchanalian flither,
  As fast as they could bicker;   445
Heigh at ae end in elbuck-chair
He sat, and royalees'd it there
Wi' jokes and ready wit, and lear,
  That flash't out quick and quicker;
His bottle-cronies' faces a'   450
Gilt rubicond, and bernish't bra,
Glister't on ilk side like a raw
  O' hairst-moons down the table;
And aye as jaip and jest he brak
On Papistrie and her vile pack,   455
As thunder on the fire-slacht's back,
Tempestuouslie there cam' a crack
  O' gaulps incomparable,
Sae that the chalmer, in and round it,
Wi' thuds o' merriment resoundit;   460
And Luckie Kay, at the rebound o't,
Sat in her chimla-nook astoundit!

Dan Momus, frae the steeple's heicht,
Pryin' and prievin' wi' his sicht,
  Saw, throu' the stany wa',   465
('Twas wi' his een like crystal clear,)
The clerk upon his tavern-cheir,
Thron'd gloriouslie amid his feir
  O' fellow-bousers braw;
He saw, and gave his wings a flaff,   470
And frae the cock's kaim flotit aff:
Scrimply there pass't a stound o' time,

113

Ere, throu' the thick stane and the lime,
He slippit like a beam throu' glass;
(For heathen gods, like ghaists, can pass   475
Throu' wa's o' stane, or yetts o' brass:)
There was a sough, like flann or flaw,
As in he whihher'd throu' the wa',
But nane his gawey godship saw;
For why? He will'd it should be swa: 480
Fornent the clerk, the burde aboon,
Himsel' he pitch't and poisit soon,
And flichter't baith his wings, whareby
Their tipsy cheeks, they kent na why,
    Were fanned wi' the flaff;   485
Than to the not'ry's een alane,
Mair bricht than pearl or ruby stane,
His frame shone out in licht serene,
    Garrin the chalmer lauff;
The jolly gossips saw the licht   490
On roof and flure refleckit bricht,
But nane, except the favour't wicht,
Kent whence it bleized on their sicht;
And he alane it was whase ear
The godkin's guid discourse did hear;   495
    'Twas ettled for nane ither;
(The rest, as he his parle out-spoutit,
Sat gazin' goutherfow, and doutit,
    Glowerin' at ane anither;)
"O thou that thus in Bacchus' chaire   500
Sits governin' in glorie there,
Direckin' wi' thy voice's rair
    The storm o' tavern-glee,
Waesucks, man! this is na the time
For sangs, and jaips, and raivin' rhime,   505
And rants and rhaposodies sublime
    That ding the saul a-jee;
A doucer and a better wark
Befits thee now, renownit clark;
Whan folks are strippin' to the sark,   510
    And lab'rin' a' their micht
To batter down a sinfu' kirk,
Up, up, and gie the Paip a jerk,
And in his droddum clap the dirk
    O' reformation richt: 515
Arise, and ring the gatherin'-bell,
And head the multitude yoursell;
Wi' hammer, halbert, maul, and mell,

March to Sanct Androis town,
And batter down baith stane and timmer,   520
O' th' brothel whare the scarlet limmer
Has toss'd her head for monie a simmer,
    And worn th' unwerdy crown;
Lay bare her pridefu' biggings braw;
Root, root her out o' house and ha';   525
Turn her adrift to rain or snaw,
    Stript naket to the skin,
That the vile vermin that ha'e crawl'd
Sae lang about her garment's fauld
May perish in the winter's cauld,   530
    And clean the warld o' dirt and sin:
Rise, then; and heave aside the cup;
And grip the knappin'-hammer up;
    March, muster, cry, Hurro!
Down wi' the mass and monkish squad,   535
Down wi' the jad in scarlet clad;
    Up, up and lay her low!"
This said, Dan Momus frae his face
His mask upliftit for a space,
That the bauld-bosom'd clerk mith get   540
A waff o' his face ere aff he set:
His face wi' lauchter's mirth-mad licht
Burn'd sae insufferablie bricht,
That, butten jeopardie, nae wicht
Could stand that lauchter-lowin' sicht;   545
Whairfore, to save the man frae scaith,
Lest lookin' lang he'd die the death,
    Dan Momus, frae the place,
Evanish't like a dead man's wraith,
Or candle blawn out by the breath,   550
Or bellerin' bubble made o' fraith,
    That does na leave a trace;
A canny waff o' sweet perfume
Was blawn in breezes throu' the room:
I wot, th' astonay'd not'ry then   555
Felt wodeness bernin' in his brain;
Upwards he boltit frae his chaire,
    As if his hand begrasp't already
An iron-geddock, swerd, or spear,
    To damnifie the scarlet lady;   560
The table stotter't on the floor
    Wi' straiks that frae his neif descendit;
Stoups, bottles, glasses, tumblin' o'er,
    Were smash't and wi' their claret blendet;

Ho, hearts! up, ane and a'! and at her!   565
Have at a fousome kirk, and batter
Her lustfu' banes untill they clatter!
 Smite! Ettle at the life!
On, on, and cry na, *Barlafummill*,
Till down amang the dirt she tummle,   570
And bury beggin'-freir and bummel;
That wi' the ruin and the rummle
 The Deil be frichtet out o' Fife!

While Momus thus in Luckie Kay's,
Blew Diston's saul up in a blaise,   575
Lo! on a nicht-cloud in mid-air,
The goddess o' men-blessin' lear
Against Sir Knicht was plottin' sair:
And monie a slee and paukie scheme
Her head did generate and freme;   580
At last she chose the stratageme
O' wauk'nin' Willie wi' a dreme.
Aff to the house o' dremes she gangs,
Whair round the wa's they stick in bangs,
 Like lempets stickin' upon rocks;   585
Or flee about on skinkin' wing,
Like butterflies in days o' spring,
 Around the flow'rs or cabbage-stocks;
She wale'd out ane, a pretty fairy,
Beltit wi' ribbons glairy-flairy,   590
And monie a tassel and fleegarie,
Whase colours aye did shift and vary;
Her body, as it mov'd, did ever
Like to an opal gleam and quiver;
(Sister to that sweet dreme that went   595
To Agamemnon in his tent:)
She tauld the friskie fairy thing
Whairtill to flee on rapid wing;
The thing at her command gaed scrievin'
Wi' sic a breesil down the heivin,   600
It beat the thunder-boltit leven:
You scarce could say, your een could see
Its motion spinnerin' fram on hie;
Ae moment its celestial stance
Was up near whair the Pleiads dance;   605
The tother, it had downwarts fled,
And hover't its slim airy head
Our Fisher-Willie's carvit bed;
By this time, Anster's steeple-bell

Had wi' her hammer chappit twell;   610
And the knicht-fisher, ere the chap,
Angarlandet wi' bien nicht-cap,
In bed lay sleepin' like a tap;
Sith he was aye ane sober wicht,
And gaed to bed guid time o' nicht,   615
As douce folks do that walk upricht:
Heigh owr the bolster, near his head,
The feeble vision took its stede;
And throu' his naistrills-valves began
To werk upon the slummerin' man: 620
Ere that his brain was clear o' dreams;
But now wi' gowden lichts it gleams,
As streamers aft throu' clearest sky
In merry-dance flash out and fly.
He dream'd that he gat wings whairwi'   625
He flew, as wi' an angel's glee,
Owr Fife frae Stirling to the sea;
And aye he look't down in his flicht
To spy her bonnie lairdships bricht
Glitterand wi' gowans and wi' licht;   630
As in a sunny simmer day,
Th' horizon's air aft seems to play,
And flicht in waves and flash away;
Sae bleme'd, unto that dreamer's sicht,
Fife's grassy hills and valleys bricht   635
Wi' gowden undulatin' licht:
Ilk laird's domain was clearly seen
Defin'd wi' streaps o' silver sheen,
That intervein'd the manors green;
A' things were goodlie, glorious, grand,   640
Exceptin' that in ilk laird's land
A great tar-barrel seem'd to stand;
And in that uglie tun stood, lair'd
Up to the chin and clotter't beard,
Greetin' and grumple-faced, a laird;   645
Sir Knicht did hing a while on wing,
Marvellin' the meanin' o' that thing;
Whan, lo! out frae his castill came,
Wi' his braid hat as red as flame,
And a' his cardinal's attire,   650
He that in his ungodlie ire,
Damn'd godlie Wishart to the fire;
A great wax-taper, redly lowin',
That frae the altar he had stowin',
He carry't in his murd'rous hand,   655

And us'd it as a kendlin' brand,
As he gaed martyrin' thro' the land:
To ilk tar-tun he pat the lowe;
At ance it flew up in a glowe;
East, wast, he in a mament flees;   660
That mament's space did weel suffees
To set the haill land in a bleis:
Three hundred pillars lang and high
O' smeik gaed curlin' to the sky:
Ah! than he saw the wretchit men   665
Wreein' and wreethin' wi' the pain,
As the flame ate them to the bane:
And siccan hidyous yells and skreiks! –
A' the warld soundit wi' their skreiks: –
Tears rappit down the dreamer's cheeks!   670
Than on *himsel* his thochts recule;
He, too, might ha'e his share o' dool;
He glancit down on bonnie Dreel;
He saw *his ain* barr'l burnin' weil,
And bleisin' a tremendous bele.   675
He saw *himsel* amid the blaze,
As round and round his head it plays! –
He waken't at the frichtsom gaze; –
His limbs were quakin' 'neath the claes, –
Albeit he was sterk carl and strang,   680
The cauld sweat frae his marrow sprang:
Ten times he turn't frae side to back,
Ere he anither souff could tak;
Its stance meanwhile the Dream did keep
Ready, whan ance he fell asleep,   685
Down on his harns again to leap: –
He slept; – he dreamit ance again;
He dreamit, that, on ocean's plain,
He in his paintit pleasure-boat,
At mid-day, whan the sun was hot,   690
Did sail for pastime and for play,
Far, far ayont the isle o' May;
The lift was clear throughout and bricht
Wi' rivers o' sun-shiney licht;
The sea in clearness seem't to vie   695
Wi' the round looking-glass o' sky;
He saw the rocks and tangly meads
Whair the big meer-swine mak their beds,
A thousand faddom deep and mair,
As clear as gin he walkit there;   700
Great skulls o' haddock, cod, and ling,

Like siller arrows frae the wing,
Gaed skuddin' thro' the mighty deep;
He heard them whizzin' in his sleep:
His nets he cast; and, lo! wi' fish   705
His nets were gluttit to his wish;
He drew them up wi' toyle and fecht;
His yawl near swampit wi' the wecht:
But sic a draft o' fishes sheen
He never saw yet wi' his een;   710
Siller lay shimmerin' on their skins;
Gowd was affrontit by their fins;
As glower'd he on his fishy heaps,
Lo! lo! cam sailin' owr the deeps
(Three frae the east, three down the Forth,   715
Twa frae the south, twa frae the north,)
Ten bonnie boaties, skimmin' licht,
Garnish't wi' gowden foolyie bricht;
And in ilk boatie's fore-stem cockit
A lang bra' bishop in his rocket;   720
A mitre prank'd his pow; his hand
Dangl'd about a crosier wand:
Sic gallant bishops wi' sic mitres
Rome ne'er admyr'd in her Sanct Peter's;
But Fisher-Willie, whan he saw   725
Thir burlie bishops big and bra',
Thrang swallowin' wi' their greedy een
His drave o' haddocks clear and clean,
He waxed wod wi' vera teen;
    But mair pertrubill'd was his case   730
Whan chasin' fast the tane the tither
They cam a' round him in a fluther,
And sieg'd his boat frae stem to ruther,
    Yelpin' and youtin' in his face:
My teinds! gi'e me my teinds, Sir Knicht!   735
I canna want my teinds till nicht!
And in a gliffin' ilka bishop
Ramm'd in his hand and cleik'd his fish up;
And aye they glampt, and aye they glaum'd,
And aye the tither teind they palm'd,   740
Till feint a haddock, ling, or potley,
Remain'd o' a' that i' the boat lay;
Whairat the mauchty Knicht took fire;
His bluid birr'd thro' his buik wi' ire;
As whan a pat wi' beef and bane   745
Is hung owr fire by Kate or Jane,
The ragin' lowes gae up its sides,

Garrin' plish-plash the internal tides,
As to the swey-crook Vulcan rides
 Curlin' in smeeky majestie;   750
The broo boils up wi' sotterin' sound;
Whummils the beef its dainty dainty pound;
Sebows and leeks dance up and bound;
And barley-pickles flee round and round
 Hilliegileerie 'mang the bree: 755
E'en sae did that fierce fisher's blood
Mount up and bubble wild and wud,
As he beheld ilk bishop's claw
Glaum at his fish and cleik them a';
Than frae his bed he spang'd and shot;   760
(Perdê! he thoucht he was in's boat
Sailin' for pastime and for play
Sax miles ayont the Isle o' May);
The bed-clais to the roof he dang;
Sheer to his feet he upwarts sprang   765
To whair his guidly sword did hang
 Aboon his head for need;
He haul'd it wraithly frae its pin;
He gript, he swang it round wi' din;
He smasht and smote thae men o' sin   770
 For their gear-graspin' greed;
He drave it on the puir cod-wares;
He gulligaw'd the posts wi' scars;
The coverlets dree'd ne'er sic wars;
 The fecht was loud and lang;   775
He slasht awa for near ane hour;
The sweat frae lith and limb did pour;
The Knicht ne'er blindit nor gave owr,
Until wi' gastly gash and clour
 Thir bishops dead he dang;   780
The like before was never kent,
That sakeless sheets should sae be shent,
And cods should dree what wraith was meant
For mensless men whase sauls were bent
 On covetize and wrang!3   785

END OF FIRST SANG

NOTES

1 Names of two cannons employed on that occasion.
2 Tassoni.
3 As illustrative of the latter dream, it may be mentioned, that Mr. D. Straton, a Fife
 Laird, was burnt by the Bishop of St Andrews for refusing him the teinds caught in
 his pleasure-boat. – See KNOX.

PAPISTRY STORM'D

Sang Second

ARGUMENT

Here sall I say how Crail's-men broke
  Out frae their beds wi' beir;
And how nae less the Anster folk
  Were pit in meikle steir;
And how they owr the muirs did flock,
  Array'd in graith o' weir;
And George Buchanan, canty cock,
  How he drew to them near.

Dan Phœbus in his eastland bow'r
Startit frae sleep 'tween three and four,
And busk't him in his dandiest duds,
For his lang journey thro the cluds;
His velvet breeks, as red as fire,   5
The snoddest pairt o' his attire,
Whilk a' the nations do admire,
  He drew up on his galliard thies:
His spanglet glairy-flairy vest,
The Ethiops' wonder east and west,   10
He button'd bonny round his waist,
  Settin' his belly in a bleis;
His coat, wi' gowden sleeves bedicht,
Whase fiery neck gleams out sae bricht,
The sterns are blindet wi' the licht,   15
  Apparyll'd his braid showthers weil;
His cockit-hat wi' canny care
He clapt upon his roseat hair;
His jewell'd shoon (a bonny pair!)
  He strappit fast round ilka heel;   20
Syn to the Hours he cry'd, My staff,
My staff, ye jads, and let me aff!

'Tis time o' day by Anster clock
That I was over India's rock!
    And, swith! they bring his staff
And throu' Aurora's gildet gate,
Whistlin', he took his gladsome gait,
And up the pend at furious rate
    Gaed spielin', spankin', aff!

The lavrick yet was scarcely singin'
When Crail's auld bell was set a ringin';
For what throu' Momus, what throu' zeal,
Clerk Diston sleepit nae great deal;
The gallant spirit in his breast
Was set against the Roman beast,
Wi' sticks and stanes to clash and clout him,
And batter down his den about him;
Forthwith to congregate the people,
He socht the bell-tow i' the steeple;
He gript it like a man distrackit;
The bell-wheel, as it gaed round, cracket,
And rattlet a tremendous racket:
Out flew, fram ilka hole and cleft,
The swallows and the dows like drift;
Frae its foundation to its spinnel
The steeple's length did dirl and dinnel;
Nae marvel then, that at the din
Scarr'd bodies frae their hames did rin;
Ae man ran out without the breiks,
Though he had kept his bed for weeks;
Ane bangit out in sic a flither,
He took ae shae, and left the tither;
On stockin' soles ran out anither;
Peter's richt leg was in a breik,
The tither leg was bare and bleak;
Out to the causeys birr'd the women;
Their weanies lay in cradles screamin';
Doors reessil'd up, and made a blatter;
Causeys did claik wi' clitter-clatter;
Ane cry'd out, *What a-deil's the matter;*
Ane answer't, *Kirkmay is a-fire!*
Anither, *Satan's in the spire!*
Ane cry'd, *The Pape, the Pape is near!*
He's landit at Sanct Androis' pier
Wi' hosts o' friers, a monstrous pack,
And tenscore Cardinals at his back!
They're arm't wi' swerds baith tane and tither;

Deil tak it, we're a' dead thegither!
They ran a' throuther in their burry,
Reel-rall, hallooin', hurry-scurry;   70
Bairns screegh'd; dogs yamff'd and youll'd outricht;
The swine ran thro' the streets wi' fricht,
And drown't themselves intill the sea;
That fricht nae langer could they dree: –
Sic dridder drear, sic panic pale   75
Took ilka livin' thing in Crail!

Meantime while thus, aside the clerk,
   Affairs gaed on wi' siccan dirdom,
Guid Fisher-Willie for the werk
Set up his spirit nae less sterk;   80
   Sae fiercelins had his wid-dreme stirr'd him:
Nae sooner clapt he on his claes,
Than, boun for bus'ness, aff he gaes;
He soucht his henchman that did stand
Wi' ane pow-axe intill his hand,   85
   Aye watchin' at his yett,
Ready, when robbers did appear,
To bring his wappen down wi' beir,
And cleeve their heads from ear to ear,
   Wi' terrible down-sett;   90
That henchman's name, as I've heard say,
Was galland Andrew Halliday;
Warder! quo he, gang straucht and tell
Dan Oliphant to ring his bell;
Alswa, bid Barclay grip his tow,   95
And gi'e the great kirk-bell a jow:
Out-ring frae kitchen and frae ha'
My burghers dear, and get them a'
   Convenit at the cross;
The weird-set day begins to daw,   100
(Its sign upon the heiven I knaw),
Whan we maun at a noble ca'
   Bring Papistrie to loss:
Thus said, Dan Andrew, at his biddin',
Unslot his yett, and out gaed whiddin',   105
His bastoun in his hand to rap
The slum'brous Barclay frae his nap:
Meanwhile the mauchty fisher-knicht
Upspiel'd his staircase fleet and licht,
E'en to the gerret's leaden heicht,   110
   Wi' swesch-trump in his hand;
Aye as he mountit ilka stair,

123

Some fairy sough'd intill his ear;
Blaw loud, Sir Knicht, and dinna fear,
    To sturtle up the land: 115
Heigh on the bartisan he stood;
He saw the day keek owr the flood;
He kent upon the eastern cloud
    Weird's lucky sign hung out;
He pat the trumpet till his mou;   120
Sae lang, sae terrible, he blew,
The dinnel'd sky dreep't draps o' dew,
    And tremblet at the tout;
'Twas heard at back o' Largo-law;
At Cupar cross they kent the blaw;   125
The lift, the lift is fa'n, but dout,
A man in Falkland streets cry'd out;
The prior o' Sanct Androis town,
Whair he on bed was sleepin' soun',
Bumbazit at the blastin' soun',   130
    Up frae his blankets jumpet;
The monks and canons on their beds
Did bang up frae the cods their heads,
And tauld in mazerment their beads;
    They thocht it the last trumpet;   135
Nae marvel, then, that men and wives,
    In Anster, and the towns about it,
Were frichtit for their vera lives
    Whan Fisher-Willie's trumpet toutit;
And, mair to magnifie their wonder,   140
At anes the bells baith up and under
Begoud to rattle on like thunder:
For in his bell-house, David Barclay
Ne'er flourished his tow mair starkly;
Lang Geordie, syn his buik was langer,   145
Tugg'd at his dancin' tow the stranger:
Ilk clapper gaif ilk bell sic paiks,
They swat on baith sides wi' the straiks;
Sae what wi' swesch-trump, what wi' bells,
The Anster folks were jimp themsells;   150
Bailie and burgher, man and woman,
Flew frae their doors like bullets bummin';
Auld Saunders Clerk, a man o' echty,
Though eild-encumber't now and wechty,
His breeks has like a lion tane,   155
And birrs them on wi' micht and main:
Jean Grieve, as frae her bed she loupit,
Puir body! owr the bed-stock coupit,

And, lichtin' on the cauld flure-stane,
Maist dislocate her henchle-bane;   160
Exceptin' her (for she lay sprauchin'),
And Robie Brown and David Strachan,
    (For they were bedrals baith),
The fient a body that had feet,
That didna skirr into the street,   165
    Effrayt, and out o' breath;
And some flew hither, some flew thither,
They overthrew the tane the tither;
Sic feerie-farie and sic flither
Were never in a' Fife thegither: 170
As when at Rome, upon the day
When Casca did brave Julius slay,
The Roman people in a fray
    Ran to the forum flockin;
The Capitol amaist was shiftet   175
Wi' crowds that hither-thither driftet;
Great skreighs were to the skies upliftet;
    Ilk house wi' fricht was rockin':
Sae to the cross o' Anster ran
Hirdie-girdie, woman and man: 180
Whan they were a' forgadder'd there,
A man stood up upon a stair:
(Nane kent him wha he was or whence;
Nane saw him e'er before or since;
Some Papists said it was the Deil: 185
Na, na; it was some better chiel;
I ken *his* grunkle unca weil:)
He cry'd, – "O, friends! I'm glad to see ye;
Sae mickle zeal and smeddum wi' ye:
Ay, ay, your heads hae' routh o' zeal   190
'Gainst Pape, and Papistry, and Deil;
Nae doubt o' that, I see it weel,
    Het on your noses burnin';
But, will-a-wins! your hands are toom
O' chappin-stick and weirlike loom,   195
To batter at the bawd o' Rome,
    And mak' her monks gae mournin';
Arm, arm your hands wi' shools and sticks;
And sweys, and cuddy-rungs, and picks;
March to the martyr-murderin' town,   200
And pu' the pridefu' biggings down;
Rive but the auld nests aff the tree,
The fient ae howdie-craw you'll see: –
But my advice is, short and lang,

Tak' your disjeunes afore you gang!"   205
This spoke, the man did disappear;
Some said he flew up in the air;
Some said he doukit down at anes
Betwixt the weil-pav'd causey-stanes,
As ghaists through treuch-stanes in a blink   210
Hame to their graves are seen to sink;
And some said ae thing, some anither;
But it was a' a perfect blether:
Ye needna mind their clash a feather.
When he was gone, they didna fail   215
To tak' his counsel, and to skail:
Aff, sae they skeygit, man and dame,
As gin cauld Hunger by the wame
Had grippit them, and nipt them hame,
    Wi' vengeance, hurry-scurry: —   220
Their ambries then they did assail;
Some ran to parritch, some to kail;
Some ran to claret, some to ale,
    And some to tartan-burry;
Some knapp'd awa' at kebbuck-stumps;   225
Some riv'd and ramsh'd at beefy rumps;
Some nibblet bits, some gobblet lumps;
Chaft-blades and chafts, and teeth and stumps,
    Now rattlet in a hurry:
Bannocks of a' kinkind o' meal,   230
Great baps and scones were swallow'd hail;
Mountains o' bread and seas o' ale
    Were down their pechans pour'd;
Frae Cellardyke to Perth or Creiff,
There never was, in my belief,   235
In capons, parritch, wine, and beef,
    Sic a disjeune devour'd!

Whan they had endit their disjeune,
They raik'd about for wappens soon;
Some ran to aiken-rungs and sticks;   240
Some ran to pinches and to picks;
Some grippet, for the greater skaith,
Great iron stanchels in their wraith;
Some haurl'd at cart and barrow trams,
For laik o' better batterin'-rams;   245
Some flourish'd sweys and masons' tools,
And graips, and forks, and guid shod-shools;
Taylors stole swerds, and sae did souters;
Plewmen cam heavy-arm't wi' couters;

Wabsters their looms in pieces brak,   250
And up the beams for wappens tak;
The bluidy butchers, and the baxters,
Had chappin'-knives beneath their oxters;
The barbers, fraithy as their suds,
Instead o' razors, flourish'd cuds;   255
Blacksmiths cam' arm't wi' tangs and nippers;
Wi' handspakes, fishermen and skippers;
Bailiies rush'd out frae council-chalmers
Wi 'halberts and wi' knappin'-hammers;
A' wi' the same fers wraith were gapin',   260
But ilk ane had a different weapon:
This man bare wood, and that bare iron,
But ilka saul wi' zeal was birrin'.

As they were armin' a' this time,
Town's-piper Jock, wi' glee sublime,   265
Gaed skrieghin' throu' the streets and skirlin',
Settin' the windocks a' a-dirlin';
Wi' spraichs o' bairns, a royat pack,
Loupin' and shoutin' at his back;
His pipes wi' sic a sequeal did squeak,   270
In the seven sterns they heard the skriek;
His drone did gruntch sae dour a sound,
Black Pluto heard it underground:
Sae what wi' gruntlin', what wi' squealin',
The causey-stanes were maist set reelin';   275
Aye at ilk corner evermair
He stopt, and gaif a hearty rair;
"Gae to the loan, and muster there!"

As whan, at michty Hector's ca',
The folks within the Trojan wa',   280
Clad in their coats o' armour bra',
   Ran frae the Scaean yett;
'Tween the wild fig-tree and the watter
The weiriors gather'd wi' a clatter;
Chariots and horse-hoofs round did scatter   285
Scamander's sand wi spairge and splatter,
   Till in mid plain they mett;
Sae, at the skriegh o' Piper Jock,
The burghers to the loan did flock;
Aye as they spank'd alang and sprung,   290
Their arms, stick, pick, and cuddy-rung,
On ane anither clank't and rung;
As whan in tail o' hairst, some day,

Whan skiffs o' wind blaw aff the brae,
A field o' beans (lang dainty strae!)   295
   Are touslet by the blast;
The bean-taps slap on ane anither,
Ilk meikle stalk assails his brither,
The reisslin' cods wag hither-thither,
   The shearers look aghast;   300
Sic like the breissil and the clatter,
As to the loan the burghers blatter.

Ere they were a' assemblet out,
   The sun rode o'er the isle o' May;
'Twas acht o' clock, or thairabout,   305
   By the school-dial near the way;
At that time in the east was seen,
Owr Innergellie's greenwood green,
A cloud o' stour, that owr the trees
Cam' swirlin' wi' the eastern breeze: 310
And westlins aye it swirl'd and blew,
And nearer aye and nearer drew,
As if a whirlwind, derf and dour,
Had ridden post frae Denmark owr,
And now was busy wi' the stour.   315
As on it swiff'd and swirl'd mair near,
A scharp-ee'd man, whase sicht was clear,
Beneath the stowry tourbillon,
Micht see slow movin' westlins on,
Shouthers and pows, an unco crowd,   320
A hundert-headed multitude,
And owr their heads lang rungs and cuds
Wavin' atween them and the cluds;
And swerds and halberts, braid and clear,
Glitterand baith i' the front and rear;   325
And the town's colours, heiz'd on hie,
Flaffin' and flamin' gallandlie;
And the town's drum, as if for battle,
Reirdin' awa' wi' furious rattle:
"The men o' Crail!" a man did shout;   330
"The men o' Crail!" cried hundreds out;
   Clerk Diston in the van!
"Harro!" the folk o' Caryl cry'd;
"Hurra!" the Anster folk reply'd;
   "Harro!" cry'd wife and man: 335
"Death to the Paip!" screamed Caryl's crowd;
"Down wi' the Paip!" skriech'd Anster loud;
"Together 'gainst the Beast!" together

They vy'd in shouts wi' ane anither,
As to embrace ilk man his brither 340
    Fordwarts they rush't and ran:
Bra thing it was, perfay, to view
Sae blithe and brisk a hallybaloo,
As intill ither's arms they flew,
And caps and cowls, and bannets blue, 345
    To spiel the lift began.
While they were thus in frisky flither,
Salutin' ilka man the tither,
And speirin' things at ane anither,
Lo! frae the country-seats around, 350
The lairds, wi' flunkie and wi' hound,
    Come daidlin', drappin' in;
For they had heard the trumpet-sound,
That had the kintra round and round
    Bedunder't wi' its din; 355
And up they bangit frae their beds,
And out at windocks shot their heads,
    Effrayt what this might mean:
They'd heard the bells far-soundin' jow;
They kent there was some hobbleshow; 360
Horses in haste were order't now,
    And whips and spurs bedien:
So down they come; and you may hear
Their bridles jinglin' loud and clear,
And flunkies' whistle, as mair near 365
    Down frae their lands they ride:
And you may see a mile awa'
Their gowden-laced waistcoats bra'
Whairon the sun-blenks, as they fa',
    Appeir to rest wi' pride: 370
I see Grangemuir; – he comes in glee;
His face, contorted funnilie,
Haulds in its faulds a prophecie
    O' meikle mirth and ploy;
I see Balcaskie; – as he rides 375
Spleen-burstin' lauchter shakes his sides;
The very naig that he bestrides
    Seems neicherin' too for joy:
See Sipsie! how he skewls his mou',
And glooms and gluntches at the crew 380
O' chisel'd saints and gods untrue,
    Whilk he in fancy views!
And look! how douce lang-headet Barns,
Wi' lades o' learnin' in his harns,

Comes trottin' cannily alang, 385
At's Latin Bible searchin' thrang
   For texts that he may use!
But the bauld laird of Innergellie,
Himsel' in green, baith back and bellie,
(His varlet flamin' out in yellow,) 390
   Comes bannin' unabash't;
See how his cheeks do storm and lour
Wi' angry puffs against the stour,
That his ain horse-cluifs, as they scour,
   Up in his face hae dash'd; 395
Mair soberlie trots Airdrie on,
And Renniehill, and Gibliston,
And lesser lairdies, four or five,
Wham here to name, or to descrive,
   I canna now be fash'd. 400

A' thae did mix, and meet and gather
Upo' the musterin'-ground thegither;
The fisher-knicht enarmed them weil
Wi' Swerds and pow-axes frae Dreel:
As they up-gript ilk man his wappen, 405
Aboon their heads a thing did happen,
   Whilk, tho' the mob were ramp already,
Render'd their hearts mair keen and crouse
T'attack within her bordel-house,
   Rome's king-debauchin' lady: 410
For, lo! fram Innergellie's trees,
Careerin' on the pirrin' breeze,
A greedy gled, intent to seize,
   Cam' wi' a soundin' clang,
And cleik't his felon claws upon 415
A laverock, that owr the loan
   Sang lustilie her sang;
As he wi' crabbit cruel claw
That innocent did gulligaw,
Some gentle cushie-dows, that saw 420
   The leesome la'rick's wae,
Aff frae their sinny dow-coat whirr'd,
And, lichtin' on the robber-bird,
Wi' peck and straik, and dusche and dird,
They forc'd and flappit to the yird 425
   That spulyier and fae:
Wi' angry bill, and wing theretill,
They wapp't and swapp't, and flapp't and slapp't
   Till, owercome at last,

Leavin' his ruffian life in air,   430
At Diston's feet he lichtet fair,
Wayme uppermost, and wamblit there
    In deadthraw grim and ghast;
The clerk took up the diein' glede,
And helm him sprowlin' owr his head;   435
    Than to the people cry'd,
"Behauld the greedy gled o' Rome,
By bills of innocents owrcome,
    In his ain heart's-bluid dy'd!
As feckless dows hae slachter'd sae   440
This grippin', grim, strang-talon'd fae,
Sae shall we, Calvin's feckless fowls,
Gie to the strumpet bluidy dools,
And cast her corp among the mools:
Tak' ye the omen, than, wi' joy,   445
And, – forward! – let us to the ploy!"
So speakin', heich aboon his head,
He swung in air the greedy gled;
The people caucht the augerie,
And testified their ready glee   450
    Wi' multi-son'rous noise;
And, "Let us march!" was cry'd aloud,
Thorough the wide-convulsit crowd,
    By monie a bellerin voice.

Anon, the marchin'-sign was gien;   455
    Bagpipes begoud to drunt and rair,
And the town's colours, in their sheen,
    Wallop't and shimmer't in the air;
Trumpets and drums, wi' blithsom brattel,
Begoud agen to blaire and rattle,   460
As if advancin' straucht for battle;
Awa' they set wi' merry cheer;
There never march'd for open weir
A troop sae lifey and sae jolly,
Sae little fash'd wi' melancholy.   465
As up they travell'd, reirdin' on,
Atween Pitkirie and the loan,
Dan Momus, god o' lauchter, over
Their hobblin' heads did hop and hover;
Sometimes, owr the hail regiment glancin',   470
Frae pow to pow he held a-dancin';
Sometimes he cock't himself upon
The peak o' the town's-piper's drone;
Sometimes, he grinnin', took a rest on

The showther o' the stalwart Diston;   475
Eftsoons he settlet, in a whip,
On Fisher-Willie's halbert's tip;
Than sought the borough's flappin' flags,
And row'd himsel' amang the rags:
He never blindit in his daffin',   480
Fliskin' like fire about, and gaffin',
Till to Dun-nino' s upponland,
Y-fere wi' that rejoicin' band
   He cam; whan, in a gliffin,
He saw the Vicar owr the Kenly   485
In fuffel'd garb, and plicht ungainly,
   Fast scamperin' and skiffin':
He was a bitter Papist black,
And sauld God's blessin' for a plack:[1]
His garments he had thrown about   490
In terrour, amaist wrang-side-out;
His loose, unbutton'd, waff briek-knees
Danglit in draperie round his thies;
His stockins, o' het haste the types,
Cam' flappin' owr his shoon in flypes: 495
'Tis addet, too, (sae, to this day,
Douce bodies in that kintra say,)
That, whan that squadron cam' in sicht
Wi' bannerols and pensels bricht,
Frichtsomely fleein' owr the heicht,   500
He had been at that vera time
Debarbin', wi' a razor prime,
   His week-negleckit beard;
He saw the troop, and, at the sicht o't,
He bangit up sae doons affrichtit,   505
Ae cheek was shav'd, the tither slichtet;
   And aff he flew afeard:
Than, hurry-scurry, hop, hop, hop,
Awa' he ran withouten stop:
Ahent his back he never looket,   510
Till he was past Strathtyrum dowcot;
His feet ne'er blindit aff their journey
Untill they landit at Balmernie;
And there he took hole like a rabbit,
And denner'd gustily with th' abbot,   515
Acquentin' him 'tween ilka gabbot,
How near he 'scap't frae being stabbit.
At a' this quakin', flichterin', rinnin',
Dan Momus' face was constant grinnin',
Whan, lo! upon the eastern heicht,   520

My grand-grand-grandsher (Taylor hight),
Appears in his braid-showther'd micht;
A merrie man, and stark theretill,
The tacksman o' Dun-nino mill;
His house stood round ahent the hill;   525
Owr a' the millers o' the shire
His buirdly stature did aspire;
And, as he by the head towr'd higher,
He shone for frankness, fun, and fire;
His hearthstane, swept and garnish'd clean,   530
Wi' yill and brandie aye was bein,
And rang wi' jokes baith morn and een;
Merry men there were aye at hame;
Whilk spread abrede my forbeir's fame:
He was the first leil laick true   535
That had read a' the Testaments throw,
    And had digest them well;
Albeit, Dan Vicar, wi' his ban',
Did blast and calumnie the man,
For readin' mair at wangyle than   540
    Lord Bishop or himsel',
For Vicar's ban', or Bitesheep's bark,
He had but little care or cark:
Sae up he comes to join the host,
(He'd got some tithand frae the coast),   545
    Wi' a' his miller-feir,
Thick Jamie Bud, lang Sandy Kay,
And three or four as stout as they,
In coats meal-melvied, powther'd gay
Wi' flows o' flour, like milky-way   550
    Whan thick sterns do appear;
Dan Momus, as he did perceive
My forbeir, smudgit in his sleeve.

    But mair he leugh, whan, frae the wast,
Stravithie's laird cam' spankin' fast,   555
To list himsel' amang that band,
And chase Corruption frae the land:
A laird he was, though somedeal auld,
In spreit yet juvenil and bauld;
Upon his face you mith discern,   560
Written quite clear to onie bairn,
A deidly hatred and a dour
To Satan, arm'd wi' monkish power:
He had a staff-swerd, straucht and lang,
That overhead he swapt and swang,   565

Develin' the air wi' monie a bang,
Whairwi' he thraten'd, in his wraith,
To dirk Diabolus to death:
At him, my grandsher and the Vicar,
As they march't up, and aff did bicker,   570
The god o' gaups did laugh and smikker;
He leugh sae loud, and lang, and sair,
That day, he couldna laugh nae mair!

Thus up, resoundin' frae the coast,
Travell't that monie-wappen'd host,   575
And keppit frae the lairdships round,
And cottar-towns throu' a' that bound,
Hinds, plewmen, lairds, and cottar callans,
That frae their spences, ha's, or hallans,
Did congregate in rairin' glee,   580
Enarm't with airn or rung o' tree,
To be partakers frank and free
O' whatsome'er that weir mith be.

As they cam' to the Prior-muir,
And saw Sanct Androis town and towr   585
    Atween them and the sea,
A wee they haltit to look down
Upon the multi-towred town,
That on her mountain o' renown
    Sat in her majestie;   590
Her sindry steeples, shootin' high,
Amid the schimmer o' the sky,
They set themsels, wi' curious eye,
    To reckon up and tell:
Her goodlie, great cathedral, spread   595
Upon the mountain's lordlie head,
In leviathan length, becrown'd
I' the middle, and at ilka bound,
Wi towr and spindyl turrets round,
    They mark'd and noted well;   600
The gowd that glitter'd on ilk spire,
The capper roofs that flared like fire,
Heigh sparklin' ower kirk and quire,
Wi' langsame gaze they did admire:
    But whan they thocht upon   605
The idolatries and sins confest,
That there did brood as in their nest;
The monie murder't saints that there,
Thro' persecutions sharp and sair,

Had to their Maker gone; 610
How poor Paul Craw, for speakin' true,
Was burnt wi' brass-ba' in his mou';
How Wishart, gentle, guid, and kind,
The friend and favourite o' mankind,
    Had, frae her causey-crown, 615
Ascendit upwarts frae his pyre
In chariot of whirlin' fire:
    Ah! martyr-murderin' town!
Thus thocht they in their hearts, and said
And cry'd, *"Aha!"*and shook the head 620
    Wi' bannin' and wi' frown;
"Thy end is come!" cry'd Barns aloud,
"Thou Scottish Babel lewd and proud!
Thou Rome o' Scotland! ah, the day
Is come, or just upon its way, 625
Whan Retribution, dour but just,
Thy gawcy glorie down shall thrust,
To rot amang the kirkyard dust
    Like carrion-corp for aye;
As asks and dragons now abide 630
Whare Babylon, in gowden pride
    Ance like a queen did ring;
Sae whair thy altars glister now,
Shall craps o' gosky dockens grow,
And jag-arm'd nettles soon, I know, 635
    The passer-by shall sting;
And schule-bairns, on a future day,
Shall be rampagin' in their play
Whare ance thy priests, in lang array,
    Their matin-sangs did sing!" 640

"As monie steeples as you see
Cockin' atween you and the sea,
Sae mony heads," cry'd out the Clerk,
"Cock on our Babylonish kirk;
They maun be a' shorn aff and clean'd: 645
Than fordwart ilka wangile friend!
Fordwart on bishop, friar, and fiend!"
This said, he northlins wagg'd his wappen,
And down the hill the host gaed stappin',
Wi' bagpipes blairing, banners flappin', 650
And a' their diff'rent armours rappin':
Syn auld St Rule cam' owr the sea,
The hill o' Boars did never see
Sae monie goodly chevalrie

Toddlin' and marchin' wi' sic glee.   655
By what time they were comin' down
The Prior-acres near the town,
The Sun, whase bernin' feet gae swift
Skelpin' alang the marble lift,
Owrspangit at ae single stend   660
The gowden key-stane o' the pend;
It was the vera ee o' the day,
    What time the carefu' kimmers keek
Aneath the kail-pat's lid to sey
The boilin' o' the beef, ere they   665
    The kettle upheese frae the kleek:
It sae bechanced at that hour,
That in Sanct Leonard's tapmast tower
Dan George Buchanan, douce and meek,
Was reading, by his windock-cheek,   670
(After a three-hours' spele at Greek,)
    His Hebrew Bible richt:
His ee was glidin' owr that part
Whair gude Josiah, wise in heart,
    A bairn in wisdom wicht,   675
Extirpate idols frae the temple,
And brized lewd priests for ane ensample;
And how, frae 'neath the burial-stanes,
He disinterr'd their murlin' banes,
And grund them into powther sma',   680
And winnow'd them i' the wind awa';
A' this he cannilie was readin',
Wi' guid sweet lear his spirit feedin',
Whan to his stoundit ear there comes
The blair o' trumpets and o' drums;   685
He frae his windock keekit out
To ken the reason o' the rout;
He saw the crowd that made the shout
    Thick on the Anster road:
Their borough-flags that flar'd and flap't,   690
Their wappens' points that overtapp't
The veil o' waffin' stour that wrapt
    That army as they yode;
He kent the shape, and swaup confest
O' learned Barns afore the rest,   695
    That, on his brankin' steed,
Seem'd the fore-rider o' that weir,
Whilst loftily his hand did rear
A flag, whairon was written clear,
    In gowden letters breid, –   700

Wreth, wreth! and bluidie fede and ill
To the vile Strumpet on the Hill!
Whairat douce George took merry cheer;
For, though to him his book was dear,
He liket FUN nae less than LEAR: 705
And mairattour, in sam' degree,
As Greek and Latin liket he,
He did dislike baith Pape and Deil;
(Thir twa thegither sortit weil:)
And aft Dan George, in mirthfu' day, 710
Was overheard to sing and say, –
"This warld'd wickedness, alace!
Like Janus, has a double face;
The rotten Deil has ane; the tither
Belangs unto the Pape his brither: 715
Their heads are double, yet but ane
Their buiks are, if I'm na' mistaen!"
Nae marvel than that George was glad
To see that Pape-assailin' squad:
  Nor laith was he, nor lang 720
To leave his Hebrew and his lear;
His shanks cam' lampin' down the stair
  As fast as they could spang:
Nae faster ran they on the day
Whan frae the Sea-tow'r, in a fray, 725
He skeyg'd frae Card'nal's wreth away,
Glad to escape his cleuks, perfay,
  Ere thrapple suffer'd wrang.

END OF SANG SECOND

NOTE

1 This vicar's name was Thomas Sclater. He was slain in Edinburgh some years later.
Knox speaks of him.

PAPISTRY STORM'D

SANG THIRD

ARGUMENT

This sang sall tell o' scrimmage fell
  Whair Lollard folks were winners;
And Papist gang, frae cudgels' bang,
  How they were famous rinners:
Syn ane and a' in Frater-ha',
  How feastit weil the sinners;
And ither things this ballad sings
  O' suppers and o' dinners.

Dan George the Kinness-burn had crost,
And near was comin' till that host,
Whan Barns spy'd, frae his upwart place,
That lamp o' learnin', George's face:
For George to him was as a brither;   5
They'd read lang Latin books thegither,
And gash'd and gabb'd wi' ane anither:
He, as he spy'd him, gaif command,
That his hail companie should stand,
And honour, as it did effeir,   10
The man o' merriment and leir:
Whairat the host upcast their caps,
And hands and lungs gaif shouts and claps;
The rocks and braes a' thairabout
Rang wi' the echo o' that shout,   15
Till, round the kirk-heugh, on the wave
It ran to Ladie Buchan's cave.

Whan they had ither greetit weil,
Quo George; My brithren, true and leill!
Great glee, perdie, my spreit doth feel   20
  To see your braw array;

You're welcome to Sanct Androis town,
T' extirpate ilka shaven crown,
And batter wi' your hammers down
　　Their idols as you may:　　　　　　　　　　25
You see them yonder, girnin' braw,
Within their niches in the wa';
You needna drede to gar them fa',
　　And kiss the ditches' dirt;
Grey-freir and black, ilk devil's whelp,　　　　30
That in our city youff and yelp,
They'll a' be better for a skelp;
　　We'll thank you meikle for't:
And in guid hour you're come, perfay,
To gi'e our filthy freirs a fray;　　　　　　　35
At twa o'clock they hald this day
　　A grand solemnitie;
Out to owr Ladie's Craig they gang
To worship there wi' prayer and sang
Their saint's auld banes, wham tempest dang　40
　　Aff frae the stormie sea:
Just lie in wait aside the wa',
Ye'll catch them marchin' in a raw
Wi' crosses, caps, and tippets braw,
　　And rotten banes, beside;　　　　　　　45
Rise and assailzie them at anes;
I fain would ken if useless banes
Will guard frae raps o' sticks and stanes
　　Their bellies and their pride;
I'll say nae mair, my brethren dear! –　　　　50
March for the ambusche and the weir;
Spulzie be your's o' crosses clear;
Baith rotten banes and ither gear,
　　May wealth o' them betide!
This said, the host wi' richt guid will　　　　55
Begoud to waigle down the hill:
They cross't St Nich'las' drubbly rill;
　　And up till th' Abbey wa'
Doucely they march't in close array;
And there, in ambuscado lay,　　　　　　　60
Till priests and freirs, baith black and grey,
　　Should ishue in a raw.

Mean time, as dinin'-time was by,
And stammachs clung, and thrapples dry,
　　They thocht on drink and meat;　　　　65
Good luck it was that frae the coast

The Commissariat o' that host
Brocht up baith sodden flesh and roast,
   Though cauld, yet guid to eat;
Sae frae their creels and wallets stout,   70
Belyve they haurl'd and draggit out
Great hams and legs o' sheep and nowt,
   And venison and veal;
And down upo' the gerss they gat,
And there in raws rejoicin' sat,   75
Smaicherin' awa at lean and fat,
   Up-gabblin', tooth and nail:
Nor did they laik delicious liquor
To gar their meat gang down the quicker,
   For weil had they taen tent   80
To bring up nappies strang and nice,
O' ilk kinkind and ilka price,
   To cherish them whan faint;
Their warst o' drinks was yill, the whilk
Dan David Barclay drank like milk;   85
   Nor did the Piper spare it;
But Fisher-Willie and the lairds
To nae sic sma' drink paid regards,
But wash'd their gebbies and their beards
   In sparklin' jaws o' claret.   90

They're comin'! cry'd a bodie out;
They're comin' now – I ken their shout;
Canons and freirs, and rabble-rout,
   Down chantin' by the mill!
I hear their aves and their trumps!   95
Cry'd Sipsies out, and up he jumps:
Banes-breakin' now, and bluidy bumps!
Exclaims the clerk, – *Hae done wi' rumps;*
   Up halbert now and bill!
Up frae the gerss their arms they get,   110
And craftilie their buschment set
On ilk side o' the southern yett
   In hidlins near the wa':
Ready, whan that the train cam out,
T' assailzie them wi' clour and clout,   115
And play their batterin'-rams about
   Upon the bellies braw:
They were nae lang in comin' down;
Cornets and caps, and cornets soon,
Grey-freir and black wi' shaven crown,   120
Tippit, and chesybil, and gown,

Cam gushin' like a stream,
Wi' trumps and cymbals soundin' high,
And chanters skirlin' in their cry,
And banners owr their beads that fly,   125
And tapers bleezin' up the sky,
Makin' the gowden sun envy
     The dazzle and the gleam:
Without the yett they were na lang,
Whan, frae their buschment in a bang,   130
Uprase that army, thick and strang,
     Wi' halyballoo and shout;
Crail's merry clerk the war-sign gaff;
He was the first wi' aiken staff
To chastify freir Tullidaff,   135
That bure on high the gowden calf,
     The idol o' that rout:
The saint's auld relics wi' the strokes
Were stricken frae their cedar-box;
Barrow and bancs wi' kicks and knocks   140
     Were daddit round about;
Then, hirie-harie! folks did rusch;
Then rag'd the scrimmage and strabusch;
Crail vy'd wi' Anster at the brusch;
     Was ne'er sic bickerin'-bout!   145
The aiken rungs on backs did batter;
The clods and stanes on crowns did clatter;
Bellies, the heicher they were and fatter,
Were dunsched in and grus'd the flatter,
     Wi' mickle pyne, but doubt: 150
Trumps, tapers, tippets, a' were marr'd;
In skreighs the singers' voices jarr'd;
The bagpipes, late that pantit hard,
     Were chok'd for want o' breath;
Sic hubbub and sic hubble-shew,   155
As scamper't aff the frichtet crew!
The grey-freir gap'd, the black-freir blew;
The canon scream'd, the shavelin' flew,
     As if 'tween life and death:
And some ran ae gate, some anither;   160
Some northlins, southlins; some in swither
Ran first the tae gate, than the tither,
Glad to escape by any whither
     That herriment and scaith.

John Tottis, though he fain would rin,   165
He couldna budge a single shin;

For Messer Barclay had him grippet
Ticht by the belt, and haurl'd his tippet,
And birs'd his beirdly pensch and nippit:
Whairat the grey-freir, Johnnie Tottis, 170
Wi' bernin' indignation hot is;
Twa wee bit bodies they were baith,
But whan their bluid was up in wreth,
As birsy's bears, and mad for scaith;
They warslet teuch wi' gurlie grapple; 175
They ettlet fierce at ither's thrapple:
They dunch'd wi' knees and elbucks baith;
Till, at the last, depreev'd o' breath,
They plumpit down frae whare they stood,
Amang the harbour's sludge and mud; 180
They row'd thegither in the slunk;
Their heads were up, their bodies sunk;
What wi' the slusch they ate and drunk,
I wat, Dan Barclay's vital spunk
    Had soon been dead and gane; 185
But Oliphant ('twas sae decreed)
Rax'd his lang arm in nick o' need,
And, grippin' Barclay by the heid,
(As fisher hauls a cod indeed),
    Upheez'd him safe again; 190
I trow, he was weel slim'd and soakit;
Great dads o' sludge amaist him chokit,
As ever and aye his mou outbockit
    The waters he had taen;
But Johnnie Tottis, feckless bodie, 195
Lay wallowin' in mis'ry muddy;
Men help't him not; but (throu' the saints)
He flounder't owr untill the Bents;
Loud gaups o' lauchter shook the bank,
As Johnnie slaister'd throu' the stank. 200

But whan that broillerie was dune,
Baith Erth below and Heaven abune
    Bare witness to that tuilzie;
For Heav'n was dim wi' stoury cluds
That up had risen wi' the thuds, 205
And Erth was strawn wi' rags and duds,
    The battle's divers spuilzie:
Here lay a cross; and here the tippet
Whairwi' wee John had been equippet;
Wide copes, great hoods a' riv'n and rent, 210
And scapularies scuff'd and shent,

And knottit girdles queer and quaint,
Lay hither-thither on the bent;
Bagpipes lay bit and bit asunder;
The drone was here, the chanter yonder;   215
A book was here, and there a bell,
A missal and a scallop-shell;
Tapers yet smeekin' on the stanes
Mixt wi' the saints' auld reekit banes;
The barrow's blads dash'd round about;   220
A trump, a taburine, and clout
    O' Tullidaff's lang gown:
The Lollard host had heartsom glee
The ruins o' that fecht to see;
And monie a gaulp and loud tehee   225
    Resoundit up and down:
Fy! fy! cry'd Dan Buchanan out,
Gae, gather up, ye impious rout,
The saints' black banes that under foot
    Lie trodden as you see: 230
Aiblins, upon some future day,
Yon henckle-bane, though mouldie, may
Be a Palladium in a fray
    To guard baith you and me:
Nae sooner said, than Piper Jock,   235
Wi' wicket murgeonin' and mock,
Pick't up the banes that lay like brock
And clappit them intill ane poke.

Their host thairafter did return
Till their first lair by Kinness-burn;   240
Thair lookin' up, whan Sipsies saw
The marble mawments carvit braw
Stuck in their niches i' the wa',
    A gloomie gluntch shot he;
I wot, he cry'd, 'tis now the hour   245
To mak yon ladies feel our power,
And bring them, in a stany shower,
    Tumblin' frae whair you see:
This said, he summon'd soon thegither
His regiment (a jolly futher!)   250
The wabsters o' the town o' Crail,
Men ferdy-limb'd and swank and hale,
Whase hearts had soukit all the haill
The pith o' parritch and cauld kaill:
Instead o' helm or morrion,   255
Thir weirlike wabsters everilkon

143

Had ane Kilmarnock nicht-cap on,
That flamit like the settin' son:
And round his head ilk ane held swappin'
A timmer treadle for a wappen: 260
Whan he beheld his yeomanrie,
Their eagerness and energie,
And how they toss't their arms on hie,
He thus accostit them: My lads!
Ye see yon girnin' Romish jads,   265
Provokin' you to gi'e them dads,
      And tumble them i' the ditches:
Let us divide our troop in twa;
Ilk half gang raikin round the wa',
Ane north, the tither westlins ga   270
      Displenishin' the niches:
Let the haill dyke be purgit clean;
Ae virgin mair be never seen! –
Farewell! we'll meet at Greg'ry's green,
      In half an hour or thairabout: 275
Sae speakin', he began th' attack;
He raucht his halbert up, and brack
      An image that stood starin' out;
She devel'd down a hideous wrack,
Her head dissociate frae her back;   280
      In splendirs flew the stane about:
Thairat, the soldiers o' his band,
Seein' their master's micht o' hand,
      Ramstam flew ragin' aff;
Some to the left, some to the richt,   285
To soop the wa's wi' a' their micht,
      Ilk wabster wi' his staff;
Nae mercy than for Papish Maries;
In flinders flew the carv't fleegaries;
Some hit the head, and some the showther,   290
Some pash'd at ance the pow to powther;
Sic clamahewits and sic baff
Were never rain'd frae feckless staffs;
In twenty minutes, less or mair,
Of a' the idols lately there   295
      Pitcht on that Abbey wa',
A man mith rax his een in vain
Ere he could spy upon a stane
      An idol heich or law;
Sic cleanly wark, and sae perfyte,   300
Wi' chappin'-sticks that sair did smyte
      Crail's merrymen did mak;

Crown'd wi' red nicht-caps they gaed out,
But wi' Victoria's joyfu' shout
   Cam crown'd wi' glory back! 305

Mean time throu' Priorie and town
The monster Fame gaed up and down
   As fast as she could post;
(Her feet laigh on the causey paikin';
Her head amang the thin clouds raikin', 310
Heigh, heigh aboon Salvador's steeple,)
Yelpin' aloud to a' the people
   The tidings o' that host;
The monie thousand gabs, within
The plumes, that sur-invest her skin 315
   Gaed clatterin' and clashin';
Ae gapin' gab did utter true;
Great lies gush'd frae anither mou':
   A third wi' baith kept gashin':
Like squibs and crackers fired aft, 320
You mith hae heard them up alaft
   Sound owr ilk chimla-tap:
What wi' their yammerin' and din,
Lord Prior James, that sat within
His palace, maist frae out his skin 325
   Wi' awsome terrour lap;
Chiefly i' th' Priorie and round it
Th' alarms and yellochins resoundit;
   For frae yon fecht that fell,
The frichten't freirs cam in about, 330
Fleein' wi' panic-skriegh and shout,
Their faces white as linen clout,
Bearin' the story o' their rout
   To cloyster, ha', and cell:
Ilk fae they saw, ilk baff they gat 335
Was by their fricht exaggerat;
   They tauld how that they met
A regiment o' giants bauld,
Like to the Anakims of auld,
Wi' clubs and wappens manifauld 340
   For deadlie battle set;
And some on faemy horses rode,
Whase manes, bedreepit red wi' blood,
   Splash't draps o't i' their een;
In iron boots some walk't afoot; 345
On dragons some flew round about;
There never was in Fife but doubt

Sic fleysome warriours seen:
As prief o' which Sanct Rule's dear banes
Were left to rot amang the stanes: 350
A mercy on us,cry'd Dean Annan,
We're gane – our kirk's nae langer stannin'!
Our anchor's lost, scream'd John Arbuckle,
We're perish'd a', baith sma' and muckle!

Amid this dridder and this flurry, 355
St Magdalen's big bell in a hurry
Begoud to reissle hurry-scurry:
That jowin' jangle was the ca',
For th' Abbey people, ane and a',
To congregate i' th' Frater-ha': 360
'Twas hour o' dine or thereabout;
Hunger was i' their wambes nae doubt,
But terrour, too, was round about;
And terrour garr'd them loup pell-mell
Frae senzie-house, kirk, court, and cell, 365
In omne-gatherum at that bell;
As whan the bees some day in June
Stravaig frae risin' sun till noon;
If mirky clouds in th' afternoon
    Come stowfin' up the west, 370
Hear they but anes the thunner-claps,
And in the leaves the plouterin' draps,
They gi'e their sma' wings sudden claps,
Amd hurry hamewarts to their scaps
    For cosy skoug and rest; 375
Sae did that Abbey people a'
Effrey't flee to the Frater-ha',
Canon, and monk, and dean, and prior,
And batie-bum, and beggin' freir,
A congregation wode wi' fear, 380
Though fat, in dulesome dreiry cheir:
The porch ne'er witness't sic a flither;
They pous'd, they jundy'd ane anither;
Their wambes afftimes were jamm'd thegither;
Mair space they had i' th' ha', though thrang! – 385
It was a dainty room and lang;
(I am a man of five feet three;
'Twas twenty times the lenght o' me:)
Guid hap, their dinner then was laid
Upon the tables lang and braid, 390
Wi' damask napery owrspread;
And gowden trunscheors like the moon,

Wi' correspondin' fork and spoon;
A wilderness o' meat was set;
Sea, soil, and sky, were here a' met;   395
Fish, flesh, and fowl, baith cauld and het;
And florentines, and pies, and tarts,
Rang'd here and there in sindry parts,
And sauces, soups, and geills, and creams,
Up-stowfin' to the roof their steams,   400
Wi' bonnie fruitage, ripe and red,
In silverised baskets spread:
And siller jugs and stoups divine
O' malvesie and claret-wine,
Shimmering like suns in order fine: 405
Temptation reel'd in tass and bicker,
Dancin' divinely 'mang the liquor;
It wad a Nazarite provokit
To break his vow and tak a bok o't,
Untill his hail-life's drowth were slockit: 410
Had I been there that nicht, I think,
Though I'm a man o' little drink,
I wadna been sae doons perjink;
But taen an over-loup for sport: –
I'd got the Paip's indulgence for't!   415

Whan they were a' forgadder't there,
Lord Prior James got on a chair,
And cry'd, *A truce to elrisch fricht!*
Let's dine, my friends, and that outricht;
Fu' stamach maks faint heart mair wight;   420
And of a' sorrows, it's confest,
A sorrow that is fu' 's aye best:
Sae down they cloytet on their seats,
And helter-skelter at the meats;
As Lybian lions, that on prey   425
Licht, after danderin' monie a day,
Ramsch skin, flesh, bane, e'en sae did they;
As windmill blades, whan wind does happen,
Rin reeshlin' round and round, and rappin',
While, ever as the shafts gae swappin',   430
The grindin'-graith below gaes clappin';
Sae quick, or rather mickle quicker,
Their chaft-blades back and fore did bicker;
Baith jaws, as if they vy'd thegither,
Sae quiver'd, nae man could tell whether   435
Gaed faster, th' upper or the nether;
Nor waur their lungs for wauchts were giftit;

The siller stoups on heigh upliftit
Were tootit in a whip and tiftit;
Eat-weil, they say, is drink-weil's brither;   440
Or rather, ane may say, its mither;
But ca' it either tane or tither,
That nicht they were leisch'd in thegither;
Had Epicurus sell been waitin'
Upon them as they pang'd their meat in,   445
He couldna weil hae blam'd the eatin';
Had Bacchus sell been there, I'm thinkin',
For pumpin' bottles and for skinkin',
For couldna weil hae blam'd the drinkin':
Sae what wi' tootin', what wi' eatin',   450
Their hearts, whan they had got some heat in,
Were stapt frae duntin' and frae beatin'.

Lord Prior James again uprase;
Ah, by Sanct Mary bricht! he says,
Me had thir Lollards no distrubill'd,   455
My denner had been nearly doubl'd;
Yet it is marvel nae the less,
That we hae made sae guid a mess,
Considerin' how our Sanct's dear banes,
Under whase shade we denner'd anes,   460
Lie now out bleachin' on the stanes:
Ah, wae is me! sic heavy dule
Ne'er yet hath happen't to Sanct Rule;
The storm that dang him frae the deep,
Upon our tangly skellies steep,   465
Was naething to the tempest black
Frae that oultrageous Lollard-pack;
That maks his banes to-day a wrack:
The barbare rocks that caught him than
In mercy, sav'd the haly man;   470
But this rock-heartit crew o' Luther
Will persecute his banes to powther;
Unless we do devise some means
Whereby to vindicate the banes;
And skail that mad ill-gainshon'd byke   475
O' Test'ment-men that doth us fyke,
To Anster back or Callardyke:
Whasa than can devise a way,
Let him up-speik as best he may,
For de'il haet mair hae I to say.   480

He sat him down to birl and quaff;

And up to speik rase Tullidaff;
I swear by him that made the moon!
The menzie o' that German loon
Hae pykin' been at this my gown,   485
    And made ae flype their plunder;
(So sayin', up to view he gaff
His lang-gown wi' its flype torn aff;
The ha' resoundit wi' a lauff
    To see it rent asunder;)   490
Yet, though my vestment thus be rent,
Sanct Geil! my spreit is yet unshent;
Thir scoundrels o' the Testament
    I challenge them ilk ane;
If no for Latin or for lear,   495
At least to joust or break a spear,
And fecht them butten fricht or fear
    Upon the gerssy plain:
This vera nicht I sall send out
A bauld defiance to the rout;   500
Cheise they a champion steeve and stout
    To battle for their wangill;
I, in my coat of airn or bress,
Sall stand to battle for the Mess,
And for our injur'd kirk's redress   505
    Sall tuilzie like an angel;
And let the fecht's conditions be;
If their priev'd knicht owr-tirvie me,
Keep they the banes but strife or plea
    Whilk this day they hae cleiket;   510
If I, wi' help o' Mary bricht,
Dumfounder to the death their knicht,
Let them gie back thir relics richt
    Within their cophine steekit;
I hae na better rede to gie;   515
If you hae better deal it free;
Gin this is best, than tak frae me
    And use the counsel as you may:
He scarce had endit, whan a gabble
O' tongues and raps upo' the tabill,   520
Frae that wine-flister't ribble-rabbill,
    Was Tullidaff's gude say.

Whan Tullidaff was dune wi' stannin',
Than up to his shanks gat John Annan;
Quoth he, "You're vera richt in plannin'   525
    How to rescue the banes;

But by Sanct Fillan! think alswa
How to rebut and schue awa
Thir damnit faes that siege our wa'
    Wi' wappens for the nanes;
Send forth a messenger to carry
The tidings to the Regent Mary;
Tell her o' a' this fiery-farie,
    Uprisen round our town;
And bid her and Lord Bishop send
Frae Falkland, whair they now attend,
A troop o' jackmen to defend
    His mitre and her crown;
Sae sall this vile canallyie-host
Be huntit downwarts to the coast;
And duds and flypes that hae been lost
    Be found again richt soon."
He scarce had ceas'd, whan John Arbuckle
Upon the tabill dang his knuckle,
    And cry'd, – "I chap this thing;
Mine be the embassage to carry
To guid Lord Bishop and Queen Mary
The tithand o' this fiery-farie,
    And jackmen thence to bring."
Up-spak Lord Prior James: "I trow,
Twa strings are best aye to ane's bow;
I do apprieve that John Arbuckle,
Bein' a man o' courage muckle,
Himsel up for this bus'ness buckle:
Mean time, at ilka abbey-yett,
Let guards and sentries round be sett;
And be ilk tow'r and turret mann'd
Wi' michty warriours out-o'-hand,
That frae nocturnal 'sault may stent
Thir rybalds o' the Testament."
He spak, and instant a' the senzie
Did ratifie it without plenzie;
Apprieval rang loud frae their menzie.

Whilst they i' th' Priorie this-gate
Were gain' on at sic a rate
    Wi' clamour and wi' feast,
Nae less the burghers throu' the town
Were yelpin', skelpin', up and down,
    Contrair the Roman beast:
For now Conspiracie stalk'd out
Nakit, without a gyzin-clout,

530

535

540

545

550

555

560

565

570

150

Red-wud for some destruction-bout;
Frae the West-port to Greg'ry's-green,
Was naething heard and naething seen,
    But tongue-strabush and war;   575
And Market-street did, like a Babel,
Wi' bladderand bodies yaup and yabble;
The South-street gowl'd wi' gibble-gabble,
    The North-street meikle waur;
The wynds were claikin' wi' the clatter;   580
The Foul-waste bumm'd wi' blitter-blatter;
Tongues never wi' sic clitter-clatter
    Did jangle and did jarr;
Wives fir'd and frenzy'd up the men;
The men inflam'd the wives agen;   585
Schule-bairns, withouten shoe or cape,
Gaed skirlin' treason 'gainst the Pape;
Auld folks, that scarce could grin or gape,
At Papistry did gleek and jaip:
The douce professors in their gowns   590
Stood preachin' on the causey-crowns,
And the puir students, (fractious lowns!)
    At ilka college-yett,
To paternosters, fiends and freirs,
Proclaimit mad and mortal weirs,   595
    Ere that the sun be set:
They spacier'd back and fore in bands,
Wi' lowin' sticks intill their hands,
Threat'nin' to hurl the bernin' brands,
    And pay the de'il his debt;   600
Till ane i' the College-wynd cry'd out,
"Aha! what deil are we about,
Tossin' our heads wi' yell and youtt,
Like Hannibal's fire-puttin' nowt,
    For nocht but idle schaw?   605
Let's down to meet the southern host,
And greet the heroes frae the coast, –
Awa' – there's nae time to be lost; –
    Aff, birkies, ane and a'!"
Incontinent he took his heels;   610
And after him an hundred chiels,
As hallockit and rais'd as de'ils,
    Ran hirdie-girdie skirrin';
"*Hurra!*" they yellochit a' throuther;
"*Hurra! Lear, Libertie, and Luther!*"   615
And split the crowd wi' shank and showther,
    Like bombard-shot a-birrin';

The rabble, whan they saw them rin,
To follow too did straucht begin;
And eastlins, like a rairin' linn,   620
    Ran down the South-street whirrin':
Tam Pethrie's horse, a scurvy hack,
Wi' lades o' camstane on his back,
    In the Eastburn-wynd was stannin';
Camstane and creels, and Tam and horse,   625
Were overturnit by their force,
    As if wi' sweep o' cannon;
And down they rushet like a jaw
Alangside o' the Abbey-wa',
Till, comin' near the burn, they saw   630
    The southern host outspread,
Busk'd in the abuilyiements o' weir,
Ensenyies waffin' lang and clear,
And halbert tall, and lance and speir,
    Hie glitterin' owr their head;   635
Whairat they gat up wi' a shout,
Strathtyrum rattlet round about:
Had Luther's sonsy sell been seen
Stappin' alang St Nich'las' green,
A greater joy there couldna been   640
    Than what did then befa',
As intill ithers' arms they rush't,
And hands were shaken, hearts were flush't,
And blobs o' joyous tears outgush't
    Beside that Abbey-wa'.   645

Mean time the sun's red steeds had haurl'd
To the north-wastern side o' th' warld
    His fiery-wheelit car;
The isles o' Lewis and o' Sky
Lay blinkin' in the beams that fly   650
    Out frae their nastrills far;
And now ae mament they did rest
On Hecla's frost-becrystall'd breast
    Their trachlet feet a wee,
Ere that they left the heevinly pend,   655
And lap wi' ane prodigious stend
    Aneath the warld intill the sea:
And Hawkey now, weel sair'd wi' food,
Within the byre forwearyt stood,
Whilst Grizzy maks the pails to flutter   660
Wi' torrents ominous o' butter.
The plewman frae his day-lang swink

Lay restin' on the kitchen-bink,
Richt glad his fire-hung pat to hear
Singin' and dringin', token clear   665
That merry parridge-time was near.
Sanct Salvador had frae his tower
Clankit aught straiks to tell the hour;
And, by that time, the host that lay
Encampit near the Kirkheugh brae,   670
What wi' the town's-folks thick and thrang,
And ither re-enforements strang,
That a' that simmer e'enin' lang
    Cam' draiglin' in wi' arms,
Had gather't and increasit sae,   675
That the hail space that stretchit frae
The Abbey-park to Kirkheugh-brae
    Was bizzin' wi' the swarms:
As bees, whan simmer overheaps
The population o' the skapes,   680
Aft emigrate and flee in heaps
    To garden-bush and flower;
Sae thick they owr the fulzies stalk,
The gard'ner, as he taks his walk,
Scarce kens agen his fav'rite stalk   685
    Wi' clusters cleedit owr;
E'en sae the space frac th' Abbey-park,
Round to the Heugh and Dennis-wark,
Was crawlin' wi' sae pang a mass,
You scarce could see a spat o' grass.   690
As now the moon had got the upper,
They 'gan to think upon their supper:
And supper frae the city cam'
Creakin' in carts, whase tree and tram
Wi' bangs o' beef and hills o' ham   695
    Did tremble and did crack;
Hurlbarrows, filled to their taps
Wi' saxpence laifs, and cakes, and baps,
Were haurlit down by baxter-chaps
    That vivers mith na' lack;   700
And carters' sleds heapt bonnily
Wi' bacon-hams baith round and high
And kebbucks curlin' to the sky
    Came draiglin' down the street:
E'en Tammie Pethrie's wrackit mare,   705
Had gather'd to her feet ance mair,
And chang'd her camstane for a skair
    O belly-timber sweet;

153

And Berwick's yill-carts were asteer,
Rumblin' wi' barls o' michtie beer;   710
That nicht his hogsheads were na sweer
    To rattle tow'rd the shore;
And ilka wine-booth thro' the town
Threw out her bottles to the moon;
Sic fludes o' liquor ne'er flow'd down   715
    The Eastburn-wynd before;
Weel you may see that siegin' host
Had skaff and skink withouten cost;
Sae down they fell to boil'd and roast
    Upon the bonnie gerss;   720
They didna stick for forks and knives;
Ilk man at's pleasure rugs and rives;
As if frae death to save their lives
    They swallow'd fast and fers;
And sic the flitter and the flutter,   725
O' multitude o' mous that smoutter,
A man mith weel had heard the clutter,
    And soundin' o' their chafts,
A mile ayont the Kenly-watter;
My faith, it was nae mincin' matter;   730
There never was sic chaft-blade blatter
    On hairst-rigs or on crafts.

END OF SANG THIRD

154

PAPISTRY STORM'D

Sang Fourth

ARGUMENT

Frae Tullidaff, a challenge bauld
   Is sent out to the host:
Arbuckle, back by sutors haul'd,
   Is in a blanket toss't;
Out to the Scores baith young and auld
   To see the joustin' post;
A battle then is sung or tauld
   Whairin sma' bluid is lost.

As on the Heugh, hard by the yett,
The captains o' the host were sett,
And round their burde on cauld and hett
   Were suppin' lustily;
(Nae licht o' candle needit they   5
For yet the gowden tail o' day
Sweipt wi' its never-settin' ray
   The rim o' th' Arctic sky;
And, mairattour, intill the East,
To see the frolick o' the feast,   10
Keek'd out, in silver cymarre drest,
   The jollie-checkit moon,
And owr the sea, and owr the sky,
And owr Sance Androis steeples high,
Flang frae her lap rejoicinglie   15
   Goupins o' glory down;
The table round the whilk they sat,
The wine-cups whilk they tooted at,
Their vera faces radiance gat
   Frae her warld-fillin' blaze;)   20
As they were pykin' thus and piddlin',
And wine-dubs round and round were driddlin',
Behauld! amid the sound o' fiddlin',

The Abbey-yett upgaes;
And frae it there did issue out   25
Sax fiddlers playin' merry bout,
And them ahent a herald stout,
    In green and yellow claes;
At's mou' he had a trumpet braw,
Whairwi' he 'gan to roust and blaw: 30
Ha, heretics! I'm come to ca'
    Your ferdiest to the fecht;
Sir Tullidaff, the warden-freir,
Albeit a feckless cuif at leir,
Yet a terrific cairl in weir,   35
    A man o' buik and wecht,
Doth by this mou' o' mine defy
The steevest o' your host, to try
In single fecht, till either die,
    The merit o' your wangill;   40
Hae ye your man by acht o' clock,
A' frack and furnish't for the shock,
Wi' him, Sir Freir, in iron frock,
    Sall tuilzie like an angel:
And let the fecht's conditions be,   45
If gude Sir Tullidaff sall die,
Keep you the banes but strife or plea
    Whilk this day ye hae cleikit;
If he, wi' help o' Mary bricht,
Dumfounder to the death your knicht,   50
Do ye restore the relics richt
    Within their cophine steekit: –
Jimp time he took to steek his mou',
Whan on the table down he threw
    Ane birrin' gauntlet down;   55
A dozen glasses by the mitten
Were into shiverssmash'd and smitten;
    Their wine flew to the moon;
Up-sprang, wi' riot and wi' rippat,
A dozen angry men to grip it,   60
    The Fisher-Knicht and Barns,
Fierce Sipsies, glumshin' in his wreth,
Clerk Diston, almost out o' breath,
And Innergellie, with an aith,
    Attestin' moon and starns,   65
That, as he was a champion fittin',
His was the combat, his the mitten: –
    Hald, hald your tirrivee,
Cry'd Dan Buchanan frae his seat,

To end this pley, and this debate,   70
Take Homer's canny classic gate,
  (A wily wight was he!)
E'en get a hat, and clap therein
Your names writ down withouten din,
  And them a' throwther whummel;   75
And whatsomever o' them a'
Our master-skinker first shall draw,
That be the man wham it sall fa'
  This furious freir to hummel;
They gat a hat, and clapt therein   80
Their names writ down withouten din,
  And whummel'd them a' throwther;
The skinker, servin' at their back,
Shov'd in his hand to pick and tak
  A champion out for Luther;   85
Behauld! the vera first he picket
(Luck rul'd it sae!) was Diston's ticket;
  He read it by the moon;
Clerk Diston's name is on the label;
Clerk Diston, soundit round the table,   90
A man mair stalwart, steeve, and stable,
To drive the freir to the Diable,
  Couldna be singlet soon:
Up frae his seat the not'ry bowtit;
"My arms!" he to the welkin shoutit;   95
"My spear! my swerd! nae mair about it;
  I'm for the battle bown;
De'il may I perish in my fecket,
By some bauld tailzeour's bodkin pricket,
If I'se na soon exhibit sticket   100
(Maugre Sanct Rule and Tam-a-Becket)
  This braggin' lurdoun loun:"
And as he spak, there fell as proof
That instant frae Hevin's spangly roof
  A starn o' shootin' licht,   105
That frae the zenith's tapmast crown
Gaed scrievin' clean across the moon;
And in the bay gaed divin' down
  That mament out o' sicht;
They kent the omen, and they clappit   110
Their hands as down the fire-ba' drappit.

Mean time Arcturus, that on hie
Glisters beside Bootes' knee,
  Like ane knee-buckle bricht,

Had been, for twa guid hours and mair,   115
Westlins o' Dairsie's forest fair,
A-chasin' Berenice's hair,
   Scarce seen for simmer's licht;
Syn they sat down to their repast,
A sign and half a sign had past   120
Across the mid-day straik, whairon
Astraddle rides the gowden sun:
And Morpheus, now i' th' lift did ramp,
Down drizzlin' frae his feathers damp
His sleepy dew-draps owr their camp: 125
Forfairn wi' toil, and drink, and sangs,
And antipapal douce harangues,
The siegers fell asleep in bangs
   Upon the gressy ground;
Exceptin' here an antrin fiddle,   130
And yonder, in the vera middle,
   A diein' bagpipe's sound;
Nae din kept soughin' i' the sky
To tell th' unpillow'd crowds that lie
   Souffin' and sloomin' round;   135
To Barns then up-spak Fisher-Willie;
Methinks it's richt, my learnit billie!
Syn baith the Bears now shine ill-willie
   Growlin' at our carouse;
To think o' dortours and o' beds,   140
Whairon to rest our legs and heads,
   Till Tullidaff us rouse:
Quoth Barns, Hech! what would Luther think
To see us as we sit and wink,
Amid sic daffery and drink!   145
   Up, then, and let us aff!
Lest that our Papish enemie
Should keek outowr the wa' and see
   How daintilie we daff!
Up than, as fast as they were able,   150
They bangit endlang frae the table,
And spers'd about in search o' beds
Throu' houses, hostillars, and sheds,
Whairon to rest their heavie heads.

Whan they were streiket down for naps,   155
They slummer'd on like vera taps,
The sounder for their claret-draps:
Except the walkrife clerk, wha lay
Doverin' and dreamin' on till day,

O' fechts, and feuds, and bluidy rackets,   160
And bucklin' habrihones and jackets,
And Tullidaff, afore his sicht,
Girnin' and gapin' like a wicht
Murder't, whase saul was on the flicht;
In brief, the harrens o' the clerk   165
Were sae commovit wi' the werk
   O' harnessin' and weir;
That in his reelin' saul ae thocht
O' parchment or o' peace was nocht,
   For dreams o' strife and steir!   170

As in and round the town they sleepit,
Than frae his cloister hidlins creepit,
Brimfu' o' zeal and courage muckle,
That michtie envoy, John Arbuckle,
On his ambassiate to carry   175
The tidings to the guid Queen Mary
Of a' this siege's fierie-farie;
And fetch frae Falkland's palace auld
A bang o' Frenchmen big and bauld,
To prick, wi' bayonet and pike,   180
Thae hereticks that did them fyke
Backlins to Crail and Cellardyke:
He frae the Abbey's wastern yett
Had scapit sly withouten lett;
   And now, ayont the town,   185
Was distant nearly half a mile,
Zig-zaggin', wi' great tent and toil,
Through the thick middens of Argyle
   Gilt glorious by the moon:
Whan frae ane little yill-house near,   190
That shone wi' candles glimmerin' clear,
Five Anster sutors in a steir,
Inflamit wud wi' Berwick's beer,
   Rush't reel-rall owr the street;
And claucht at random on the freir;   195
I wat, he soon was put in fear;
His skrilles, and skreichs, and skellochs dreir,
   Maugre his cloak's deceit,
Made soon th' ambassadour to kythe;
Whairat the tipsy sutors blyth   200
   Gat out their nippers straucht,
And, wi' their iron grapples, grippit
His flesh, and unto troublance nippit,
Garrin' him scream a hideous rippet;

As aye they hotch'd and laucht;   205
Untill the pangs o' back and thie
Made frae his saul the cork to flee;
And a' the secrets frank and free
O' that Guise-fleechin' ambassie
    Cam gushin' frae his mou';   210
Than wox the saucy sutors glad,
And bad their captive be na 'fraid;
Him they'd convoy, without debaid,
To whair he should, for what he said,
    Get guerdon as was due;   215
They dragg'd him to the Fisher-Knicht;
(Wham up they rapt ere mornin'-licht);
They tauld their captive's fenzied plight,
    His journey and its drift;
"E'en tak a blanket," quoth the Knicht,   220
"At ilka corner plant a wicht;
Mak the thief wallop out o' sicht
    Reboundin' up the lift;
Till 'mid the starns he stick and settle
Atween the Great Bear and the Little: 225
Sae punish'd be the man that gangs
To bring out Guise's bluidy bangs
'Gainst his puir countrymen for wrangs!"
They gat a braid, strang, dainty blanket;
Ae wicht at ilka neuk stood plantit;   230
The fifth man took his stance aloof
To mark whan i' the starry roof
    Th' ambassadour should stick;
They whummel'd him to heevin' alaft;
Ten times he birr'd up; but as aft   235
Amid the keppin' garment saft
    His buik reboundit quick;
Ilk time they garr'd him upwarts bicker,
Erthlins he tummil'd down the quicker;
The aftener he to heevin' cam naur,   240
He seem'd to hate it aye the waur;
Untill the sutor-folk at length
    Wi' flings fortravail'd and forfairn',
Found to the wastin' o' their strength
    He would na stick and be a stern!   245

Whilst near Sanct Androis town this wark
O' blanket-heezies stout and stark
Was gaen on in th' Abbey-park;
    Lo! on the heevinly plain

Twa heathen gods were seen thegither   250
Scrievin' awa wi' ane anither;
The god² that had a double mither,
    And she³ that had na nane;
Quoth he, "Perdie, I'm vext to see
A worshipper maist dear to me   255
Yonder out-owre the siller sea
    About to daur the death;"
Quoth she, "Perfay, I'm vext likewise
To see ane clerk wham I do prize
Resolvit soon in Mars's guise   260
    To jeopardie his breath:"
Quoth he, "Do you then tak guid tent
Your parchment weriour be na shent;
My bottle-champion, be it kent,
    Nae dammishment shall dree:"   265
Quoth she, "Do you then look till't weel
Your drinkin' wicht 'scape head and heel;
My witty clerk frae straiks o' steel,
    I warrant, sall 'scape free:"
Thus they up in the sky thegither,   270
Claver'd awa wi' ane anither.

But soon the red-hair'd maid, that sleeps
With her auld grasshopper⁴ i' the deeps,
Keek'd upwarts thro' the rowin' sea,
And saw the Hours wi' gigglin' glee   275
Thrang harnessin' the steeds, that bear
Her bernin' chariot throu' the air;
Up hurry-scurry in her sark
She spangit for her daily dark;
She was in sic a flichterin' fricht,   280
Lest she should hender mornin'-licht,
She took nae time to girdle richt
    Her jupes about or gown;
But naket (save her sark) and bare,
She skeygit uplins throu' the air;   285
And, mountin' up her chaise's chair,
    Drave aff her horses soon;
Apollo leugh, and shook his sides
As aff in naket glore she rides;
E'en Jove himsel', wi' roguish eye,   290
Keek't through a peep-hole in the sky
To see her, jiggin' truttie-trottie
Without her jupes or little-coatie.

161

The day-daw scarce begound to glisten,
Whan frae his pallet up-sprang Diston;   295
The windocks scarce wi' beams did lauff,
Whan bangit up Sir Tullidaff;
Twa ferdy faes, destin'd ere nicht
To try ilk ither's utmost micht,
For makin' baith their sauls tak' flicht,   300
Ilk had ane omen to betaken
The doom that owr his pow was shakin':
As Tullidaff drew up his breiks,
Ilk button that his finger seeks,
As if forleitet by its steeks,   305
   Upon the flure down-drappit;
The mair he fummelt and he fykit,
Fient haet ae button would keep sticket,
Sae that his garment, wild and wicket,
   Aye at his heels did flap;   310
Whairas, e'en o' their ain accord,
The Clerk's, as gin they kent their lord,
Stole up without a single heeze,
And cannilie, unto his thies,
   Did circumjack and clap!   315

Envestet were thir warriours baith
Soon in their buliements and graith;
(The warden's trunk-hose to his fecket
Wi' gowden corken-priens was pricket:)
Whan they were clad in claise and shoon,   320
To diff'rent things they turnit soon,
To pit their sauls in better tune:
Sir Frier began wi' blitter-blatter
His pray'rs to saints to pitter-patter,
And muse on mass and haly watter;   325
But Diston, butten fear or flutter,
To fit him for the battle's clutter,
Betook himsel' to rows and butter.

Let's leave them thair at mass and meat,
And look about anither gate;   330
Sanct Salvador's lang strappan steeple
Had peltit five hours to the people;
The streets were fu' o' mornin'-licht,
And windocks' lozens yellow-bricht
Wi' blinks back-bleezin' on the sicht: 335
Whan the town-crier wi' his clap
Gan throu' the streets to reird and rap;

And the town's-drummer wi' his drum
Begoud to brattle and to bum;
And the town's-piper wi' his drone 340
Garr'd sleep frae ilk ee-lid be gone:
First the tae man, and then the tither,
And sometimes a' the three thegither,
Yammer't upon the causey-crowns;
Ho! men and wives, and student-lowns! 345
Auld folks and bairns, and learnit gowns!
Up frae your lazy beds, and see
The jollie justing and the spree
Upon the Scores about to be!
Whairat baith learnit and unlearnit bodies 350
About them rapplet fast their duddies,
And, headlins hurryin' frae their doors,
Out-ran in thousands to the Scores;
As fast as water frae a spout,
Dickeman's-wynd spew'd hundreds out; 355
Great bangs the Castle-wynd out-bockit;
The Butts wi' bodies maist was chokit;
Sic hobblin', hurryin', and happin',
Wi' elbucks jundyin' and rappin',
Coat-tails and women's gowns flip-flappin', 360
At fair or sermon ne'er did happen:
Bar'l-belly'd men and great-wambe women
Stood jammit i' the Butts, and screamin',
Till, wi' their batterin'-rams afore them,
They smash'd the smaiks that maist did smore tham: 365
Lean skraes o' men, and sclender wives,
Were glad to get out wi' their lives:
But in the Castle-wynd mair space
And breidth they had to run their race:
In brief, wi' bodies fleein', flittin', 370
The town seem'd desolation-smitten;
Nae livin' thing, save cat or kitten,
Upon the lanely hearth-stane sittin':
Nae toomer was the city, than
Whan the great laird o' Montalban, 375
On his Boyardo fair and fleet,
Past the West-port, and up the street
Rade on – in mickle maze I ween,
For fient ae face was to be seen
In windocks or at doors; 380
Baith great and little, a' were out
To see the famous tiltin'-bout
'Tween Ariodant and Lurcan stout

163

The heralds had the rink-room metit,   385
The barriers set, and lists completit;
And gapin', glowerin', round about,
Wi' skirl, and skry, and rallion-shout,
Stood thick and far the rabble-rout;
As whan a fisherman, some day   390
In August, near the Isle o' May,
Lichts on a skull o' herrings thick,
Amid whase millions, flikkerin' quick,
His coble seems to stand and stick;
As far as he can cast his een,   395
Guid fish and sea are only seen;
The finny folk, as if in daffin',
Out-loup upon his ee-brees baffin';
He, in his glad heart, fa's a-lauffin',
And blesses Neptune for sic skaffin'.   400
Sae thick, around the rink-room, stood
That monie-headit multitude:
The heralds were nae little fash'd
To keep the lists frae bein' crash'd
By waves o' folk that drave and dash'd.   405
At length a trumpet in the wast
Was heard out-bellerin' a blast;
And, in a jiffie, ere it ceas'd,
Anither beller'd in the east:
The crowd, distract at ilka blast,   410
Look't ae-half east, the tither wast;
And eastlins, lo! there did appear
Heich on a steed, that nicker'd clear,
Sir Tullidaff, the michtie freir,
Waggin' in's hand a ten-fit speir: 415
He was enguardit, fore and back,
By Papist-priests, a rotten pack,
Canons and freirs, baith grey and black;
On ilka hand there wagg't and wav'd
Shav'n-crowns, clean clipt, and trigly shav'd,   420
That glisten'd in the mornin'-licht
Like marble knublocks burnish't bricht,
Or rowan-stanes upon the shore,
Amang the jaws that splash and roar:
Mairfurth, their wembes had sic a wecht,   425
Walkin' to them was but a fecht;
At ilka stap they puff't and pecht:
Tippets were there, cowls, cornets, caps,

Rockets, and lang-gowns wi' their flaps;
The Paip's ain livery, gawcy-gay,   430
Frae a' the cloisters' kists that day
Shone out in Tullidaff's array:
This in the east; – but in the wast
Nae less a pomp cam' streamin' fast:
    The Clerk on's battle-horse,   435
Wi' a' his merrymen defendit,
That in a huddle round attendit,
Burghers, and lairds, and plewmen blendit,
And royat bairns that spang'd and stendit
    Wi' a' their micht and force: 440
Him, as he rode on in the middle,
Encompass't men wi' pipe and fiddle,
That garr'd resound maist a' the widdle,
Skreighin' and screedin' fiddle-diddle:
Aye, as they saw at ilka stap   445
His spear to waver and to wap,
As if for laik o' fae to stick
Auld girnin' Juno to the quick,
    Their craigs wi' gaulps did rattle;
What wi' the scraighs o' lauchter there,   450
And janty faces shinin' fair,
'Twas clear they were the men o' lear;
And Luther's gklad ghaist in the air
    Gaed wi' them to the battle.

As nearer to the lists they ride,   455
The meikle menzie on ilk side
Did break in twa, and clean divide,
    To gie them passage in;
Whan baith had ridden up the gap,
Again the crowd, like water-jaup,   460
Thegither rush'd, and clos'd the slap
    Wi' hussiling and din:
But whan the Papists, rang'd in raw,
Their chief within the barriers saw,
His courser bardit trig and braw   465
    Wi' gowd and crimson-claith;
His ten-fit tram of aiken spear
Terriblie wallopin' in air,
Enouch e'en wi' its wind to scare
    A Lutheran to the death;   470
They couldna bide that sicht without
Clappin' their hands wi' pridefu' shout,
And yellochin' a' round about,

As if the triumph's meed
Were theirs already butten doubt: 475
But soon frae Luther's gleesome rout
Contrair there cam' a rattlin'-bout,
    A counter-clap indeed,
That swallow'd up the Papist din,
And shook the Paip's strang-hauld o' sin,   480
Garrin' Sir Freir growe in his skin
    Wi' ane prophetic dreid.

Ane herald bare upon his head
(Like to a baxter bearin' bread)
The cedar kist, a precious lade,   485
    O' mickle werth and wecht;
Whairin the banes that host had cleikit,
Though yellow-reestit sair and smeekit,
Again were closit in and steekit,
    The premium o' that fecht: 490
Sir Constable arrang'd in order
Ilk thing within the barrier's border;
Firm on their weir-steeds for the faucht,
Ilk man fornent the tither straucht,
Sat meditatin' deeds o' maucht: 495
Good luck, their helmets hid their chouks,
Whilk grinn'd and glowr'd sic crabbit looks,
Sic terrible and grim rebukes,
That, had they but seen ane anither,
Baith knichts had likely swarf'd thegither,   500
And drappit down wi' perfect drither.
Within their rests their trams o' wood
Stood tremblin', as if slauchter-wode,
Bernin' up i' the air for blood:
At last, as sign o' battle's bressil,   505
Ane trumpeter garr'd reird and reissil
His dainty, muckle-mou'd, brass-whistle,
And cry't, "Sanct Andrew shaw the recht!
Now, aff, ye deevils, to the fecht!"
And at it, swap! baith horse and man,   510
Windflaucht thegither rasch'd and ran:
As whan twa fiery dragons dart
In heevin' ilk ane frae diff'rent airt,
And dash their hissin' heads thegither,
As if t' upgabble ane anither;   515
Heav'n rattles wi' the dunnerin' dush,
And round is fill'd wi' fiery frush;
The scouther'd Ram in terrour shakes

Frae's smeekin' fleece the bernin' flakes;
The Great Bear gowls; the Lesser quakes: 520
Sae clos'd wi' bustyious bang and baff,
Clerk Diston and Freir Tullidaff:
And sae, as arms on arms were batter'd,
The spunks, and sparks, and splinters blatter'd,
And the hail barreis clash'd and clatter'd;   525
The sky sough'd wi' ane eerie bum,
And th' earnest people, all and some,
Sat tremblin', doitrify'd, and dumb,
To see what awfu' end mith come:
But sae it happen'd that nae scaith   530
That renk, wrocht either dool or death;
They were sae cas'd in weirlike graith,
Scart-free and haill they 'scapit baith:
Yet did their spears sic straiks let gird,
They near down-devel'd to the yird   535
The dinnel'd warriours wi' their dird:
Ilk fallow's heels clean gat the upper,
His back-neck down upon the crupper:
Yet soon again their heads up-bangit,
Their steeds were turn't, and forwart spangit,   540
Their bridles rang, and armour clangit:
They clos'd; they clash'd; but, de'il-ma-care,
Fient haet o' dammishment was there,
Exceptin' that the not'ry's spear,
    As good luck did direck it,   545
Did pierce the Papist's frock o' mail,
And brak a big wanrestfu' beal,
That near his lunzie, live and hail,
    Grew up aneath his jacket;
For monie a year that boil had thriven,   550
And monie a twinge its master given,
Untill at length, throu' cuirass riven,
    In ran the airn by chance,
And lat out baith the wind and matter,
That lang had lodgit in that tetter;   555
My certie! mair the man was better
    Of war's than surgeon's lance!
He felt at ance his eased smart,
And thank't his faeman in his heart
For cure o' that mal-easy part,   560
    And hummit, Praise be blest!
Then, musterin' micht for thwack and thump,
He cry't, "Have at you, Lollard rump!
For curin' me o' my sair lump,

That lang has been my pest." 565
Incontinent wi' fire-slacht speed,
They join'd, they grapplit steed to steed;
Baith spears, as feckless for the fede,
   They drappit hither-thither;
Wi' hands and arms alane they foucht: 570
They grippit, graspit, warslet, wrocht,
And, with enormous raxes, soucht
   T' unsaddle ane anither;
As weel they mith hae try'd to stir up
A rootit aik-tree, or a fir up, 575
As aff frae saddle, out frae stirrup,
   T' up-heize the tane the tither;
Sometimes they twinet breast and back
Sae close, they for a minute stack;
Sometimes, down headlang wi' a crack, 580
Baith totterin' knichts were like to swak
   Upon the yird thegither;
What might hae happ'd, nae man can say;
They mith hae warstled on a' day,
Had not ane goddess till the fray 585
   Down frae the sky come linkin',
And cast her cantrip owr her knicht;
(Some said they saw the vision bricht
Down slidin' on a beam o' licht,
   And owr the barreis blinkin':) 590
Her gramowrie she cast; and, swith!
Her weary knicht's ilk limb and lith
Gat tenfauld poustie, powr, and pith,
   To give his fae a jee-up;
He gripp't the grey-freir by the waist, 595
And, wi' a rousing rax, that maist
   Had haurl'd an aiken-tree up,
He frae his saddle heiz'd him hie,
And held him in his hand a wie
Mair easy than a bairn in glee 600
   Haulds simmer butterflie up:
Than, wi' a dardum and a dirdum,
Yirdlins he daddit him and birr'd him:
But what befel him thus-gate daddit,
In the neist sang ye'll find it addit: – 605
My Muse is jankit now and jadit!

END OF SANG FOURTH

168

NOTES

1 Suburb of St Andrews, so called.
2 Bacchus.
3 Minerva.
4 Tithonus.
5 See Orlando Furioso, 5th Canto.

PAPISTRY STORM'D

SANG FIFTH

ARGUMENT

Heils-over-head Sir Freir is cast,
  Whilk Papists' wreth does raise;
But hameward soon they scamper fast,
  In terribill amaze:
Their gates are then assail'd at last,
  Wi' fludes o' faemin' faes;
A ghaist is seen; and omens ghast
  Betaken comin' waes.

Their steeds, amid that battle's bustle,
Camstarie turnin' wi' the justle,
  Back-spangit baith at anes,
Near whair the herald on his head
(Like to a baxter bearin' bread)   5
The barrow bare wi' a' its lade
  O' cedar-kist and banes:
And sae it fell, and sae it happit,
That, as Sir Freir was erthlins swappit,
Richt down upon the kist he drappit: 10
As whan a tumbler at a fair,
Whair thousands round him goave and stare,
Up-wreils and whummles i' the air,
  Heels-over-gowdie whurlin';
Till, a' his birr exhaust, the man,   15
Mair dizzy than he first began,
Down frae the sky as fast's he can
  Comes whazelin' and hurlin';
Richt sae the freir i' th' ether whummlet,
In super-sault, than erthlins tummlet: 20
Swap on the barrow down he rummlet;
The herald wi' the daud was hummlet;

Nae wicht that wecht could bide;
Fertor in flinders flew around;
The kist, it boundit on the ground, 25
Scatterin', throu' a' the barrei's bound,
  The banes frae side to side:
Whilk, whan the vexit Papists saw,
That shame they couldna stand at a',
To see their knicht in the dead-thraw, 30
  And their belovit banes,
That us'd to shine in shrinin'-box,
Now dash't and casten at the cocks,
  Amang the sand and stanes:
They couldna thole ae moment langer; 35
They over-loup'd the lists in anger,
And dash't them down wi' clash and clanger;
  And down intill the course,
Wi' hirdie-girdie hurly-burly,
And countenances sour and surly, 40
  They drang wi' pith and force;
As when at Dort and Zuyder-see,
Whan western winds gowl dreidfullie,
A sea-dyke, under stress o' sea,
  Is bursten by its blatter; 45
Great swallin' surges frae the deep
Come swingin' in wi' frichtsome sweep,
To drown hail cities in their sleep,
And to the weathercocks, to steep
  The steeples in salt-water: 50
E'en sae the flude o' Papists brak
The pales, and pour'd, wi' crash and crack,
On the rink-room their creishy pack
  Wi' clamour and uproar,
Up frae the grund their knicht to tak 55
(That lay bumbazet on his back,)
And cleik the heukle-banies black
That sparpled lay about like wrack
  Or tangles on a shore:
They scarce had time, 'mang sand and stanes, 60
To glaum and glammach for the banes,
Whan frae th' opposin' side at anes
  Down-lap douce Luther's thrang,
Makin' the rails to flee asunder,
And rollin' in wi' sound o' thunder 65
T' attack in monie a score and hunder
  That break-faith Papish gang:
As when i' th' Pentland firth twa tides,

Owr wham a diff'rent tempest rides,
(This ane the wast-wind lamps and lashes,   70
That ane the east-wind drives and dashes
    Baith in to Stroma's strand,)
They meet and curl their heads in wreth;
Cauld Stroma's isle is fill'd wi' fraeth;
The skipper caucht sees nocht but death,   75
    And wrack on ilka hand;
But frae his wee house, Johnie Groat
Keeks out, and blesses his glad lot
    That he's in bigget land:
E'en wi' sic wreth commix and mingle   80
Upon the crowdit rink-room's chingle,
Papists and faes in dreidfu' pingle:
Sir Tullidaff, that lay down-knocket,
Was maistlins smother't up, and chokit,
Wi' heaps that owr him flew and flockit;   85
The weir-steeds round and round were blokit;
Nae man thocht now on banes or kist;
    Heukbanes and shrine were now nae miss't;
    Their sauls were sae in ire:
Ae Lollard-man got ere he wist   90
A lounder frae a Papish fist,
    That garr'd his een glent fire;
Ae Papish wratch gat on his pechan
Sae devilish a dandiefechan,
    It dang clean in his stammach;   95
Ae wee short canon, fat and fodgel,
Gat on his bare pow wi' a cudgel,
    It garr'd him yesk his drammach:
Was naething gain but knocks and nevels,
And clamehewits, baffs, and bevels;   100
The hail ring focht like vera devils;
Neifs flew, like shot impell't by powther,
Mortallie fast frae ilka showther;
At shaven-crowns some fechtars slappit;
On bany skulls hard knuckles rappit;   105
At cheeks and noses ithers swappit,
Sae that the dreidfu' blude down drappit;
And some fell'd ane, some smash't anither;
They baff't, buff't, cuff't, the tane the tither;
Was never sic hillie-belew and flither   110
Within a' Christendie thegither:
Heav'n hielde us a' frae sic a drither!

Dan Momus, frae his cloudie chair,

Whair he was sittin' i' the air,
Observin', butten cark or care,   115
   This rumpus and this rook,
Unseen, cam fleein' frae his heicht,
And 'mang the fechtars down did licht:
That mament he to human sicht
   Pat on ane human buik;   120
He borrow't John Arbuckle's face,
His belly, too, o' richt guid case,
His sonsy over-lardit thies,
His coots, his elbucks, and his knees,
   His gown and ither gear;   125
The vera buttons, claith and steeks,
Were just the same as Johnie's breeks;
The hairs upon his chafts and cheeks
   Fient ane were less or mair;
Tak the hail widdle a' thegither,   130
Nae things were liker ane anither,
Than this puir shadow, slim and bruckle,
To solid-backit John Arbuckle,
O' double chin and belly muckle:
Amid the fecht he plumpit richt,   135
Yet not ae body saw him licht;
The carls, atween the wham he squeez'd,
Felt na, as down his frame he feez'd;
Nae sooner in but seen; behauld!
His head, as if wi' cudgel maul'd,   140
Show'd on its tapmast crown a bump
A bonny weel-dissemblet lump,
As if just risen frae the thump:
A streap o' blude that rill'd as red
As ony man's blude ever shed   145
   Strinkel't his ilka haffet;
The swallin' seem'd as gin it had
That mament got a dainty dad,
And that the rung that gae the blad
   Was just up-liftit aff it: 150
Whairat th' Eidolon wi' the pain
Yelloch't wi' a' his micht and main:
A thousand nowt in Falkland plain,
Gather'd for sale to southron-men,
   Upon a market-day,   155
E'en were they a' at anes to rout,
Couldna hae bellow't sic a bout,
   As that fause freir, perfay;
Not Mars, whan he at Troy was woundit,

173

Sae terrible a scroinogh soundit,   160
Whan the hail Hellespont reboundit,
And ky on Ida's taps confoundit
    Ran down the hills for fray:
Was never heard sae fell a shout
In Fife, and a' the land about;   165
The sky kept half a minute dirlin';
Sclates cam aff roofs o' houses hurlin';
A man, up at the Milton-dam,
Swaif't, and fell down intill a dwam;
He lay an hour ere back he cam!   170
As whan a bairn a ba' doth fling,
In a round-heapit barley-bing,
    Some day in funnie glee;
The pickles, whair the ba' doth licht,
Are dashit round about on flicht,   175
And up the barn fly out o' sicht
    E'en to the riggen-tree:
Sae-wyse the Papists, as befel
That terrible warld-waukin' yell,
Did scatter aff, and skail pell-mell,   180
    As fast as they could flee:
The freir they ne'er look't i' the face;
They took nae time to speir his case;
The nearest to him first up-banget;
They thocht themsels baith shot and hanget;   185
The farrest aff, as much fear-fangit,
Like run-de'ils boltit aff and spangit:
Nae wicht had pow'r to ask his brither,
De'il, man, what means this flicht and flither?
But drivin', daddin' ane anither,   190
    As fast as legs could loup,
In bangs successive aff they shoalit,
And east the Scores in surges rollit,
    Mair as they mair had skoup;
Terrour flew owr them wi' his whip,   195
And scourg'd their pows as they did skip;
He leisch'd the blude out o' their faces,
Sendin' it down to ither places,
    That of it mair had need;
Feet flew and flicker'd derf and dire;   200
Knee-pans and knees amaist took fire
    Wi' spankin' and wi' speed:
They'd nccd o' speed; for, at their back,
Wi' hoot and whoop and lachter's crack,
Their faemen, Learnin's gleesome pack,   205

Triumphantlie did rattle,
Kickin' the blindin' stour on hie,
And hurlin' sticks and bits o' tree,
And knockin' wi' baith leg and knee
Upon the fatlings aff that flee   210
    Mair fast than frae a battle;
The Fisher-Knicht, wi' halbert's prob,
Their hobblin' hender-ends did job,
As on they wallop and they bob
    Afore him wi' a brattle;   215
The rink-space soon was toom'd o' men;
Baith tane and tither aff were gane;
Dickeman's-wynd again was chokit;
The Butts wi' bodies up was blockit;
The Castle-wynd in screighs out-bokit   220
    Thick, thick, on Greg'ry's green
Monks, canons, freirs, that thither flockit
To save themsels and cowl and rocket,
Within the yetts, that stood unlockit
To catch the skails, that maul'd and mockit,   225
    Cam rushin' in bedien;
The yetts resoundit wi' their shout;
For ane that gat in o' that rout,
Ten fuffin' stood a while thairout:
As keps a lang ae-archit brig   230
A blashy spate o' waters big
    Whan Lammas rains fa' fast;
Aboon the brig the fludes stand heapit;
Below they're rather laigh and neapit,
    Though down they guller fast: 235
Sae a' without, wi' folks was floodit,
But a' within, was nae sa crowdit;
    Till by and bye in time,
As ae fat bang dang in anither,
The yets, that gap't t' admit that fither,   240
Swallow'd the haill o' them thegither,
    Baith shaven-crown and waim.

Whilst at the yetts gaed on this steir
Upon the renk the warden-freir,
Forleitet by his Papish feir,   245
    Lay doitrify't and doytet;
His saul, frae whan it swarf'd awa,
Dumfounder't wi' the daddin' fa'
Had never hame return't at a',
    Syn on his back he cloytit: 250

175

He restit canny at his ease;
Whan owr him faes ran chasin' faes,
   He kent na o' their clutter;
Else had he felt the smaiks that time
March owr the mountain o' his wyme,   255
He'd nicket them for that sam crime,
And briz'd their bodies into slime,
   As ane would brize fresh-butter:
Aside him stood his steed o' weir,
That owr him nicker'd strang and clear,   260
Strivin' to rouse his master dear: –
As he in dwalmin'-fit lay there,
Behauld! king Bacchus in the air
   Descry'd his drearie dools,
And cry'd, Allace me and alack!   265
That thus my knicht sould lie in wrack
Sae lang, owr-whelmit on his back,
Reckless o' hippocras or sack,
   Like corp meet for the mools:
He mauna die on that cauld field;   270
His weird is no the ghaist to yield
   'Mang stanes and dirt sae sunken;
But canopy'd by dreepin' table,
Whan's back-bane is to sit unable,
To yesk his saul awa' in glore   275
Upo' the death-bed o' the floor,
   For-wakit and for-drunken;
Meantime, to help him frae his dwam,
He wad be nae waur o' a dram:
So down he flew, and, as he flew,   280
His radiant shape he did transmew
Into a Tavernar most true,
   Just girt for operation:
His bloizent face, begildet fine
Wi' rubicunditie divine,   285
Spak volumes in the praise o' wine,
   Wi' obvious celebration;
Ane apron cinctured his waist,
Whairtill a gowden cork-screw lac'd
   Divulg'd his occupation;   290
His richt-hand grippit firm and fast
A brandy-bottle, big and vast
   As onie in this nation;
His left the glitterin' glass did grip,
Whairfrae his bumbaz'd knicht mith sip   295
   Tebbit and animation:

So down he lichtet at his side,
And frae the bottle o' his pride
   He jirbles out a dram,
And lifts it to the grey-freir's neis;   300
To the freir's harns the fragrance flees;
   That mament back he cam!
He gript it like a man delierit;
He tootit aff the glorious spirit;
   He drownit dead his dwam!   305
"Anither tass," he cries, "and than" –
He gat it frae the tapster-man;
Nae mair about it; up he sprang
Upon his weir-steed wi' a bang,
Mair ferdie, and mair swank and strang   310
   Than when a-field he drew;
His steed he punzied wi' his heel,
And east the Scores as mad's the de'il,
Makin' the chuckie-stanes to reel,
   He gallopit and flew;   315
Three minutes' time was scantlins past,
Whan Luther's people stood aghast
   Within the yett, to view
Baith founder't Tullidaff and horse,
Wham they had left upon the course,   320
Postet and set in tenfauld force,
   The tuilzie to renew,
And frae the stranghaulds to rambarre
The shock o' that near-comin' war:
"Come on, ye dowfarts! ilka ane;   325
Fecht me wi' swerd, or stick, or stane;
Come on, I will recule for nane!"

Quo' the bauld laird o' Innergellie
To gley-mou'd Sipsie, – "My dear billie!
Saw you not late yon flastin fellie,   330
Wi's circumbendibus o' bellie,
   Spread flatlins on the yird?"
Quo' gley-mou'd Sipsie, – "By Sanct Geil!
I now believe in gramarie weel;
And that yon dampnit Papish chiel   335
Is friendit by man's fae the de'il,
   That he so soon hath stirr'd!"
Quo' wise Stravithie, – "I na thocht
That pray'rs to saints or demons broucht
Help till ane founder't man in oucht,   340
   Till now that I behauld

Yon bannock-hive set up again,
Thro' help o' Satan or Sanct Blane,
To daur and challenge us, like ane,
    Sae boysterous and bauld."   345

Thusgates the lairds did tove and crack
As that fierce freir, on courser's back,
    Did barricad the Pends;
Whilst i' th' Cathedral-yett John Annan,
The dean o' puissant pith, was stannin',   350
And, like a dainty bombard-cannon,
    That ither port defends.
By this time Greg'ry's-green was pang
Wi' multitudes that, thick and thrang,
Frae ilk inlett ran in ding-dang: 355
And the South-street, frae th' Eastburn wynd
Down to the Pends, was pav'd and lin'd
Wi' pows o' bodies a' kinkind:
Sanct Androis town, though wonder-auld,
Did never in her day behauld   360
A gadderin' sae big and bauld:
Not e'en that glad mid-simmertide,
Whan the great Kirk was sacrify'd;
What day our good king Robert Bruce,
Wi' a' his feir o' courtiers crouse,   365
Abbots and deans, and bishops douce,
Drest in their dalmatykes sae spruce,
    Their rings and ither braws;
Wi' the hail pick and wale o' Fife,
Gentle and sempill, man and wife,   370
Frae town and hamlet, swarmin' rife,
    Appear'd within the wa's;
Grund-flure and gall'rie, nave and wing,
Seem'd but ane universal bing;
Yet, though the kirk inside was thrang,   375
Without there was a michtier bang;
Windocks and doors were cramm't and heapit
Wi' wichts that glowrit in and gapit;
The roofs, ilk spire, the great mid-steeple
Were buzzin', and owr-clad wi' people: 380
And whan they skail'd, that michtie flock,
(I've read it in ane auncient boke,)
The kirk-yard's coffins yald and broke
Aneath the press o' livin' fock!
That was a day for folk nae doubt,   385
But this day that I speak about

Was famouser for rabble-rout:
Like swallin' jaws on rough shores jappin',
Loud, loud their tongues, withouten stappin',
Gaed on thegither, reirdin', rappin': 390
Rich were their mou's o' gibe and jaip,
And fulmination 'gainst the Paip;
Sedition set ilk gab a-gape:
Dowr were their threats and their grimaces,
Gurlie and crabbit-like their faces, 395
As glunsch'd they at the Papish places,
Bannin' within their hearts and sauls
The vera stanes intill the walls.
And now, respondent to their minds,
Their hands wagg'd wapons a' kinkinds; 400
And sic varietie o' graith,
Gather't for sailzie and for skaith,
And wieldit by sae wud a band,
Was never seen in onie land;
Cauld airn was now distinctly seen 405
In sindry shapes baith blunt and keen;
Timmer in baston, cudgel, rung,
Owr-head was swappit now and swung;
And stanes were bicker't aff and flung.
Chiefly upon the champions twa, 410
Stanc'd ilka ane to guard his wa',
The tempest o' the weir did fa';
Great cuddy-rungs and gnarlet cuds,
Wi' soundin' harness-thumpin' thuds,
Cam' peltin' on their backs in cluds; 415
The causey-stanes were fierce up-rippet,
And in strang neifs be-grasp't and grippet,
And hurl'd wi' vengeance and wi' rippat:
Stanes, sticks, and bricks, as thick as shot,
Rain'd aff ilk hero's iron coat, 420
And at his feet did rap and stot;
As when upon a Christmas cloud
King Johnie Frost doth ride abroad,
    And frae his wallet flings
Owr a great city's houses' taps 425
His hail in mickle rattlin' draps,
That aff the eaves upo' the street
Come stottin' at the burghers' feet,
    And settle there in bings;
Sae stanes, stobs, sticks, come peltin' aff 430
Dean Annan and freir Tullidaff:
But nae the less, for a' that stour,

179

They stand immoveable and dowr,
And naething reck that 'saultin' shower.

But whan bauld Innergellie saw   435
How thir twa bangsters foil'd them a',
And row'd the surge o' weir awa'
    Aff frae the Papish houffs,
His lip wi' wreth wox big and red,
And to the fisher-knicht he said,   440
"Ah! shame on mine and on your head!
    Twa caitiff cowart couffs!
That here behauld, but care or cark,
Yon fat-envelop'd chieftains stark,
Twa blaitie-bums in iron sark,   445
    Withstandin' a' our feir;
While we, wham for our rigs and lands
Weil it becomes to use our brands,
And shaw ensample to the bands,
Stand taiglin', daiglin' wi' our hands,   450
    And whillie-whain' here:
Ah! ill we do deserve to dine,
And gust our gabs wi' dribs o' wine,
If we, to th' eyes o' lawly hine,
Eschew the feats and wark divine   455
    O' hardiness and weir;
Gang you then, and wi' fearsome dunt
Attack Sir Tullidaff in front,
Whilst I the kirk-yard-dyke shall mount,
And sailzie wi' impetuous brunt   460
    Dean Annan in his rear:
And never may we tout again
A tass o' claret or champagne,
But sit dry-mou'd wi' drinkin' men,
If we do not wi' micht and main   465
    Dumfounder dean and freir."
Sae speakin', wi' a machtie spang
Up on the kirkyard-dyke he sprang;
Atap o' the wa' he stood nat lang,
But down intill the inside flang   470
    Himsel' wi' awsome beir;
His armour, as he fell, did clank;
His feet amang the grass-graves sank;
He fand himsel', baith front and flank,
Ere well he wist, wi' Papists' rank   475
    Surroundit far and near;
Round him they rush'd, and push't, and pecht

To overturn him wi' their swecht,
Or wi' their bellies' waddlin' wecht,
   Ere he was well awere, 480
To gruss him down intill a graff,
   Withouten kist or bier;
He at their waddlin' troop did lauff,
And wi' his prickin' gude pyk-staff
Made them rebound and wintle aff, 485
To shelter them frae buff and baff
   Within the kirk and queir.

Dean Annan a' this time was thrang
Rebuttin' his confrontin' gang,
And keppin' on his cuirass strang 490
The stanes that on him dush't and dang;
   Ah! little did he think,
That in his rear a warlike man
Was meditatin' wicket plan,
And comin' up as fast's he can 495
   To gie his back a clink!
The craftie laird did soon draw near,
And, hidlins hoverin' in his rear,
Wi' searchin' een, like pawky scout,
Explor'd his rearward round-about, 500
To find some part defenceless out
   Whairthro' to prick and punzie;
He soon discern'd, wi' gleesome heart,
Ane out-post, ane unguarded pairt,
That seem'd to court cauld iron's smart, 505
Stretchin' itsel' for straik o' dart,
   Frae neck-bane down to lunzie;
"*Sanct Clune*," he said, "direck my dird,
And bring this fallow to the yird!"
That mament he a straik let gird 510
That throu' the faeman's breeches birr'd,
   And in his breech did settle;
The man, bumbazit at the smart,
Cast round his richt hand to the part,
And fand intrench'd the dulefu' dart, 515
That sent a prinklin' to his heart
   Mair fierce than burr or nettle:
His heart, being dirlet to the quick,
Gaes whiltie-whaltie, fast and thick,
   Wi' quiverings and quakes; 520
His een, bein' in the mirligoes,
Ae single styme afore his nose

They couldna see for glaiks:
Sae down he tummlet in a drow,
And owr-and-owr did wreil and row;   525
His frichtit ghaist, un-housit now,
    A while his flesh forsakes; –
Strange! that ae punzie on the back
Should sooner bring that carl to wrack
Than sticks and cudgels, monie a hunder,   530
Hurl'd at him wi' a hideous lounder,
And peltin' on his front like thunder:
Sic droll bout-gates, sic sma' mean means,
Bryng michtie kings, and dukes and thanes
Aft to their laighest marrow-banes!   535

As he lay wamblin', dead amaist,
Forleitit by his ain dear ghaist,
Behauld! the faemen wham he fac'd,
    And frae the yett aff-fendit,
Seein' its buirdly bulwerk gane,   540
Grew galyard now, and crouse ilk ane,
And throu' the yett wi' micht and main
    Merrilie spang'd and stendit.
There let them spang and stend a wee
Till we look round about and see   545
How Tullidaff is comin' on
Wi' the Fisher-knicht and ither fone.
The Fisher-knicht, whan that he saw
His brither laird owr-loup the wa',
And, Alexander-like, furth-shaw   550
    Example in that strife,
Now thocht it guid time to begin
To shaw (his saul bein' in that pin)
He car'd as little for his skin
    As onie man in Fife;   555
He saw how Tullidaff the proud
Sat on his weir-steed vap'rin' loud,
Obstructin' in his prideful' mood
    The Pends to all and each,
Cryin', – "Ye dowfarts! ilka ane,   560
Ha! fecht me now wi' swerd or stane!
Come on, I will recule for nane!"
    And sic like flastin' speech;
Whilk raisit till ane unco heicht
The crabbitness o' that guid knicht,   565
To see himsel and a' his micht
Sae mockit and sae put to sleicht

By sic a bladderand freir:
Instant he frae his henchman's hand,
That near him did perfurnish'd stand 570
　　Wi' a' his battle-gear,
Grippit and grasp't wi' michtie strength
A pow-axe of enormous length,
　　Whase vera sicht strack fear;
Its airn, curv'd like a three-nichts' moon, 575
Heich quivered his head aboon
　　A dozen fit and mair;
The folk that stood about the knicht
Flew back wi' driddour and wi' fricht,
As they beheld the monstrous sicht 580
　　Rise owr them in the air;
Its vera sough did freeze their bluid,
And on their scalps, that birsy stood,
　　Garr'd prinkle ilka hair:
Wi' baith his arms up i' the sky, 585
Typhœus-like, he held it high,
And, thro' the press advancin' nigh
　　To that big braggart there,
He brocht it down wi' siccan force
Upon the forehead o' his horse, 590
A thunderbolt wi' fudder-flash
Couldna hae gien sae fell a smash,
　　Or made sae loud a rair;
The weir-steed's skull was yerk'd in twa;
Ae half flew to the western wa'; 595
The ither half, baith bluid and bane,
Was daddit to the eastern ane,
And stack upon ane ayslar stane:
Sae swift and swipper was the deed,
That for a little while the steed 600
Withouten either harns nor heid
　　Stood, after he was slain,
Immoveable in that same stede,
Ere he perceiv'd that he was dead,
　　Or that his head was gane: 605
But by-and-bye, on side and back
He devell'd wi' a deadly swack;
Sir Tullidaff, amid the wrack,
　　Down to the ground came tumblin',
Wi' a' his cumbrous battle-graith, 610
His wecht o' flesche and armour baith,
　　About him rattlin', rumblin';
The monie-archit pends a' round

183

Wi' clang and bang did ring and sound,
As down he dunner'd on the ground;   615
But it sae chanced that his horse
(Whilk now was but ane headless corse)
Had drappit on his schank and thie,
And briz'd them sair and heavilie,
   Wi' mickle pyne and stress,   620
Sae that th' o'erwhelmit freir in vain
Wrigglet and warslet fast and fain
To get his shank-bane eas'd again
   Frae sic a sair distress;
And skelloch'd at ane awfu' rate,   625
As onie man in sic a state
   Would do to get redress:
His faes they did na care a dout
For a' that he did yell and yout,
But owr him wi' a boastfu' shout   630
   They ran wi' fitterin' feet;
In ae half-minute frae his fa',
The pends were cramm't frae wa' to wa',
As in they bangit, great and sma',
   Outrageous fram the street;   635
The portals o' the houffs o' sin
Were now wide ope to let them in,
And shouts without and screams within
   Proclaimit round about
That now was come the weird-fix'd hour   640
Ordain'd to break the Papish power,
And frae her lust-engend'rin' bower
   To haurl the Harlot out:
That hour, it's said, the mickle bell
In the great steeple, o' itsel',   645
Did toll a heavie dismal knell,
As harbinger t' announce and tell
   The waes that did owr-hing:
And Arnold's nakit ghaist was seen
(They said, that saw it wi' their een,)   650
Loupin' hip-hop frae spire to spire,
And skiftin' owr the roofs like fire,
   Like ane unsettlet thing;
And aye he blubber't and he blobbit
And, *Fare ye weil!* aye sich't and sobbit,   655
   And sair his hands did wring;
Than south to France he turn'd his ee,
And loupit clean out-owr the sea
   Wi' ane amazin' spring:

And, frae the marble that did pave 660
The mools o' Lamberton's cauld grave,
Big bluidy draps, wi' elritch grane,
As if the man below did mane,
Barst out and smotter't a' the stane:
Ilk buried bishop seem'd to howl, 665
Ilk image did respond and yowl,
Ilk gallerie sent out a gowl,
And the great altar gave a growl!
Sic awfu' signs, that awfu' hour,
Portendit the approachin' stowre, 670
The rushin' down o' kirk and towr,
And downfa' o' the Papish power!

END OF SANG FIFTH

PAPISTRY STORM'D

SANG SIXTH

ARGUMENT

This canticle's the best ava;
　　There's fechtin' and there's thwackin';
Canons and freirs frae kirk and ha'
　　Are peltit and sent packin';
Pu'pits and beelds are hackit sma';
　　There's guttin' kists and hackin';
And as the finish, to crown a',
　　Down comes the steeple crackin'.

The sun was cockin' now upon
The vera pin o' Mid-day's cone,
And frae his beryl-bernin' throne,
　　That loftily did low,
Scatter't his great spring-flude o' beams,　　　　　5
That whiten'd a' th' Eastnook wi' gleams,
And made the Firth's clear glassy streams
　　In siller dance and row;
Nae cloud owr-head the lift did dim,
But i' the western weddir-glim　　　　　　　　　　10
A black up-castin', with ane rim
　　O' darkness, lace'd the yerth,
Betakenin' by the vapour's form,
That in th' Atlantic flude a storm
　　Was lab'rin' for a birth.　　　　　　　　　　　15

The hour o' denner now was come,
And men grew hungry all and some,
　　And cravin' in their crap;
Frae five o'clock that they had risen
Sorry a flow had cross't their gizen　　　　　　　　20
　　O' solid or o' sap;

In Lothian, and in ither pairts,
They denner'd weil, wi' cheirfu' hearts,
  On tailyies fat and fine;
But in Sanct Androis town that day,   25
Man, wife, nor bairn, as I've heard say,
  Had na' a heart to dine;
They were sae bent on cloister-guttin',
And hackin' images and cuttin',
Ae thocht on beef or yet on mutton   30
  Nae man could safely spare;
He that was yesterday a glutton,
This day he didna care a button
  For belly or for fare:
Hunger and Anger are near-kin,   35
Whilk made them that bauld wark begin
Wi' greater dirdom, wraith, and din,
Than they wud dune wi' panget skin
  Plumpet wi' vivers rare.

Sae in within the yetts they ran   40
Ramstam, rampagin', wife and man,
Thousands, wi' bitter winze and ban,
  Cast at the rotten bang,
That now, confoundit wi' the steir,
Took to their heels in deidly fear,   45
To shelter them in kirk or queir
  Frae that in-pourin' thrang;
Canon, the greasy monk, and prior,
Arch-dean, and ilka-colour'd freir,
The Pape's hail fam'ly, fat and fere,   50
  Did in a mass forgather
Within their sacrify'd abodes,
Scougin' themsel's frae stanes and clods,
Aside their shrines and velvet-cods,
Their Lares and their household-gods,   55
  Frae siccan stalwart weather;
As Trojan wives, upon the nicht
Whan Priam's palace bleezit bricht,
Huggit and kiss't (a doolfu' sicht!)
Altars and posts in ghastlie fricht,   60
  Makin' loud scriechs and manes;
Saewise that cowl'd and girdlet fither,
Astoundit wi' dumfounderin' drither,
Ran throu' the Hey-kirk hither-thither,
  Huggin' their beilds and banes: 65
The doors were steek'd and boltit hard;

Wickets and windocks firmly barr'd;
But throu' the doors and wa's they heard,
    Ascendin' from without,
The terrible stramash o' tongues,   70
And winzes flung fram angry lungs,
And shouts o' men wi' picks and rungs,
    That huddlit round about;
Ilk man encouragin' his feer,
Cryin' aloud, To weir! to weir!   75
Down wi' the Harlot and her geir!
    Assailzie! Strike! Destroy!
Whilst throu' the windocks they did spy
Weir's wild wud wappens wavin' by;
Cuds, swerds, and halberts, heavit high,   80
Whase shadows 'tween them and the sky
    Forebodit noucht but noy;
And surly faces, warst ava,
Horribly glumschin' ane and a',
    Or girnin' into joy,   85
As they look't up ilk lofty wa',
Takin' their meiths for its downfa',
    That they may strike and stroy.

Thairat th' assailzie did begin
Wi' gallyies o' loud-blairin' din;   90
A thousand sticks, a thousand stanes,
Are throu' the windocks dash't at anes;
The garnish't glass, the birnish't lozens,
Are knocket in, and dash't in dozens;
Great iron-sweys, great timmer-trams,   95
And meikle smitin' batterin'-rams,
Swinget about by angry squads,
Gaif ilk besiegit door sic dads,
They garr'd them crack and flee in blads;
Man, wife, nor bairn, of a' that host,   100
Was idle, or was aff his post;
The little bairns threw little stanes,
And play'd upon the paintet panes;
The wives, as rampant in their mettle,
With idle foolitch neifs did ettle,   105
And wi' their flytings fir'd the battle:
The men – here sax, there seven or aucht,
A batterin'-ram wi' a' their maucht,
Were swappin' 'gainst a portal straucht;
Here scores their pinches and their picks   110
Atween the ayslar stanes did fix,

188

And rugg't and rave them out;
Wi' batter-ax some brak in sma'
The carvit wark and pillars bra,
Sendin' the glory of the wa',   115
    In fritter't frush about;
Some to the windocks up did clamber,
And daddit in, wi' chappin'-hammer,
    The staney-frames and lead;
Some delvit down wi' spades and shools,   120
Deep, deep amid the yerth and mools,
Strivin' wi' howkin' and wi' diggin'
To bring th' upsettin' pridefu' biggin'
    Laigh down amang the dead:
And some gat ladders large and lang,   125
On whilk they mountit and did spang,
Chasin' ilk ither in a bang
    Up to the roofs on hie;
Owr whilk frae end to end they spread,
Like flock o' locusts black and braid,   130
And rave frae rafter and frae riggin'
'The capper that owr-clad the biggin',
    Glitterand owr land and sea.

But, saftly, Muse! and tak mair time;
Be mair partic'lar in your rhime;   135
I wish to ken what chiftain first
Intill th' expugnate kirk did burst?
What man assailzied with ane kick
The water-vat, and garr'd it quick
Gang rowin' aff its silver styk?   140
Wha the Hey-altar over-coupit?
The graven idols aff wha soupit?
Wha tumbled down the Card'nal's pupit?
And monie ither famous thing,
Worthy o' you to say and sing,   145
Albeit I be to write inding.

The batterin'-ram wi' jowin' jerk
Nae sooner brak the door o' the kirk,
Whan Caryl's bauld through-gain' clerk
    Burst in wi' sudden spang,   150
His left hand holdin' up on-heicht
The borough-colours wavin' bricht;
A halbert in his stalwart richt
    Up-stannin' clean and lang;
He paus'd a wee on the dure-stane   155

189

Crying, "Hurra! my merry men!
Ha! Satan's toy-shop now is taen!
  Look up and see your spulzie!
March, birkies, ben, and follow me!"
Sae sayin', wi triumphant glee,   160
He wav't his pennon up on hie,
  The sign o' march and tulzie;
Whilk whan the Papish folk beheld,
A gallyie o' fierce wraith was yell'd
  Frae a' within the kirk,   165
Mixt wi' shrill skellochs o' despair
As they espy'd gambadin' there
  That lion-lookin' clerk:
Yet, nat the less for his bauld look,
Great shoals o' freirs, frae ilk kirk-neuk,   170
Men o' weil-biggit frame and buik,
  Cam down upon him ruschin',
Ettlin', wi' fuffin' and wi' pain,
To ding th' assaulter back again,
And hurlin' at his head a rain   175
  O' creepie, stool, and cushion:
He lower'd down his braid-cheek't wappen,
And round and round he held it swappin',
To catch the fallows that mith happen
  To come within his cleik;   180
Will Cranstoun, that deil's-buckie chap,
(A tap-thrawn monk wi' roundit cap,)
Was the first man that caught a wap;
  He gat in on his cheek;
Wi' its strang swing, the girdlet brither   185
Flew frae ae pillar to the tither,
  Syn in a stound did drap:
Tam Guillaum in his heavy gown
(A bummill kent throu' a' the town)
Was the neist man whase shaven crown   190
  Was hansel'd wi' a swap;
The bummil felt the swap sae sair,
Backlins he stagger't wi' a rair
To Gamyl's tomb, and hid him thair
  Fram onie mair wanhap;   195
And twenty mair sic rotten whelps
Gat on the haffets famous skelps,
That made them utter yells and yelps
  And tummle into trances;
Sae that the not'ry throu' the wrack   200
O' strewit shavelings in a crack

March't wi' his legion at his back
  With iron-gads and lances;
By this time, too, wi' dreidfu' din,
The windocks a' were driven in,   205
  And heaps o' ragin' bodies
Cam streamin' in throu' ilk fenester,
Loupin' ilk man than tither faster,
Red-wud for mischief and disaster,
  And brandishin' their cuddies;   210
Sae that the kirk's ilk batter'd side
Fram a' her raggit loop-holes wide,
Lat in ane over-flowin' tide
  O ragin'-wud assaulters;
That forcit into sma'er space   215
The Paip's canallyie scant o' grace
Garrin' them fecht i' th' middle place
  For heartstanes now and altars:
And now the hail kirk east and wast
Was but ane hurlie-burlie vast   220
O' fechters and defenders fast
  A' toylin' at the tulyie;
The Cross-kirk too was just as thrang
O' bangsters that did ither 'mang
  In hideous tulyie-mulyie;   225
Terrible thumps were gien and taken,
Whairby ten thousand ribs were shaken;
Nac man did spare his faeman's bacon;
  Nae man cry'd, Hoolyie! Hoolyie!
Braid showther-blades now gat their paikin'; 230
Back-banes wi' bastinads were shaken
  Down, down to their foundation:
Ilk wappen that cam frae the coast,
Was now in action by the host,
Swung round their huddlin' heads and tost 235
  In windy agitation;
Battens and a' kinkind o' sticks,
Clodmells and barrow-trams and picks,
And handspakes that gave lounderin' licks,
  Flicker'd in fierce vibration;   240
The vera wind o' siccan werk
Blew down the mouse-webs black and mirk,
That had, up on the tap o' th' kirk,
  Twa hunder year been stickin';
What wi' the mouse-webs fram on hie,   245
And stour that frae their feet did flie,
Around their heads a canopie

O' mistie motes did thicken;
Sae that, half-hidden in the dark,
They labour'd at the fechtin'-wark,   250
But ilka man took weil his mark,
And, as he lounder't strang and stark,
    Kent weil wham he was lickin'.

Around the bonnie siller-platter,
That did contein the Heilie water,   255
Twal canons bare the brunt and blatter
    By William Lauder backit,
Whase face wi' crabbitness did grin,
And his flyte-poke aneath his chin
Priev'd he was in an angry pin   260
    To be thus-gate attacket;
The laird o' Barns discern't ere lang
That canker'd carl amid the gang,
Wha wi' his accusation dang
    Gude Wishart to the dede;   265
The mem'rie o' that wicket thing,
And cruel martyrdom inding
Was to his mind a ready sting,
    To prick him up to fede:
Ah, cruel wratch! he thus began,   270
Yet dost thou live, thou wicket man?
Whan he wham thy black tongue did ban
    Lies down amang the dead!
Ah! happy me, if I can pay
Sma' vengeance for that michtie wae: 275
He drew his swerd out, saying sae,
    And wi' a sturdy straik,
First his richt ear he clean aff-cleft,
And then he sneddit aff his left,
Leavin' o' baith his lugs bereft   280
    The head of that vile rake:
The wratch ran quiverin' aff and quakin',
Leavin' his lugs to save his bacon;
    Happy it sae had endit,
For had he gat his just desert,   285
His tongue, the rogue's maist peccant pairt,
    Had frae his mou' been rendit:
But whan Kilbrachmont by that taken
The water-ewer saw forsaken,
    Nor langer weil defendit,   290
He rush'd upon it with a spang,
And wi' a monstrous kick down-dang

The styk o' silver rich and lang
    That did up-hald the platter;
The vat flew mair than twenty paces,   295
Strenkellin', a' round, the fechtar's faces,
    Wi' its out-waffin' water;
The stick, extirpate wi' the blaw,
Clean owr the flure frae wa' to wa'
    Gaed rowin' wi' a clatter.   300

Whilst styk and vat was dingin' down,
A troop, saul-thirsty for renown,
The scholars of Sanct Androis town,
Ilk ane in dud o' scarlet gown,
    Gaed 'tween the wa's and pillars,   305
Ravagin' on, a furious squade,
The Regent Douglas at their head,
Seekin' for beelds to ding them dead,
That they mith spread their name abroad
    As famous image-killers: 310
Ilk tirlie-wirlie mawment bra,
'That had, for cent'ries ane or twa,
Brankit on pillar or on wa',
    Cam tumblin' tap-owr-tail;
The gifts o' Cardinals and Paips,   315
Owr-fret wi' spanglet gowden-caps,
    And siller vest or veil,
Aneath the straik o' learnit gown,
Cam divin' on the pavement down,
Ilk ane upon its marble crown   320
    Smashin' itsel' to splinders;
A saint or image in a niche,
That wont to glitter there sae rich,
Enflamin' folk to sic a pitch –
The sorrow ane was left o' such;   325
    The haill were frush'd to flinders:
Much glory frae that plunder-bout
Ilk learnit gown, withouten doubt,
    May challenge and may claim;
Exceptin' Crail's bauld wabster-band,   330
For idol-breakin' strength o' hand,
Nane may the guerdon sae demand,
    Or share sae weil the fame.

Meantime a fier o' lairds, close groupit,
Besiegit weil the mickle pu'pit;   335
It was the Cardinal's ain kirk-loom;

He brocht it in a ship frae Rome;
'Twas a' owr-carv'd wi' saints and fairies,
And tirlie-wirlies and fleegaries,
And cardinals'-hats and Virgin Maries;   340
Fram it he us'd, on gala-days,
Busk't in his bravitie o' claes,
To pitter-patter and to phrase:
The vera sicht o' that vain loom
Recallit Beaton up and Rome;   345
The lairds wox wudder aye and wudder;
They drew their swerds, and, in a pudder,
Attack't it fierce as fire or fudder;
They hack't it sae wi' swerd and dirk,
Splenders and bits at ilka yerk   350
Gaed fleein' round throu' a' the kirk;
Never was sakeless dask o' timmer
Sae persecute and put to cummer;
What wi' their gulligaws and gashes,
The pu'pit had been driv'n to smashes,   355
And not ae scrap had 'scap'd that stour
To busk the bein' ha' o' Balfour,[1]
Had not a laird cry'd, "Hoolie! hoolie!
Hae mercy ilk man wi' his gullie!
Leave but a crumb o' this kirk-loom,   360
Memorial o' the power o' Rome,
And my Lord Card'nal's bottom-room!"
This said, they a' their showthers stoopit,
And whummel'd up the muckle pu'pit.

Thus they; but battle's fiercest beir   365
Was ragin' the Hey-altar near;
That was the crater o' the steir,
The vera navel o' the weir;
Lord Prior James had stood there lang,
Rallyin' and gen'rallin' his gang;   370
But seein' Papists' side gae wrang,
Out at the Chanc'llor's-door he flang:
A howdle o' hog-showtherin' freirs,
Augustines, Carm'leits, Cordeliers,
    He bauldly left ahent,   375
To be that altar's body-guard,
And bide the buff o' lout and laird,
    As he flew owr the bent:
Than skippers, tailzeours, lairds, and hinds,
Fludes o' mad burghers a' kinkinds,   380
Dissim'lar men, but sim'lar minds,

194

In formidable sailyie,
Cam' whurrin' in like cats on rattens,
Swappin' their handspakes and their battens,
    And ither mad artailyie;   385
Then mells cam' down on gowden pyx;
Cud quarrell'd it wi' crucifix;
And crosiers and candlesticks
In th' air excambied furious licks
Wi' aiken-rungs and chappin'-sticks: 390
    Was never sic a squabble!
Hood, cord and round-cap, cowl and clout,
In tatter-wallops flew about;
Trodden were wafers under-foot;
And than sic skellochin' and shout,   395
Frae conquerin' and conquer'd rout!
    Was never sic a yabble!
If e'er there was sic strife and clatter,
Fracas o' tongues and bellerin' blatter,
    'Twas at the towr o' Babel!   400
The Cross-kirk rang wi' scolds and flytes;
The Main-kirk rang wi' slaps and smites;
    Pell-mell, thwack! hiddie-giddie!
There were sic gouffs, and youffs, and swaks,
On heads and bellies, sides and backs,   405
If onie whair are heard sic cracks,
    'Tis in a blacksmith's smiddie!
Not frae the blacksmith's study rush
Sae thick the sparks and hammer-flush,
As then did devel, dunt, and dusch,   410
    Makin' the ee-sicht giddie;
Aiblins they'd focht till candle-licht,
Had not a stieve braid-showther'd wicht,
My great-great-grandsher, in his micht,
    Ran on them wi' a spang;   415
Meal-melvied as he was, I wot,
The meal cam fleein' aff his coat,
    As up the kirk he sprang;
He caucht John Caldcleugh by the thrapple,
And made him tirvie down and tapple   420
    Head-foremest wi' a bang:
He clench't Tam Tottis (Johnie's brither),
And garr'd him waigle hither-thither,
    Syn on the flure him flang:
Arch-dean John Wynram he did grip;   425
He caucht Prior Guthrie on the hip;
He garr'd fat hoastin' Forman skip;

Principal Cranston he did trip;
He wi' his fingers' furious nip
    Half-strangled Canon Strang: 430
Great Ajax, whan he waxit daft,
Bang'd na the puir sheep owr the taft,
As my great-grandsher bang'd and baf't
    That rotten Papist gang:
Sic doings were owr het to last;   435
The Papists could na bide that blast;
Astonay'd, gumple-fac'd, aghast,
Out at the Dortour-door, fu' fast,
Hurry-scurry, they birr'd and brast,
    Wi' blastin' and wi' puffin';   440
The Chanc'llor's dure was pang'd alsae;
Ilk man, brain-mad to get away,
Kickin' the neist to garr him gae,
On's mooly-heel rapt horny tae;
    And out-ran, fisslin', fuffin':   445
Meantime my grandsher and some others,
The Laird o' Grange, and John Carruthers,
In chevalrie twin-bairns and brothers,
    The altar fierce attacket;
Missal and mawment, pyx and tass,   450
The haill machinery o' the mass
    Were soupit down and swacket;
The marble slabs, the gowden-gilt,
And frettit-wark was stroy'd and split;
That great show-shop of idol-ware,   455
Gather't for near four hundred year,
Graham's, Gamyl's, Pai's, and Arnold's gear,
Rome's michtie mummery heapit there –
    Was in a mament wracket!
The kirk, meantime, was turnin' thinner   460
O' vile mass-worshipper and sinner;
They saw their Capitol now shaken,
Their great Palladium tash'd and taken;
Sae, out at ilk door, quiverin', quakin',
    They birringly did bicker;   465
Men never, wi' sic whoslin' breath,
Fram th' instantaneous grip o' death
    Flew furiouser or quicker:
Doors wadna serve to let them gang;
Furth at the windocks too they sprang;   470
Terrible stends they took and lang,
    To 'scape frae that kirk-bicker;
In kirkyard or in abbey-ground

They tarry'd not ae single stound;
They couldna think their heads their ain   475
Ere they were fairly fled and gane:
Sae out at ilka abbey-yett
Baith south, and east, and wast, they sett
    Out-owr the kintra fast;
Strathtyrum's bonnie banks were black   480
Wi' freirs, all-fleein' in a pack,
Wi' tatterwallops at their back,
    And faces clean down-cast;
Some took the road to Cupar-town:
Some to the Anster coast ran down;   485
Some bicker'd to Balmer'nie; some
To Falkland, ere they stap'd, did come;
Some landit up at Tullilum
    Wi' stammachs clung and clappit;
For therty miles a' round about,   490
The land was cover't wi' that rout,
    That ran and never stappit;
The roads and fields, as if wi' buds,
Were strawn wi' rags and bits o' duds,
    That frae their showthers drappit;   495
Sic wrack, and ruin, and deray,
Was never in Scotland syn that day
When scatter't Southrons in dismay
Frae Bannockburn's eventfu' day
    Ran on and never stappit.   500
As they were fleein' thus abread,
Kirk-spulyie, herriement, and raid,
    Gaed on mair fast then ever;
In the Main-kirk three thousand folk
Carv't wark and arch and pillar broke;   505
Through the Cross-kirk twa thousand ran
Batterin' awa', ilk angry man,
    Wi' hammer, axe, and lever;
A thousand bodies on the riggin'
Tirr'd and unroof't the pridefu' biggin';   510
Great faulds o' capper aff were flypit;
Great sheets o' braid lead aff were rippit;
The folk aboon in joy down-lookit
Throu' holes that their ane hands had howkit,
    Hallooin' them below;   515
The folk below cast up their een,
Gazin' on sky and heevin's sheen,
Throu' sky-lichts whair late nocht was seen
But ceiling dark and rafter-treen, –

And shoutit back, Hurro! 520
Sae ilka man provok't his brither,
And the hail tot gaed on thegither,
Vyin' in strife wi' ane anither
     At ravagin' and ruggin';
Nae thing was prosperin' there and thrivin', 525
But tirlin' roofs and rafter-rivin',
And pullin' down and puggin';
Weil as they thriv'd aboon in plunder,
I think, they prosper't better under;
For now the vestry was attacket; 530
Presses and kists were hew'd and hackit,
Wi' huge rapacitie and racket;
Out-flew unwillin' to the licht,
The gard-rob's bravities sae bricht,
For Haly-days stor'd up aricht; 535
Hands of unhallow't men out-dragget
Pai's velvet-cods wi' silver taggit,
And wi' their swerds them hash't and hagget
Makin' them shabby cods and ragget.
The bawdekyns and cloth o' gold, 540
Stoles, towals, vestments manifold,
The snaw-white albs wi' their parures,
Fannouns and ither garnitures,
The chesybyls wi' spangles thick,
And Beaton's ain dear dalmatick, 545
The hail o' them, by lawit fists,
Were haurl'd and howkit frae their kists:
For Paip's anathema or ban
Car'd not a bodle onie man;
And monie ane that day did herrie 550
Braw spulyie frae the vestiary;
The piper o' the brogh o' Crail
Ran aff wi' ae priest's-vestment hail;
The town's-drummer o' Cellardyke
Stole Beaton's ain dear dalmatyke; 555
(He wore it lang on king's birth-days,
Like a cur-sackie owr his claes,
Whan drummin' throu' the public ways;)
Twa Regents o' Sanct Androis town,
(Their names I sanna here set down,) 560
Stole ane a stole, and ane a gown;
But David Barclay had mair sense;
In spulyiein' he shaw'd craft and mense;
For albs or priestly vestiments
     He didna care a plack; 565

198

He saw the styk o' th' water-ewer
Glitterin' temptation on the flure;
He cleek't it up, and to the dure
    He bangit in a crack;
And hame as fast as feet could carry   570
He hurry'd frae that fierie-farie;
That siller styk, for monie a year,
Dan David, 'mang his ither gear,
    Fu' carefullie did keep;
His bairn's-bairns lang stor'd it well;   575
But now it's gane – as I hear tell;
Tairge them about it now – they'll say,
O' sic ane styk untill this day
    We never heard a cheep!
Time, thus, wi' meikle greedy mou',   580
Swallows up auncient things and true,
And leaveth nocht to modern hashes
But idle tales and empty clashes.

Whilst Barclay wi' the silver styk
Was owr the King's-muir runnin' quick,   585
    The kirk was a' displenish't;
Of idols there remain't not ane;
Priest's-claes and busking-clouts were gane;
Capper and thack-lead aff were tane;
    Kirk-guttin' clean was finish't;   590
Except bare wa's and lime and stane,
O' that kirk's brav'ries left was nane;
    Her glorie was diminish't;
Neth'less the meikle middle tow'r,
Wi' her lang spindly sisters four,   595
Stood glowrin' a' the kintra owr,
Up-struttin' in their pride o' pow'r
    As gawcy as afore;
As lang as they stood brankin' sae
Nae man could safelie brag and say   600
That down unto the grund that day
    Was brocht the Papal glore;
The gildit crucifix that shone
The great mid-steeple's tap upon,
Sae lang as it near heevin should stand,   605
'Twas but a sign to sea and land,
That, shelter't underneath that taken,
Rome's power, though shatterit and shaken,
    Yet in our land micht live;
And aiblins on some after-time,   610

199

Blude-nurs'd by Guise micht yet sublime
   Ereck her head and thrive;
Thairfor, out frae the huddlin' crowd
Ane College-regent bangin', stood
Heigh on a graff-stane up, and loud   615
   Bespak the listnin' people;
Gae, get Deaf Meg and Crookit Mou';
Stech their how hungry stammachs fou;
And wi' them batter till it bow
   The meikle middle steeple;   620
Gif ance yon cross were yerdlins come,
Than, than, I'll think the pride o' Rome
To be doun-cast, and seal'd her doom
   Within our land for ever;
And our twa friends, I'll whisper you,   625
Dinnelin' Deaf Meg and Crookit Mou'
Allenarlie that feat can do;
   There's nane can crack sae clever:
Nae sooner was the hint thrawn out,
Than sax-score fallows swank and stout,   630
   Down till the Castill flew;
And wi' great poust o' arm and leg
The dinnelin' and dure Deaf Meg,
And her sour sister lang and big,
   Out frae their port-holes drew;   635
In twenty minutes a' the men
Return't mair hearty back agen,
Wi' cords and cables, micht and main,
Haulin' the iron sisters twain,
   Wi' whoopin' and halloo;   640
In thirteen minutes they were plantit
Wi' mickle mou's that gap't and gauntit,
Threatnin' wi' their first puff o' breath
To blaw the bottoms out aneath
   The steeple's buirdly length;   645
They needit but ae single spark
To kendle them for that dure wark,
   And try their spit-fire strength;
Out frae their throats wi' frichtsom gowl,
As if a' Scylla's dogs did howl,   650
Baith fire and soot and shot did rowl;
Meg never frae her chokit thrapple
Garr'd sae the bullets roar and rapple;
Crook-Mou' did never in sic ire
Vomit, wi' hurly-burly dire,   655
Her stammach-fu' o' airn and fire:

The pond'rous steeple wi' the brattle
Did vibrate back and fore, and rattle;
Frae her four stuttin' pillars stout
Lumps of out-batter't stane fell out   660
    Enwrappit wi' their lime;
And meikle pieces mair and mair
Down tumblin' laid the inside bare,
As the re-loadit sister-pair
Aye guller't out wi' awfu' rair   665
    Their charges ilka time.

As thir twa bombards on the ground
Were thunderin' wi' an awesome sound,
Up i' the sky, wi' michtier clutter,
The clouds begoud their voice to utter,   670
And correspondinglie to mutter;
For now the vapours dark and dim,
That a' day in the welkin's rim
Had nurs'd themsels owr ocean's brim
    Wi' waters frae her wave,   675
Now up the sky had spread and run,
And wi' ane horrid tempest dun
Had worry'd up the splendid sun,
Narrowin' the ether's bricht expanse
Into a black-hung uglie trance   680
    As gloomie as the grave;
Great, gourlie, goustrous-lookin' clouds
Seem'd jundyin' i' the air wi' thuds,
And on the towns, and fields, and woods,
Out frae their fissures pour'd the floods   685
    They'd borrow't frae the sea;
Whilst thunder-vollies, peal on peal,
And fudder-flashes mixt wi' hail,
Garr'd bodies tremmle and turn pale,
    And kye on mountains flee;   690
And little fishes, in the deep,
Down to their laighest bottoms creep,
And there their tangly coverts keep,
That they mith not behauld the sweep
    O' fire-slaucht from on hie;   695
Owr auld Sanct Androis city maist
The fury o' that storm did rest;
Owr her Hie-kirk, maist dark and dour
The thunder-vapour seem't to lowr,
As if upon the mid-most tow'r   700
The cloud concentratit its power;

Men lookit up wi' fear and dreid
On the pit-mirkness owr their heid,
Expeckin' some fell thing indeed;
And as they lookit, in a stound,   705
There cam a crack, that wi' its sound,
Garr'd dinnel a' the houses round,
    And the haill hill to shake;
At that sam mament rent asunder
Frae cross aloft to bottoms under,   710
By the tremendous pith o' thunder,
The cannon-batter't steeple fell,
Spire, arches, bartizan, and bell,
Wi' roarin' ruin terribell,
    Maist like to ane earthquake;   715
Masses o' stane, enormous blads,
Down on the kirk, wi' dunderin' dads,
    Tremendouslie cam tumblin';
That wa's, roofs, pillars did confound
In ae destruction round and round;   720
Makin' the haill kirk-yard rebound
    Wi' rattlin' and wi' rumblin':
A cloud o' limy stouff and stour,
In spite o' the thick-gushin' shower
    Flew whirlin' up to heevin,   725
As fain the thunder-cloud to meet
And gratulate on hie, and greet
    The fiery-winget levin';
Wi' rubbish and wi' frush that flew
Dinnelin Deaf Meg and Crookit Mou'   730
Were maistlins bury'd up, I trow,
And whelmit clean frae bodies' view;
    But it was wonder-luck,
That wi' the smashery o' stane,
Man, wife, nor bairnie, there was nane   735
Murder't, or maimit, or owr-tane,
Wi' breakin' or o' skull or bane;
    Nae wicht was scaith'd or struck;
Sic tent they'd taken ane and a'
To stand a gudly space awa   740
Frae that descendin' steeple's fa',
And keep themsels scart-free and hail
Frae banes-breakin' or ither bale.

Whan they beheld that steeple's ruin
The yird wi' smokin' shivers strewin',   745
They kent richt weil their endit wark,

The consummation o' their dark;
And hamewarts bairn, and wife, and man,
Helter-skelter they skelp't and ran,
The faster for the hail and rain   750
That peltit on their pows wi' pain;
As they intill their chambers gat,
Down to their suppers then they sat:
They'd need o' cheese and bread, I wat,
After the lang darg they'd been at.   755

But whan the Pape in Vatican
Heard o' the puir freirs how they ran,
And how, despisin' bull or ban,
Fife's fechtin' bodies, wife and man,
    His kirk had spulyied sae,   760
Three days he in his mournin'-chalmer,
Sat greetin' wi' ane eerie yamer
Makin' the Tiber ring wi' clamour
    And echoes o' his wae;
The College, too, o' Cardinalls,   765
They cast aside their fal-de-ralls,
And spacier'd weepin' throu' their halls
    In doolfu' claes o' black;
And ilka monk wi' grane and gaunt
Made a heart-rendin' mulligrant,   770
    And pat on claith o' sack;
As throughout Scotland there was joy,
And gladness at that spulyie-ploy,
Sae throughout a' the Papal lands,
Was noucht but grief and wringin' hands,   775
And sichan' 'mang the monkish bands,
    Allace me! and Allack!

FINIS

NOTE

1   The dining-room of Balfour-house is still decked with the beautiful remains of this
celebrated pulpit.

TAMMY LITTLE

A JUVENILE JEU-D'ESPRIT

By the Author of "Anster Fair"

Wee Tammy Little, honest man!
  I kent the body weel,
As round the kintra-side he gaed,
  Careerin' wi' his creel.
He was sae slender and sae wee,   5
  That aye when blasts did blaw,
He ballasted himself wi' stanes
  'Gainst bein' blawn awa.
A meikle stane the wee bit man
  In ilka coat-pouch clappit,   10
That by the michty gowlin' wind
  He michtna down be swappit.
When he did chance within a wood,
  On simmer days, to be,
Aye he was frichtit lest the craws   15
  Should heise him up on hie;
And aye he, wi' an aiken cud,
  The air did thump and beat,
To stap the craws frae liftin' him
  Up to their nests for meat.   20
Ae day, when in a barn he lay,
  And thrashers thrang were thair,
He in a moment vanish'd aff,
  And nae man could tell whair;
They lookit till the riggin' up,   25
  And round and round they lookit,
At last they fand him underneath
  A firlot cruyled and crookit.
Ance as big Samuel past him by,
  Big Samuel gave a sneeze,   30
And wi' the sough o't he was cast
  Clean down upon his knees.
His wife and he upon ane day
  Did chance to disagree,
And up she took the bellowses,   35
  As wild as wife could be;
She gave ane puff intill his face,

And made him, like a feather,
Flee frae the tae side o' the house,
  Resoundin' till the tither! 40
Ae simmer e'en, when as he through
  Pitkirie forest past,
By three braid leaves, blawn aff the trees,
  He down to yird was cast;
A tirl o' wind the three braid leaves 45
  Down frae the forest dang,
Ane frae an ash, ane frae an elm,
  Ane frae an aik-tree strang;
Ane strak him sair on the back-neck,
  Ane on the nose him rappit, 50
Ane smote him on the vera heart,
  And down as dead he drappit.
But ah! but ah! a drearier dool
  Ance hapt at Ounston-dammy,
That heise'd him a'thegither up, 55
  And maist extinguish't Tammy;
For, as he cam slow-daunderin' down,
  In's hand his basket hingin',
And staiver'd ower the hie-road's breidth,
  Frae side to side a-swingin'; 60
There cam a blast frae Kelly law,
  As bald a blast as ever
Auld snivelin' Boreas blew abraid,
  To make the warld shiver;
It liftet Tammy aff his feet, 65
  Mair easy than a shavin',
And hurl'd him half-a-mile complete,
  Hie up 'tween earth and heaven.
That day puir Tammy had wi' stanes
  No ballasted his body, 70
So that he flew, maist like a shot,
  Ower corn-land and ower cloddy.
You've seen ane tumbler on a stage,
  Tumble sax times and mair,
But Tammy weil sax hundred times 75
  Gaed tumblin' through the air.
And whan the whirly-wind gave ower,
  He frae the lift fell plumb,
And in a blink stood stickin' fast
  In Gaffer Glowr-weel's lum. 80
Ay – there his legs and body stack
  Amang the smotherin' soot,
But, by a wonderfu' good luck,

His head kept peepin' out.
But Gaffer Glowr-weel, when he saw   85
  A man stuck in his lum,
He swarf'd wi' drither clean awa,
  And sat some seconds dumb.
It took five masons near an hour,
  A' riving at the lum   90
Wi' picks, (he was sae jamm'd therein,)
  Ere Tammy out could come.
As for his basket – weel I wat,
  His basket's fate and fa'
Was, as I've heard douce neighbours tell,   95
  The queerest thing of a'.
The blast took up the body's creel,
  And laid it on a cloud,
That bare it, sailin' through the sky,
  Richt ower the Firth's braid flood;   100
And whan the cloud did melt awa,
Then, then the creel cam' down,
And fell'd the town-clerk o' Dunbar
  E'en in his ain guid town;
The clerk stood yelpin' on the street,   105
  At some bit strife that stirr'd him,
Down cam' the creel, and to the yird
  It dang him wi' a dirdom!

THE EPITAPH FOR TAMMY

O Earth! O Earth! if thou hast but
  A rabbit-hole to spair,   110
O grant the graff to Tammy's corp,
  That it may nestle thair:
And press thou light on him, now dead,
  That was sae slim and wee,
For weel I wat, when he was quick,   115
  He lightly prest on thee!
                                   Φιλοταιγμων.

206

THE TANGIERS GIANT

By the Author of "Anster Fair"

TO THE EDITOR OF THE EDINBURGH LITERARY JOURNAL

MY DEAR GIGANTIC MR EDITOR,
METHINKS I have in secret observed, that you and others of strutting corporeal altitude are apt to think more highly of yourselves than you ought to think, from the accidental circumstance of your Typhœan stature – that you, in short, are apt to look down somewhat contemptuously on myself, and on all the rest of lowly, modest, and Zaccheus-statured mankind. It is then for the express purpose of *humbling you*, and the other towering *gigantaccli* of the Six-Feet Club, that I have indited the following verses. I trust you will accept of them as a stroke of humiliation – as one of the *fulgura* of Apollo levelled at your ambitious and sun-challenging heads: – for you will not fail, I think, to perceive, that, in comparison with *my Giant*, you and all others of similar stamp and mould are but

> ———"as that small infantry
> Warr'd on by cranes!"

I expect, therefore, that, for the humiliation of the lofty-headed, you will transmit a copy of the "Tangiers Giant" to each member of your assuming and over-lording Six-Feet Club of Edinburgh – Believe me, notwithstanding your height, to be, my dear sir, most faithfully yours,
W.T.

> In Tangiers town, as I've been tauld,[1]
> There lived intill the times of auld,
>   A giant, stout and big,
> The awfuest and the dowrest carl
> That on the outside o' this warl'   5
>   E'er wallop'd bane or leg.
> When he was born, on that same day
> He was like other weans, perfay,
>   Nae langer than ane ladle;
> But in three days he shot sae lang,   10
> That out wi' 's feet and head he dang
>   Baith end-boords o' his cradle.

And, whan the big-baned babe did see,
How that his cradle, short and wee,
   Could haud him in nae langer,   15
His passion took a tirrivee,
He grippit it, and garr'd it flee
   In flinders, in his anger.
Ere he was span'd – what beef, what bane! –
He was a babe o' thretty stane,   20
   And buirdlier than his mither;
Whan he for's parridge grat at morn,
Men never heard, syn they were born,
   A yeut sae fu' o' drither!
When he'd seen thretty years or sae,   25
Far meikler was his little tae
   Than our big Samuel's showther;
When he down on a stool did lean,
The stool was in an instant gane,
   'Twas briss'd clean down to powther.   30
When through the streets of Tangiers town
He gaed, spasiering up and down,
   Houses and kirks did trummel;
O' his coat-tail, the vera wap
Raised whirlwinds wi' its flichtering flap,   35
   And garr'd auld lumm-heads tummel.
Had ye been five mile out o' toun,
Ye might hae seen his head aboon
   The heighest houses tow'rin;
Ilk awsome tramp he gaif the ground,   40
Garr'd aik-trees shake their heads a' round,
   And lions rin hame cow'rin'.
To show his powstie to the people,
Ance in his arms he took the steeple,
   Kiss'd it, and ca'd it "Brither";   45
Syn from its bottom up it wrung,
And in the air three times it swung,
   Spire, bell, and a' thegither,
And when he'd swung it merrilie,
Again upon its bottom he   50
   Did clap it down sae clever;
Except a sma' crack half-way round,
The steeple stood upon its found
   As stout and staunch as ever.
Ae king's birthday, when he was fu',   55
Twa Tangier blades began to pu'
   His tails, when on a sudden,
Ane by the richt leg up he grippit,

The tither by the neck he snippit,
    And sent them skyward scuddin';   60
On earth they ne'er again cam down:
Ane in a tan-pat i' the moon
    Fell plump, and breathed his last;
The tither ane was jammit ticht
'Tween twa stars o' the Pleiades bricht,   65
    Whair yet he's sticking fast.
Ae day when he stood near the sea,
A fleet o' Tyrian ships in glee
    Was sailin' gawcy by –
He gript ae frigate by the mast,   70
And frae the deep in powstie vast
    He raised her in the sky:
And then the great ship up he tummell'd;
Her mast was down, her hulk up-whummell'd,
    Her keel hie i' the lift;   75
Captain and cargo down cam rummelin',
Marines and men and meat cam tummelin'
    Down frae her decks like drift.
He had ane mammoth for his horse,[2]
Whairon wi' michty birr and force   80
    He rade baith up and down;
My certy! whan on him he lap,
For hill nor tree he didna stap,
    For tower, nor yet for town.
From Calpe till the Chinese wa'   85
He travell'd in a day or twa;
    And, as he gallop't east,
The tower o' Babel down he batter'd;
For five mile round its bricks were scatter'd –
    Sic birr was in his beast!   90
But whan he came to Ecbatan,
A terribler strabasch was than;
    He souchtna street nor yett;
But hurly-burly, smash, smash, smash,
Through wa's and roofs he drave slap-dash,   95
    Down-dundering a' he met;
What wi' his monster's thunderin' thud,
And what wi' brasch and smasch and scud
    O' rafters, sclates, and stanes,
Ten thousand folk to dead were devell'd,   100
Ten thousand mair were aiblins levell'd,
    Half-dead wi' fractured banes!
He travell'd, too, baith south and north,
Baith hinges o' the warld, forsooth;

At Thebes³ he brak his fast,   105
And at the blithe Cape o' Good Houp
He took his denner and a stoup
   O' wine for his repast;
He try'd, too, on his fearsome horse,
His way up to our Pole to force,   110
   To spy its whirlin' pin;
Up to the Arctic ice-ribb'd flood,
Nichering he cam, as he were wud,
   Wi' dirdom and wi' din:
As north he rode, he didna wait   115
To mak a brig ower Helle's strait,
   Like Persia's pridefu' king;
He loupit from Abydos' strand,
And thwack on Sestos' beach did land,
   Makin' hail Europe ring!   120
As up through Thrace his beast did cour,
He kick'd up sic ane cloud o' stour
   From his gambading hoof,
The King o' Thrace, whan he in's ha'
Sat dining wi' his princes braw,   125
   Was chokit wi' the stoof!
But whan he reach'd Siberia's shore,
His monster, wi' a grewsome roar,
   Down squish'd amang the snaw;
The beast was smored, and ne'er gat out;   130
His rider, wi' ane damnit shout,
   Sprang aff, and spreul'd awa.
His end was like his lawless life;
He challenged Atlas in some strife,
   T' up-haud Heiven on his head;   135
He tried the sterny Heiven t' up-haud; –
Down cam the lift; and wi' a daud
   It smored the scoundrel dead!

THE MORAL

From this dour giant we may see
How little bulk o' limb and thie   140
   The human race bestead;
A wee bit man wi' meikle sense,
Is better than ane carl immense
   Wi' nonsense in his head!

Banks of the Devon, Clackmannanshire,
   September, 1830.

NOTES

1   For this giant of 90 feet or more, we have somewhat like classical authority. Says an old author, – "Gabinus, the Roman historian, makes mention of the sepulchre of Antæus, near Tingi, (or Tangiers,) as also of a skeleton, *sixty cubits* long, which Sertorius disinterred, and again covered with earth." – Strabo, lib. 17. cap. 3.

2   An enormous animal of this class was disclosed by the melting of the snow in 1801, upon the snow-buried confines of Siberia. How the monster got there – how it was entombed there – appeared inexplicable to the philosophical enquirers of that period, and is only to be explained by the story of the text.

3   Egyptian Thebes, surely.

APPENDIX

MAGGY LAUDER

The text of the traditional Scots poem, 'Maggy Lauder', which inspired Tennant to write *Anster Fair*: attribution of authorship to Francis Semple (1616–1682) has no manuscript authority. 'Maggy Lauder' first appeared in print in David Herd's *Ancient and Modern Scottish Songs and Ballads*, first published in 1776.

Wha wad na be in love
    Wi' bonny MAGGIE LAUDER?
A piper met her gaun to Fife,
    And speir'd what was't they ca'd her;
Right scornfully she answer'd him,   5
    Begone, you hallanshaker,
Jog on your gate, you bladderskate,
    My name is MAGGIE LAUDER.

MAGGIE, quoth he, and by my bags,
    I'm fidging fain to see thee;   10
Sit down by me, my bonny bird,
    In troth I winna steer thee;
For I'm a piper to my trade,
    My name is ROB the Ranter,
The lasses loup as they were daft,   15
    When I blaw up my chanter.

Piper, quoth MEG, hae you your bags,
    Or is your drone in order?
If you be ROB, I've heard of you,
    Live you upo' the border?   30
The lasses a', baith far and near,
    Have heard of ROB the Ranter;
I'll shake my foot wi' right goodwill,
    Gif you'll blaw up your chanter.

Then to his bags he flew wi' speed,   25
    About the drone he twisted;
MEG up and wallop'd o'er the green,
    For brawly could she frisk it.

Weel done, quoth he, play up, quoth she,
  Weel bob'd, quoth ROB the Ranter,   30
'Tis worth my while to play indeed,
  When I hae sic a dancer.

Weel hae ye play'd your part, quoth MEG,
  Your cheeks are like the crimson;
There's nane in Scotland plays sae weel,   35
  Since we lost HABBY SIMPSON.
I've liv'd in Fife, baith maid and wife,
  These ten years and a quarter;
Gin you should come to Enster fair,
  Speir ye for MAGGIE LAUDER.   40

[Editorial note: 'Enster' is the local pronunciation of 'Anster'.]

NOTES

ANSTER FAIR

The text is that of the 1812 edition, while also including the few stanzas which were added or substituted in the edition of 1814. Other 1814 emendations are indicated below. Such honorific names as 'monarch', 'muse', 'lady', 'dame', 'king', 'heaven', 'knight', 'earl', 'liege', 'squire', 'esquire', 'nobleman', 'lord', 'fair', 'bride' and 'bridegroom', such collective nouns as 'piper/pipers', 'graces', 'heralds', 'monks', and 'trumpeters', and such place names as 'loan' and 'abbey', appearing in lower-case in 1812, are all capitalised in 1814, but their occurrence is so frequent that only the present general indication can be made. In 1812 nearly nearly all personal names are printed in upper and lower case: exceptions are those of the hero and heroine (ROBERT, RANTER, MAGGIE, MAG, etc.). In 1814 this use of capitals and small capitals is extended to the other personal names. In 1812 'Scot' as a personal name is so spelt in the text, but appears in the Arguments as 'Scott': in 1814 it is altered to 'Scott' throughout. In 1812 the neuter possessive pronoun regularly appears as 'it's', a spelling still in use in the early nineteenth century, but by then becoming old-fashioned (see the *Oxford English Dictionary*). The more modern form, 'its', is adopted in 1814. Some manifest printer's errors in the 1812 edition are corrected in the present text: these are recorded below.

Title Page
In each of these epigraphs from the Latin, Tennant gives only part of the original sentence, thereby slanting them towards his own ends. In the first quotation, from Plautus, *Casina* 4. l.2, the sentence depends on a pun, since 'ludus' which normally means 'game' (in the sense of Olympic games) can also mean 'to make game of someone', 'poke fun at', *ludum facere* with that 'someone' in the dative (and the dative of 'an old man' follows in the next line of the original Latin, which Tennant omits). However, the last word that Tennant prints, *ludificabiles*, is actually a joke-word coined by Plautus, meaning 'to make a person an object of sport'. While the original Latin text, translated absolutely literally, means 'By Pollux, I don't believe that the games at Nemea or at Olympia or anywhere else are as lively as the game made here of our old man', what Tennant wants his truncated three lines to mean is something like 'By heaven, I don't believe the European or Olympic games or games wherever are as comical as the fun and games played in here'.

In the second quotation, Tennant amends Phaedrus, *Fab.* 4. 2. 2, leaving out the first line of the sentence. In the full original version, the translation is,

'You think I'm joking, and the pipes I play on, with nothing better to do, are truly frivolous'. But reduced to Tennant's single line, the translation reads, 'With nothing better to do, I play the pipes'.

Canto I

Argument. This is omitted, as are those of the cantos following, from 1814.

1–6. The epic poems alluded to in the first six lines are Homer's *Iliad*, Virgil's *Aeneid*, Ariosto's *Orlando Furioso*, and Milton's *Paradise Lost* and *Paradise Regained*.

17. Parnassus.

18–20. Pindar, the greatest of Greek lyric poets, whose future was said to have been foreshadowed in youth by a swarm of bees resting on his sleeping lips.

18. 1814, harp-fing'ring

24. 1814, scorn (1812 printer's error: sdein)

28. 1814, A pickle parsley got for all his pains

35. Homer.

37–40. Ovid's story of the wooing of Atalanta.

103. 1814, Yet with her teeth held now and then a picking,

111–12. 1814,

> While she, though their addresses still she heard,
> Held back from all her heart, and still no beau preferr'd.

113–18. 1814,

> What, what, quo' MAG, must thus it be my doom
>   To spend my prime in maidhood's joyless state,
> And waste away my body's sprightly bloom
>   In spouseless solitude without a mate,
> Still toying with my suitors, as they come
> Cringing in lowly courtship to my gate?

121. 1814, For was e'er heiress with much gold in chest

129–68. The suitors' surnames were well-known in the Anstruther district.

136. 1814, He is a pompous fool – I cannot think of him.

157. 1814, But oh! his mouth a sorry smell exhales

165. 1814, Auchmoutie too, and Bruce that persecute

171. *The Iliad*, XVIII, 442.

183. The fabulous Arabian bird was reputed to lay an egg of myrrh once in every six hundred years.

195–6. The goddess of the rainbow.

198. 1814, Plucked from their sockets, sure by genie-power

201–8. Camoens, *The Lusiads*.

216. 1814, As e'er

261. 1814, may (1812 printer's error: my)

282. 1814, whip-wielding

311–12. Midas, King of Phrygia, judging a musical contest between Apollo and Pan, decided in favour of the latter, whereupon Apollo changed the king's ears into those of an ass.

338. 1814, Forgot to patter in such pelting wise

353. 1814, silver harness'd

368. 1814, The Scottish beau

376. 1814, each nose.

385. 1814, Ho! beau and pipers
418–21. Virgil, *The Aeneid*, IV, 252.
432. 1814, borne

Canto II.

2. King James I of Scotland (1394–1437), the reputed author of the allegorical love-poem *The Kingis Quair*.
47. 1814, stems (1812 printer's error: sterns)
68. 1814, And grow, by bousing
107. 1814, sapient tongue
112. Henry Wardlaw, bishop of St Andrews from 1404, founded the University of St Andrews in 1410.
116. The birthplace of Aphrodite, goddess of love.
121–8. Ovid, *Fasti II.*, 303–356. Faunus (the Latin Pan) catches sight of the Lydian princess Omphale walking with Hercules, then a slave to the lady, and lusts for her. He follows them to the vineyards of Mount Tmolus, and there in a cave Omphale, indulging in transvestism, compels Hercules to change clothes with her. After dining, she and her slave fall asleep on beds placed side by side. In the dark, Faunus creeps in, feeling for Omphale, and, deceived by the clothing, is somewhat puzzled by Hercules' hairy legs. Hercules, jerking up, knocks Faunus off the bed, almost senseless. The attendants rush in with torches, and everyone doubles up with laughter at the discomfited and groaning Faunus.
129–30. 1814,
      Nor come they only down; in chaise or gig
      The endoctrin'd sage professors lolling ride
145. Stanza 18a added 1814, after Tennant's appointment as schoolmaster in Dunino.
160. 1814, A good Crail capon
166. 1814, strangely glad
260. 1814, with brows of brass
279. 1814, Dunkeld
284. 1814, grow king
299. 1814, Lochaber-axe
396. 1814, foamy bosom
430. 1814, isles of fish
462, footnote. 1814, Anster House was destroyed to its foundation in 1811.
468. 1814, entangled reel
478. 1814, That
504. 1814, and men dash hard on men.
514. Sir David Lyndsay of the Mount (1490–1555), whose play *The Three Estates* was performed before King James V in Cupar, Fife, in 1535.
562. Playing-cards.
567. A Fife game played on a 'Tod-brod' (Fox-board) with wooden pins.
572. 1814, enchanting

Canto III

2. Mount Ida, overlooking the city of Troy.
34. 1814, Full merrily
96. 1814, haughtiest

107. 1814, sides (1812 printer's error: tides)
133. 1814, Woe
139. 1814, Coan. A light transparent dress manufactured on the island of Cos.
151–8. Queen of Nineveh and Babylon, whose famous walls were built at her command.
195. 1814, shrilling noise
197. 1814, humm'd and squeal'd
224–6. The beautiful nymph, Daphne, pursued by the god Apollo, escaped his unwelcome attentions only by being transformed into a laurel tree.
251. 1814, Donkeys in dozens
371. 1814, terror
387–8. 1814

> All drench'd with sweat, internally so warm,
> They loudly bray before, and belch behind:

391. 1814, SCOTT
400. 1814, RANTER
423. 1814, commingled
424. 1814, Cursing
439. 1814, sputt'ring shell
466. 1814, SCOTT
479. 1814, halloo'd (1812 printer's error: hallow'd)

Canto IV

Stanza 1a. 1814, substituted for Stanza 1.
26. 1814, Than through
119. Misprinted in 1812 as 'eying'.
193–200. Virgil, *The Aeneid*, iii, 775.
321. 1814, people's sight
328. 1814, Gapes
400. Homer, *The Odyssey*, X, 19.
497. 1814, electric
536. 1814, jetty-feather'd
632. 1814, Haughtily heav'd
654. 1814, wag feet, arms, and trunk
655–6. 1814,

> As if they strove, in capering so brisk,
> To heave their aged knees up to the solar disk.

679. 1814, Racked and convuls'd, the ingorging surges roar

Canto V

2. 1814, Beattie Laing
2, footnote. George Sinclair (1618–1687), *Satan's Invisible World Discovered* (1685).
101. 1814, Who sith that death
130. Sir Michael Scott of Balwearie in Fife, one of the most learned men in thirteenth-century Europe, was popularly regarded as a magician or wizard, a superstition given literary expression during Tennant's young manhood in Walter Scott's *The Lay of the Last Minstrel* (1805).
198. 1814, Heaven's tapestry

449–64. For further evidence of the fairies' healing powers see the introduction to the tale of Tam Lin in Walter Scott's *Minstrelsy of the Scottish Border* (1802).
513–60. For the traditional story of Sir Michael's metamorphosis, see the notes to *The Lay of the Last Minstrel* and James Hogg's fantasy-novel *The Three Perils of Man* (1822).
573. 1814, mountainous and high
576. 1814, strangely

Canto VI

Stanza 1. 1814, replaced by Canto 4, Stanza 1, 1812.
22. 1814, Whirling
58. 1814, All-smoking
177. 1814, 'While in each well-proved street and alley strait
200. 1814, each fire in sky seem'd burning
223. 1814, Through
225. 1814, tapestry
269. St Regulus, a Greek monk credited with bringing the bones of St Andrew to Fife around the year 350 A.D.
595. 1814, *supplest*
607–8. Cf. the lines of the old song, 'Oh, the monks of Melrose made guid kale,/ On Friday when they *fasted*'.
657. 1814, And now, my lord, O King, we must away
681. 1814, of their short surprise

PAPISTRY STORM'D

The text is that of the first (and only) edition, Edinburgh 1827. The title-page describes the volume as 'Imprentit at Edinbroch,/ Be Oliver and Boyd, Tweedal-Court./ Anno Do. M.DCCC.XXVII', and the author is given as 'M. W. T.' (?Master William Tennant).
Dedication. The Latin might be translated as 'To the memory/ of David Lyndsay, Fife poet/ of greatest renown,/ this poem, however insignificant,/ in order to mark our love and respect,/ is dedicated'. Tennant had already followed Lyndsay in writing on Cardinal Beaton, and it is Lyndsay's presentation of Catholic clerics as foolish clowns in *The Three Estates* which seems to have provided the model for the way they are drawn in the present work.
A Proemium. When Tennant claims John Knox as his predecessor in writing humorously about 'Papish disasters, distresses, and discomfitures', he would appear to be recalling most particularly the earlier author's *magnum opus*, *The History of the Reformation in Scotland*, first written between 1559 and 1561, and revised and expanded in 1566, with a fifth book (perhaps by another hand) added later, the whole being published in 1644.

Sang First

Argument, IV. St Andrews, called 'the Roman city' because it was the principal centre of Roman Catholic worship in Scotland.
V. The god of mirth.
1–28. The attack on Catholic church property, following Knox's anti-Catholic

218

sermon in St Andrews on 11 June 1559, is a matter of historical record, but the mustering of Protestant supporters from all over Fife to effect this 'reform' is an invention by Tennant, as is his statement that St Andrews Cathedral was destroyed at that time. While some of the characters in the poem are historical, many are fictitious.

29–50. Homer, as author of *The Iliad.*

82–83. Cardinal Beaton was murdered in St Andrews by a band of Protestant assassins in 1547.

84–115. John Knox (1505–1572) had been a Catholic priest for some fifteen years before he became sword-bearer to the Protestant preacher George Wishart in 1545. After Wishart was burned as a heretic in St Andrews in 1546, at the instigation of Cardinal Beaton, the head of the Catholic Church in Scotland, and after Beaton's subsequent murder, Knox joined the assassins in the Castle of St Andrews in April 1547, and it was there, a month later, that he first received a 'call' to the Protestant ministry. Captured by the French allies of the Catholic queen-regent, Marie of Guise (or Lorraine), Knox was imprisoned in the French galleys until 1549, and after his release he spent most of the next decade in exile, as a Protestant minister in England and on the Continent, and as the author of anti-Catholic publications. Returning to Scotland in 1559, when the Protestant Lords of the Congregation were already in rebellion against the queen-regent's government, he began a Reformation campaign with a sermon in Perth, as a result of which all the churches and monasteries in the district were defaced or destroyed. Similar scenes occurred in Fife, first in Crail and Anstruther, then in St Andrews.

90. The Pope.

126. A notorious cardinal (1542–1621), the principal anti-protestant theologian.

185. An associate of Knox, who likewise joined Beaton's assassins in the Castle of St Andrews in 1547, John Rough (b.1510) was a Dominican who embraced the Reformed faith. Becoming a Protestant preacher in England in 1547, he was martyred in London during the reign of Mary Tudor ('Bloody Mary') ten years later. His introduction into the present work as a living person therefore represents a chronological error on Tennant's part.

235. Younger brother of George Ramsay of Dalhousie.

236. Sir William Kirkcaldy of Grange (d.1573) was implicated in the murder of Beaton, taken prisoner in the Castle of St Andrews, and served in the French galleys. Opposed to the marriage of Mary, Queen of Scots and Lord Darnley, he was outlawed for failing to attend the wedding. He was involved in the murder of Rizzio. At Carberry Hill he shared command of the Confederate Lords, but although hostile to Mary's second husband, Bothwell, he was loyal to the Queen herself and held Edinburgh Castle in her name in 1573. When he was forced to surrender he was publicly hanged at the Market Cross of Edinburgh.

241. The Anstruther baronet, whose seat was an old castle one and three-quarter miles north-west of Pittenweem.

253–57. Laird of an old mansion in the southern extremity of Crail parish.

258–62. James Melville, implicated in the assassination of Beaton, fled to Britanny, and was the only one of the associates who did not eventually return to Scotland.

263–66. An estate one and a quarter miles east north-east of Colinsburgh.

270–309. Pallas Athene (Minerva), goddess of wisdom. Reputedly born from the head of Zeus (Jove), she thus had only one parent (1.277).

321–23. The Battle of the Frogs and Mice, popularly attributed to Homer during antiquity, is a mock-epic in Greek, probably composed in the fifth century B.C., which describes a war provoked by the drowning of a mouse.

324–26. Alessandro Tassoni (1565–1635), author of *La Secchia Rapita* (1622), an Italian mock-heroic poem in *ottava rima* on a war fought over a bucket.

392. Crail.

409. The Duke of Guise, leader of the ultra-Catholic faction at the French court, and his sister, the queen-regent of Scotland, widow of James V and mother of Mary, Queen of Scots.

648–69. Cardinal Beaton.

Sang Second

Argument, VII–VIII. George Buchanan (1506–1582), who was to become Principal of St Leonard's College, University of St Andrews, in 1566, and tutor to King James VI in 1570, was recognised in his own day as an outstanding scholar and the greatest living Latin poet. Although Mary, Queen of Scots was his patron after her return to Scotland from France in 1561, he savagely attacked her in his later Latin prose. There is no contemporary evidence associating him with the events in St Andrews in 1559 which followed Knox's preaching there.

1. The sun-god.

107. Possibly Barclay of Garthy, who in 1560 signed 'the last band at Leith'.

279–87. The Iliad.

611–12. Educated in France, where he studied medicine at Montpellier, and in Prague, he served the King of Poland for ten years before 1432. As a follower of Hus and Wycliff he was burned at the stake in St Andrews, probably in 1433.

613–17. Martyred in St Andrews in 1546. Tennant pictures him ascending to heaven like Elijah.

Sang Third

324–6. History reveals that the Lord Prior of St Andrews at this period was not a cleric but a layman, no less than Lord James Stuart, the illegitimate half-brother of Mary, Queen of Scots and a leading advocate of Reform (later Earl of Moray, and later still the regent of Scotland).

351–2. A canon of St Andrews who became Principal of St Leonard's College in 1544. He attacked the sermons of John Rough and publicly disputed with Knox.

353–4. A Grey friar who, along with the sub-prior of St Andrews, had engaged in doctrinal disputation with Knox.

Sang Fourth

375–8. Commander of the French forces in Scotland throughout 1548, relieved 1549.

Sang Fifth

359–84. The consecration of St Andrews Cathedral in the reign of King Robert I.

649–59. A former bishop of St Andrews.

661–64. The bishop at the time of the cathedral's consecration.

Sang Saxt

Argument, V–VIII. The destruction of church furnishings has an historical basis, but the fall of the cathedral steeple at this time is an invention of Tennant's.

194. A former bishop of St Andrews.

257–87. John (not William) Lauder (?1490–1557), secretary to Archbishop Forman of St Andrews, 1517–1521. Archdeacon of Teviotdale, 1536. Secretary to Archbishop David Beaton of St Andrews, 1531–1546. Clerk and notary of the officials' court of St Andrews. Lauder was sent to Glasgow to assist Archbishop Dunbar at the trials of Russell and Kennedy, both burned at the stake, in 1539. He was prosecutor at the trial of George Wishart at St Andrews, 1546.

301–33, 386–94, 446–569. The *Historie of the Estate of Scotland* says that 'the sermon by Knox was scarcely downe when they fell to work to purge the kirk and break down the altars and images of all kinds of idolatrie . . . and before the sun was downe there wes never an inch standing bot bare walls. Bot the idols that were in the Abbey were brought to the north part of the said Abbey, in the same place where Walter Milne was burned (a year or thereabouts before) and there they burned the whole idols'.

307. John Douglas (?1493–1574), provost of St Mary's College, 1547. Rector of St Andrews University, 1551–1773. A reformer, he was involved in the drawing-up of *The Book of Discipline*, and was nominated 'tulchan' Archbishop of St Andrews by the Earl of Morton in 1571. (In *The Concise Scots Dictionary*, the figurative meaning of 'tulchan' is given as 'a substitute, a person appointed nominally to an office, the power and emoluments being diverted to another'.)

425. John Winram (?1493–1582), sub-prior of the Augustinian priory of St Andrews, 1536. He summoned a convention of Black and Grey friars before which Knox and Rough appeared, and he engaged in a disputation with Knox, along with John Arbuckle. Later he embraced the Reformed faith and became Superintendent of Fife and Strathearn, 1561–1572 and 1574–1575, and of Strathearn only, 1572–1574. He helped to draft the *Confession of Faith*.

427. Sir Robert Forman of Luthrie carried messages between the Catholic queen-regent and the Protestant 'Congregation'. He succeeded Sir David Lyndsay as Lyon King-at-Arms in 1558.

457. Former bishops of St Andrews.

709–97. Tennant is correct in ascribing the destruction of the cathedral to the elements, but over-dramatic in attributing the disaster to the effects of a single overwhelming storm in 1559. The cathedral was still standing in 1561, when a Privy Council ordinance scheduled its destruction, and it was unroofed about that time. Sixty years later the Scottish weather had triumphed over ecclesiastical architecture, Habbakuk Bissett referring to 'the auld Rewynous wallis of the Cathedrall and sumtyme maist Magnifik kirk of the Archbishoprie of St Androis'.

TAMMY LITTLE

Text as in *The Edinburgh Literary Journal; or, Weekly Register of Criticism and Belles Lettres*, No. 88, 17 July 1830. There is no external evidence to corroborate the sub-title. The Greek signature means 'Playful' or 'Sportive'.

THE TANGIERS GIANT

Text as in *The Edinburgh Literary Journal; or, Weekly Register of Criticism and Belles Lettres*, No. 102, 23 October 1830.

GLOSSARY

a', all
abee, let alone, bear with
abuilyiement, dress
ae, one
aff, off
ahent, behind
aiblins, perhaps
aiken-rung, oaken-staff
air, early
airn, iron
airt, direction
aits, oats
ajee, ajar
allenerlie, only
alswa, also
ambrie, cupboard
ane, one
anes, once
artailyie, artillery
ask, lizard
assaillyie, assail
astonay'd, astonished
athort, across
atween, between
aucht, eight
auld, old
aye, always
ayont, beyond
ayslar, ashlar

baff, beat, strike, stroke, blow
baird, bard
bairn, child
baith, both
bale, sorrow, misery, evil, disaster, destruction
bang, throw violently
bannock-hive, corpulence, induced by hearty eating
barlafummle, call for a truce

bap, roll
barreis, barriers (the lists)
bastoun, baston, heavy staff, baton
batie-bum, simpleton, inactive fellow
bauld, bold
bawdikyns, cloth of gold
baxter, baker
beal, boil
beck, curtsey, cringe
bedien, quickly, forthwith
bedral, beadle, sexton
begoud, began
beik, bask
beir, noise, cry, roar
bele, beller, bellow, roar
belyve, immediately, quickly
bicker, fight, skirmish
bien, wealthy, plentiful, well-provided
bigent, first-year student
bigg(ing), build(ing)
billie, fellow
bink, bench
birkie, lively (young chap)
birr, force, fury; whirr
blad, severe blow
blaitie-bum, stupid ass
blatter, rattle
bleeze, blaze
bleme, blossom
blether, nonsense
bloizent, swollen, disfigured
bodle, copper coin (two Scots pence)
body, person
bonny, pretty, attractive
bordel-house, brothel
bousy, big, fat, drunken, corpulent, puffed-up
bout-gates, deceitful course, evasion
bown, prepared, ready, in order

223

bowt, spring, leap
brae, slope
braid, broad
brand, sword
brank, bear oneself proudly
brast, burst
brattle, clatter
bra(w), handsome
bree, broo, brow
breeks, breeches, trousers
breik, breech
breird, germinate
breissil, come on in a hurry
brewster, brewer
brize, press
brock, fragments
brogh, burgh, town
brogle, botch, bungle
broillerie, state of contention
bruckle, brittle
brulyie(ment), broil, battle
brym, fierce, violent
brusch, rush, gush
bud, gift, bribe
buik, bulk, size, quantity
buirdlie, well-made, stately
bum, hum, buzz, drone
bumbazed, stupefied
bumill, bummell, bungle; idle fellow
burde, board
buschment, ambush
bustyious, boisterous
butten, without
byke, habitation; nest of bees, wasps, ants

callan, stripling, lad
camstane, limestone; white clay
camstarie, riotous, quarrelsome
canallyie, the mob
cantrip, magical trick
canty, lively, cheerful
capper, copper
carl, man, fellow
cark, load, burden, care, anxiety
cauld, cold
cauldrife, chilly
causey, roadway, street, pavement
certie, certes, assuredly
chaft(bane), jaw, cheek(bone)

chap, knock, rap
chiel, fellow
chingle, shingle
chouk, cheek
chuckie-stane, pebble
circumjack, fit, apply
claes, clothes, bed-clothes
claik, gossip
clamahewit, stroke, drubbing
clatter, talk idly
claucht, clutched
claver, prattle
cleedit, clad
cleik, catch
clew, cleave, fasten; claw, talon
clitter-clatter, idle talk
clother't, clotter't, clotted, caked
cloytet, fallen heavily
clour, strike, stroke, blow
clud, cloud
clung, empty
coble, small boat
cod(ware), cushion, pillow(slip)
collieshangie, uproar, squabble
contrair, contrary, opposed to
coot, ankle
corkin-prien, corking-pin
coup(it), upset
covetize, greed
crabbit, bad-tempered, cross
crack, boast, brag, converse
craft, croft
craig, rock; throat
crouse, brisk, lively
croyl, dwarfish, deformed
cud, cudgel
cuddie, donkey
cuif, incompetent
culyie, coax, cajole, fondle
cummer, female friend, gossip; vexation
cur-sackie, overall, pinafore, smock
cushie-dow, pigeon

dad(dit), blow, stroke, stricken
daffery, daffin, romping, folly
daidle, saunter
daigle, trifle
dalmatyk, white dress worn by a bishop
dammishment, stupefaction

dander, saunter
dandiefechan, hollow
dang, beaten
darg, dark, work
daw, dawn
deadthraw, last agonies of death
debaid, delay
deil ane, not a single
deil's-buckie, perverse person
deray, disorder
derf, bold, hardy, severe, cruel, sullen
descrive, describe
devell, (to give a) stunning blow
ding-dang, pell-mell, helter-skelter
dinnel, make a great noise; thrill, tingle
dird(rum), stroke, uproar, tumult
dirl, thrill
disjeune, breakfast
distrubill'd, disturbed
dvitrify'd, stupefied
doken, dock-leaf
dole(some), deceit(ful)
dool, grief
doons, not very (much)
dortour, bedroom
douce, sweet, pleasant, comfortable
douk(it), duck(ed)
dour, stubborn, relentless
dover, doze off, wander, walk unsteadily
dow, dove
dowfart, dull, spiritless, stupid
downa, dare not
doytet, stupid, confused
draigle, draggle, bedraggled
drammach, meal and water mixed; pulp
drave, drove
drede, dread
dree, endure
dreep, drip
driddler, drither, fear, dread
droddum, the breech
drow, fainting fit
drowth, thirst
drubbly, turbid
drunt, drone
dub, small pool
duds, clothes

dunder, dunner, clatter, make a thunderous noise
dusche, crashing fall
dwam, dream, faint
dyke, wall

eastlins, eastward
ee-bree, eye-brow
een, eyne, eyes
effeir, fear; become, becoming
effrayit, afraid
eild, age
elbuck, elbow
elrisch, preternatural, frightful, uncouth, austere
ensenyie, sign, standard, badge
ereck, erect
erthlins, earthwards; along or towards the ground
ettle, aim, propose, design
everilk, every
excambied, exchanged

faddom, fathom
fae, foe
fa'n, fallen
fashery, vexation
faucht, fecht, fight
fause, false
fear-fangit, captive to fear
feckit, woollen garment with sleeves and buttoned front
fede, feud
feeze, screw, twist
feir, band
fellie, fellow
fenester, window
fenyied, pretended
ferdy, strong, active
fertor, shrine, reliquary
fient a, not a single
fiery-farie, bustle, show, pretended bustle
fire-slacht, lightning
firlot, fourth part of a boll of six bushels
fizz, rage
flaff, flap, flutter
flann, gust of wind
flast, gasconade

flaw, gust of wind
fleegarie, whim, gew-gaw
flinder, splinter
flotter, overflow
flure, floor
fluther, flutter
flype, fold
flyte, scold
fodgel, plump, buxom
fone, foes
foolyie, leaf, gold-leaf
fordwart, forward
forfairn, forlorn, worn out
forleitit, forsaken
fornent, opposite to; concerning
fortravail'd, greatly fatigued
fousome, filthy
frack, ready, active
fraith, froth
freir, friar
freme, strange, unlucky, adverse,
    unfriendly
frush, dash, break in pieces; brittle,
    fragile
fudder-flash, lightning-flash
fuff, puff
fuffel'd, dishevelled, disarranged

gab, gabbed, mouth, chattered
gabbot, gobbet
gaff, babble, chatter, guffaw
gaif, gave
galliard, gallant, lively, spruce, gay,
    bright
gallyie, roar, cry
gambade, leap, caper
gant, gaunt, yawn
gar, make, cause to
gash, prattle
gate, way
gauf, gaulf, guffaw
gaukit, stupid, clumsy
gaup, gape, stare open-mouthed
gawcy, handsome
gawntress, gantry
gebbie, mouth; stomach
gee, mood, caprice, fancy, fit of sul-
    lenness or temper
geill, jelly
gerss, grass

ghaist, ghost
gin, if
girn, grimace
gizzen, throat
glaik, trick, deception; silly, thought-
    less person
glaikin, looking foolishly or idly; tri-
    fling with
glaik'd, glaikit, foolish, stupid,
    thoughtless, irresponsible
glairy-fairy, gaudy, showy
glamour, gramourie, enchantment,
    magic
glammach, snatch, grab, devour
glamp't, glaum'd, snatched, grabbed,
    devoured
gled, kite (bird)
gleek, look, peep
gley-mou'd, squint-mouthed
gliff, look; frighten, startle
glore, glory
glowr, scowl
glunch, scowl
goave, vacant stare
gosky, rank, luxuriant
gouff, golf
goutherfow, amazed
gowan, daisy
gowden, golden
gowl, howl, yell
graff, grave
graip, grope; fork
graith, equipment, furnishings
grandsher, grandfather
griding, striking
Grizzie, name for a brindled cow
growe, grue, gruss, feel horror or terror,
    shudder with fear
grunkle, crinkle, wrinkle, crackle
gruntch, grumble, object, refuse
gruntle, grunt
grush, gruss, crush
guid, good
guller, roar, shout, bawl
gulligaw'd, wounded, cut, hacked,
    gashed
gumple-fac'd, dejected
gurlie, stormy, threatening, bitter
gyzin-clout, masquing-gear

habrihone, habergeon
haffet, (blow to) side of head
hail, whole
hairst-rig, harvest-field
halflin, adolescent
halie, holy
hallan, screen
hallockit, giddy, hare-brained
hammerflush, sparks which fly from red-hot iron when beaten with a hammer
handsel, hansel, (give a) gift
harns, harrens, brains
hash, cut into small pieces, slash, mangle, chop, spoil, deface
Hawkey, name for a cow
heels-over-gowdie, head-over-heels
heise, heize, hoist, lift up
heich, high
hench, haunch
hender(-ends), latter(-parts)
herry, herriment, pillage
heuchle-bane, heukle-bane, hip-bone
heugh, pit, mine-shaft, quarry-face
hiddie-giddie, topsy-turvy, confused
hidlins, secretly, stealthily
hielde, cover, conceal, hide
hight, named
hilligilleerie, topsy-turvy
hine, far
hirdy-girdic, uproar, confusion, disorder
hoast, cough
hobbleshow, hubbleshow, uproar, confusion, hubbub
hog-shouther, push or jostle with the shoulder, shove about
hoolie, hoolyie, gently
hotch, heave with laughter
houff, inn
houp, hope
how, empty, hollow
howdie-craw, hooded crow
howk, dig
howdle, swarm, crowd
huffy, proud, choleric
hurl, dash, hurtle, fall from a height

ilka, each
ill-gainshon'd, mischievously disposed

ill-willie, malevolent
inding, unworthy
ingyne, brain, intelligence
iron-geddock, small staff or goad of iron

jad, jade
jank, give the slip
japper, breaker
jaw, wave
jaw-hole, primitive drain; sewer
jee-up, move on
jiffie, trice
jig, dance, play the fiddle
jimp, neat, graceful, slender
jirble, spill
joe, sweetheart
joyeusitie, pleasure
jow, toll, swing, swell, surge
jundy, push, shove
justle, jostle

kail, broth
kaim, kem, comb
kebbuck, a whole cheese
keek, peep
kenn, know
keppit, caught
kimmer, see *cummer*
kinkind, kind, sort, description
kintra, country
kirk-ayle, church-aisle
kirk-rapyne, church-plunder
kist, chest, coffin
kleek, hook
knap, knock, strike, rap; blow
knublock, knob
kye, cattle
kythe, appear

lade, load
laick, layman
laif, loaf
laigh, low
laird, estate-holder
lair'd, buried
lamp, take long steps
landwart, rural
lang(syne), long (ago)
lauchter, laughter
laverick, lavrick, lark

law, low; mountain
lawit, common
lear, learning
leich, leisch, lash
leifsum, pleasant
leil, loyal
leugh, laughed
leven, lightning
lift, sky
limmer, scoundrel, loose woman
linn, waterfall
lith, small part of the body
loan, interval between fields
lounder, severe stroke, blow
loup, leap
lour, frown
lowe, flame
lown, boy
lozen, pane of glass
lubbard, lubber, lout
lunyie, loins

magistrand, final-year student
mairattour, moreover
mal-easy, physical or mental illness or distress
maucht(y), might(y), powerful(ly)
maugre, ill-will, in spite of
maun, must
mawment, idol
mazerment, amazement, perplexity
meer-swine, dolphins, porpoises
meikle, mickle, great, much
meiths, marks, signs, landmarks, boundaries
melvied, soiled with meal
menzie, company, crowd
meridian, mid-day, noon (meal)
metit, meted
mirligoes, objects indistinctly seen
mith, might
mither, mother
moolert, crumbled
mools, earth of the grave
mooly-heels, chilblains
mou', mouth
mouldwarp, mole
muir, moor
mulligrant, complaint, lamentation

murgeon, contortion, grimace
murl, crumble, reduce to fragments, ruin

naig, nag (horse)
naistrill, nostril
nappie, strong ale
naur, near
neapit, at the lowest point of the tide
neevil, strike with the fist, blow with the fist
neis, nose
neist, next
neuk, corner
nicker, snicker, neigh
niddle, fiddle, toy, potter
nieve, fist
nowt, cattle

ouf(es), elf, elves
our, owr, over
owr-tane, overtaken
owr-tirvie, turn upside-down
outbock, vomit out
oxter, armpit

paidle, paddle
paik, stroke; beat, drub
Paip, pope
parle, speech
parochin, parish
parritch, porridge
pat, put; pot
paukie, sly, artful
pech, pant
pend, arch
perfyte, perfect
perjink, exact, precise
peuggin, puffing; expressing impatience, disgust, disbelief
pensch, paunch
pickle, predicament, awkward job; small amount
pingle, strive, strife, broil, battle
pirr, breathe gently
pit-mirk, black as the pit
plenzie, complain
plewman, ploughman
plowter, splash, puddle about
ploy, piece of fun

poke, bag, paunch, small sack
potley, type of fish
pous'd, pushed
poustie, powstie, power, strength, force
pouther, powther, powder
pow, head
preclair, supereminent
prick, pierce
prinkle, tingle, thrill, prickle
prieve, prove
puir, poor
punzie, pierce, sting
pupit, pulpit
pyne, pain
pyrnit, striped with colours

queir, quire, choir
quhair, book

raik, advance quickly
rafter-treen, wooden rafters
rallion, clattering, noise
rambarre, keep off, bar
ramp, wild, bold, unrestrained
ramsch, brusque
ramstam, headstrong, rash, unrestrained
rappit, dashed, thumped, struck, thudded
rapplet, shot up
rashies, rushes
rax, reach (out), stretch
recht, right
recule, recoil
rede, advice, counsel
reel-rall, confusion
reesil'd, beaten soundly
reird, noise, shouting
reissilin', rustling
reprime, repress
rigadoon, brisk dance
riggin-tree, rafter
ring, reign
rink-room, space for coursing
rippet, noise, clamour
rive, tear apart
roarie-buckie, whelk shell which makes a roaring sound when held to the ear
rocket, bishop's surplice

rout, rowt, roar, rumble
routh, plenty
row, roll
royat, extravagant, nonsensical, wild, stormy
rum-deil, queer devil
rung, cudgel
ruther, outcry, uproar
rybald, dissipated (person)

sae-wyse, thus
sailyie, sailzie, attack
sakeless, innocent
sark, shirt
sayar, seyer, poet
scap, scape, skape, skip
scouther, burn, scorch, singe
screigh, screech
scrievin, grazing, peeling, tearing off, scratching, scraping
scrimply, shortly
scroyl, worthless fellow
scroinogh, shriek, yell, lament, loud noise
sebows, syboes
senzie-house, synod-house
sey, test, try
shae, shoe
shank, leg
shent, destroyed
shod-shool, wooden shovel shod with iron
shog, shake, jog, sway, swing, rock, wobble
shool, shovel
showl'd, distorted
showther, shoulder
sic, siccan, syk, such
sich, sigh
siller, silver, money
sinny, sunny
sith, since
skaff(in), food, provisions
skail, spill, scatter
skair, timid, shy; frighten
skellie, skelly, squint; a rock
skelloch, shrill cry
skelp, slap
skelpie, person of little worth
skeygit, cleared off

skewl, turn aside, deflect, screw up, twist

skiff, move gently and smoothly along

skink, pour, drink

skinkle, sparkle

skirr, scour

skoug, hide, shield, protect

skoup, run hither and thither, bound, dart

skrae, lean person

skreek, shriek

skrill, shriek

skry, cry, proclaim; noise

skull, multitude of fish

slee, skilled

slunk, wet and muddy hollow

smaicher, nibble, munch

smaik, rogue, rascal

smaickerin, mean or contemptible behaviour

smeddum, courage

smeek, smeik, smoke

smiddie, smithy

smidge, smudge, laugh in a suppressed way, titter

smikker, leering smile

smirkle, smirk, smirch

smotter, spatter, soil stain

smoutter, eat often

smore, smother

sneck, latch

snod, smooth, neat, trim, orderly, comfortable

sonsy, friendly, hearty, honest, attractive

sotter, boil and bubble

souff, breath

sough, sound of the wind

souter, cobbler

Southron, English(man)

spacier, walk, pace

spain, wean

spang, jerk, sharp blow

spank, move nimbly, briskly

sparpled, dispersed

speik, speech

speil, spele, climb

sperse, sprinkle, scatter

spindyl, thin, slender

spinnel, slender spire

spinner, run or fly swiftly; spiral

splinder, splinter, fragment

spraich, sprauch, scream, cry, shriek, weep and wail

spree, boisterous quarrel

spreit, spirit

spreul, sprawl, rush, struggle, scramble

spulzie, spoil, plunder

spunk, spirit

squish, crush, squash

stabasch, tumult, uproar

staiver, totter

stalwart, strong, stormy

stang, sting

stank, swampy place

steek, steik, stitch

steeve, rigid, stiff

steir, disturb(ance)

stend, spring, bound

sterk, stark

stern(y), star(ry)

sticket, stabbed

stoof, stouf, stowf, walk with a lazy, heavy step

stot, bounce

stotter, stagger

stound, moment; throb, thrill, ache, stun

stour, dust, disturbance, force, violence

strabusch, tumult, uproar

strae, straw

straik, stroke

stramash, uproar, commotion, row

stranger, stronger

straucht, straight

stravaig, wander

streap, rill

streik, stretch

strenkell, sprinkle

styme, particle

supersault, somersault

swa, so

swack, swak, fit

swaif, swoon

swank, lithe, agile, strong, smart

swarf, faint, swoon, stupefy

swap, strike, throw, brandish

swat, sweated

swaup, countenance, facial resemblance

swecht, swing, force

sweer, reluctant

swerd, sword

swesch-trump, war-trumpet

swey, vacillate, sway, swing

swey-crook, moveable iron bar from which pots etc. may be hung over a fire

swink, toil, struggle hard

swipper, nimble, sudden, hasty

swith, quickly

swither, dither

syn, since

taburine, drum

tacket, small nail, hobnail

ta'en, taken

taft, wall round an enclosure

tailyie, piece of meat

taigle, entangle, muddle, confuse

tairge, cross-examine

taiver, wander, bewilder, annoy

tane, (the) one

tartan-purry, dish of boiled oatmeal mixed with chopped red cabbage or boiled with cabbage-water

tass, cup, goblet

tash, stain, smudge, blemish, spoil, damage

tatterwallop, rags, tatters

tauld, told

tebbit, sensation, energy, strength

teen, rage, harm, hurt, sorrow, grief

teinds, allocation of the tenth part of a parish for the support of religion

tent, care

tether, halter; bind, confine

tetter, hinder, delay

thack-lead, leaden roofing

thae, those

than, then

thegidder, together

thie, thigh

this-gate, thus-gate, thus, in this way

thole, endure

thrang, busy

thrapple, throat

threugh-stane, gravestone

throuther, mingled indiscriminately

tiftet, drunk

timmer, wood(en)

tirl, rattle

tirlie-wirlie, commotion, disturbance, noisy quarrel

tirr, beat, thump, shake

tirrivee, fit of passion

tirvee, tirvie, fall, cause to fall; tantrum

tithand, tidings

tither, (the) other

tongue-ferdy, active in speech

toom, empty

tot, sum total

tourbillon, cloud of dust

tout, toot, drink down

tove, chat, talk, gossip

tow, rope

trachle, exhaust with travel

transmew, transmute

tram, shaft

trig, neat

trunscheour, plate, trencher

tuilzie(-mulzie), quarrel, broil, struggle

tunakyl, tunic

unka, extraordinary

unsicker, unsure

unwerdy, unworthy, unbecoming, unfit

upppunland, in the country (as opposed to the town)

up-wriel, writhe upwards

vivers, viands, food

wa', wall

wab, web

wabster, weaver

wae, woe

waesucks, alas

waff, glimpse

waigle, waggle

wale, choose

walkrife, wakeful

wally, strong

wamble, wriggle, writhe

wame, belly

231

wangil, wangyle, evangel (the Bible in English)
wanhap, misfortune
wanrestfu', restless, unsettled, uneasy
wap, wrap
wappen, weapon
warstle, wrestle
wast, west
wat, wet
water-jaup, water-splash
waucht, gulp, swig
waur, worse
weanies, little children
wechtie, weighty
weddir-glim, the horizon
wee, wie, small
weegle, wiggle
weel I wat, well I know
weir, weiriors, war, warriors
weird(-set), fate(-appointed)
whazel, wheeze
whid, run, scamper
whihher, bluster or rage like the wind
whilk, which
whillywha, wheedle, coax, cajole
whillie-whaltie, beat rapidly
whummle, whummill, overwhelm
wicht, strong, valiant
wicket, wicked, bad-tempered, vicious
widdle, bustle, tumult

wid-dreme, nightmare
windflaucht, quick as the wind
windock, winnock, window
winze, curse
wist, know
wode, wud(ness), mad(ness)
worsit, worsted
wrack, wreck, suffering, punishment, vengeance
wraithly, angrily
wree, wry
wrocht, wrought

yald, gave way; alert, active
yam(m)er, cry, yell, shriek
yauff, bark, yelp
yelloch, scream, shriek, yell
yerk, beat, strike, jerk
Yerth, Earth
yesk, hiccup, belch, vomit
yett, gate
yeut, yout, cry, shout, roar, yell
Y-fere, in company with
yirdlins, earthward; along or towards the ground
yill, ale
yode, went
yokin', rough handling
youff, swipe, thump